Leftovers

Over a decade ago, Jorge Castañeda wrote the classic *Utopia Unarmed*, which offered a penetrating and comprehensive account of the Latin American left's fate at the end of the Cold War. Since then, the left across Latin America has travelled in paths no one could have predicted. Latin American nations from Mexico to Argentina wavered for years between leftism and American-supported neoliberalism, but in recent years the left has experienced a tremendous resurgence throughout the region. However, the left is not unified, and as Castañeda, Morales, and their contributors show, it has followed two distinct paths—a more cosmopolitan style leftism, exemplified by Brazil and Chile, and a left fuelled by populist nationalism that has clear debts to Perón or Cárdenas, and is most evident in Venezuela, Mexico's PRD, Bolivia, and Argentina. *Leftovers* comprehensively updates this very important story, with country and area specialists contributing.

Jorge G. Castañeda, Mexico's Foreign Minister from 2000 to 2003, is Global Distinguished Professor of Politics and Latin American and Caribbean Studies at New York University.

Marco A. Morales is a doctoral student in political science at New York University.

D1595833

Leftovers

Tales of the Latin American Left

Edited by
Jorge G. Castañeda
and Marco A. Morales

Routledge
Taylor & Francis Group

NEW YORK AND LONDON

First published 2008
by Routledge
270 Madison Ave, New York, NY 10016

Simultaneously published in the UK
by Routledge
2 Park Square, Milton Park, Abingdon, Oxon OX14 4RN

Routledge is an imprint of the Taylor & Francis Group, an informa
business

Typeset in 10/12pt Sabon by Keyword Group Ltd
Printed and bound in the United States of America on acid-free
paper by Edwards Brothers, Inc

Library of Congress Cataloging in Publication Data,
Leftovers : tales of the Latin American left / edited by Jorge G. Castañeda
and Marco A. Morales.
p. cm.
Includes bibliographical references and index.
[etc.]
1. Latin America—Politics and government—1980- 2. Right and left
(Political science) I. Castañeda, Jorge G., 1953- II. Morales, Marco A., 1976-
JL960.L44 2008
320.53098—dc22
2007048649

ISBN10: 0-415-95670-6 (hbk)
ISBN10: 0-415-95671-4 (pbk)
ISBN10: 0-203-92673-0 (ebk)

ISBN13: 978-0-415-95670-3 (hbk)
ISBN13: 978-0-415-95671-0 (pbk)
ISBN13: 978-0-203-92673-4 (ebk)

Contents

Figures

Tables

Acknowledgements

In many ways this project evolved parallel to a graduate course on the Latin American Left taught at New York University between 2005 and 2007. Many of the questions that this volume seeks to address were shaped by the discussions that took place in the classroom. The thoughtful comments of students were always challenging and called for thinking about the recent rise of the left in Latin America—and its consequences—from different angles.

The core of this book has been fed by many hands. We are indebted to the young scholars who agreed to undertake this project with us and who were excited to bring their expertise and research to bear—sometimes going the extra mile and collecting new data—in order to enhance our understanding of the Latin American left. Special thanks to Patricio Navia and his innate wit for titles.

Our gratitude goes also to NYU's Center for Latin American and Caribbean Studies (CLACS) that has provided consistent support for teaching and a resourceful environment for extra-curricular activities.

We also want to thank Routledge, especially Michael Kerns and Felisa Salvago-Keyes, who were always on top of things to get the book finished in a timely fashion.

Needless to say, this endeavor would have been tedious had it not been for the countless hours of amusement provided by the ingenious leaders of the left in Latin America. Our eternal gratitude to them ... and to the voters—not weapons—who led them to power.

Abbreviations

ALBA	Bolivarian Alternative of the Americas (Alternativa Bolivariana de las Américas)
APRA	Peruvian Aprista Party (Partido Aprista Peruano, earlier Alianza Popular Revolucionaria Americana)
ARI	Peru's Revolutionary Alliance of the Left (Alianza Revolucionaria de Izquierda)
CAFTA–DR	Central America–United States–Dominican Republic Free Trade Agreement
CAN	Andean Community of Nations (Comunidad Andina de Naciones)
CUT	Brazil's United Workers' Central (Central Unica dos Trabalhadores)
DEA	United States Drug Enforcement Agency
EZLN	Zapatista Army of National Liberation (Ejército Zapatista de Liberación Nacional)
FA	Uruguay's Broad Front (Frente Amplio)
FARC	Colombian Armed Revolutionary Forces (Fuerzas Armadas Revolucionarias de Colombia)
FMNL	El Salvador's Farabundo Martí National Liberation Front (Frente Farabundo Martí de Liberación Nacional)
FREPASO	Argentina's Front for a Solidary Country (Frente por un País Solidario)
FSLN	Nicaragua's Sandinista Front for National Liberation (Frente Sandinista de Liberación Nacional)
FTAA	Free Trade Area of the Americas
FV	Argentina's Front for Victory (Frente para la Victoria)
GDP	Gross Domestic Product
IMF	International Monetary Fund
IU	Peru's United Left (Izquierda Unida)
MAS	Movement Toward Socialism (Movimiento al Socialismo) in Bolivia and Venezuela

MBR-200   Venezuela's Bolivarian Revolutionary Movement
           (Movimiento Bolivariano Revolucionario)
Mercosur   Common South American Market (Mercado Común
           del Sur)
MST   Brazil's Landless Movement (Movimento dos Sem Terra)
MVR   Venezuela's Fifth Republic Movement (Movimiento Quinta
           República)
NAFTA   North American Free Trade Agreement
OAS   Organization of the American States
PAN   Mexico's National Action Party (Partido Acción Nacional)
PCM   Mexico's Communist Party (Partido Comunista Mexicano)
PDVSA   Venezuelan Oil Company (Petróleos de Venezuela, S.A.)
PJ   Argentina's Justicialista Party
PRD   Mexico's Party of the Democratic Revolution (Partido de la
           Revolución Democrática)
PRI   Mexico's Institutional Revolutionary Party (Partido
           Revolucionario Institucional)
PSDB   Brazilian Social Democratic Party (Partido da Social
           Democracia Brasileira)
PT   Brazil's Workers' Party (Partido dos Trabalhadores)
UCR   Argentina's Civic Radical Union (Unión Cívica Radical)
WTO   World Trade Organization

Part I

Revisiting the Utopia

Chapter 1

The current state
of the Utopia[†]

Jorge G. Castañeda and Marco A. Morales

As one of the first comprehensive academic pieces dealing with the Latin American left, *Utopia Unarmed* (Castañeda 1993) became a classic reference for those studying Latin American politics, and especially those interested in the Latin American left. Written at a time of economic, social, and political distress in the region, *Utopia Unarmed* concluded with a diagnosis of the Latin American left—adequate for the beginning of the 1990s—and a prognosis for the years to follow. The recent surge of the left in Latin America calls for a necessary endeavor: revisiting the analysis in *Utopia Unarmed*. Many things happened in Latin America since 1993 that changed both intra-country and inter-country dynamics. In more than one way, the Latin America that *Utopia Unarmed* analyzed has undergone profound changes, some of them unforeseeable a decade and a half ago.

For one, Latin America had first-hand experiences with financial crises that had long-lasting effects in some economies. The 1994 Mexican crisis, later followed by the 1997 East Asian crisis, and the 1998 Russian crises reverberated in the economies of the region. These events ended in the Argentine moratorium before the International Monetary Fund (IMF) that resulted from an unsuccessful experiment with a *convertibility plan* that pegged the Argentine peso to the U.S. dollar. Neither these crises nor their effects can be fully understood independent from the more-open-and-less-regulated-economy reforms implemented in the region throughout the 1990s.

Perhaps one of the most unexpected developments of the last decade happened on the trade front. The North American Free Trade Agreement (NAFTA) was negotiated, approved and entered into force on January 1, 1994, creating the largest trading block in the globe. Only months after that, the first Summit of the Americas endorsed a proposal of then U.S. President Clinton to create of a regional tariff-free zone: the Free Trade

[†] Sections of this text draw on a piece published in the Spring/Summer 2007 issue of the *Brown Journal of World Affairs* under the title "The Left Turn Continues." We thank Alejandra Lecona for superb research assistance.

Area of the Americas (FTAA). Needless to say, the negotiations missed the final agreement deadline initially projected for 2005. Its fate was inevitably tied to the success of the World Trade Organization's (WTO) Doha Development Round, which should have also been accomplished by 2005. The WTO negotiations stalled and the prospects of completion seem feeble at best after the collapse of the negotiations at the V Ministerial Meeting in Cancún, Mexico.

Meanwhile, the United States has engaged in a series of bilateral Free Trade Agreements (FTAs) with some countries in the continent—most notably the Central America–United States–Dominican Republic Free Trade Agreement (CAFTA–DR)—which might have contributed to a watered-down mandate to conclude negotiations on the multilateral front. But countries in the region have also negotiated their own trade agreements, and widened the influence of other trade-enhancing previous arrangements such as Mercosur and the Andean Pact. In the meantime, Cuba and Venezuela established the foundations for the Bolivarian Alternative of the Americas (ALBA), an international alliance designed to counter the free-trade efforts in the region. Thus far, Nicaragua and Bolivia have adhered to the pact. While it is too soon to tell whether it will prosper as an alternative to FTAA, it is clear that it has broken down the consensus necessary for FTAA or any WTO-based trade agreement to have continental effects.

The human rights and democracy agenda also took an unexpected turn. The Organization of the American States (OAS) approved the Inter-American Democratic Charter in 2000, which incidentally saved Venezuela's Hugo Chávez from being overthrown by a coup. The Spanish Judge Baltazar Garzón reignited the debate over human rights violations in dictatorships by issuing an order in 1998 for the arrest of former Chilean dictator Augusto Pinochet and investigations related to disappearance of Spanish citizens during the Argentine dictatorship. And the rise of the Zapatista movement in Mexico in January 1994 brought the "indian question" to the forefront of the human rights causes, to name a few developments. All of this, coupled with the domestic protection of human rights, has forced a "broader definition" of democracy and citizenship in the hemisphere.

Notwithstanding these advances, the social structure of the region has had few improvements. Some poverty-reducing programs have been relatively successful in Mexico (*Progresa/Oportunidades*), Brazil (*Bolsa Família*) and Chile (*Chile Solidario*). Still, the rest of the countries in the region have been unable to cope with this problem over the past fifteen years. Inequality, as well, remains a pending task and a pressing one since Latin America is still the region with the worst income distribution in the globe. The low growth rates throughout the 1990s and the mild recoveries of some economies during the last five years have not contributed to a better distribution of income. And the parallel task of improving the conditions of ethnic minorities and underprivileged groups also has a long way to go.

As has been the case throughout the past century, Latin America's relationship with the United States has had some interesting developments. While the Clinton administration had a somewhat elaborate perspective on the topic (which incidentally led to military interventions in Haiti), the salience of Latin America in U.S. foreign policy has decreased, mostly as a result of other global developments. Undoubtedly, the most significant of them was 9/11, followed by the wars in Afghanistan and Iraq. This clearly was the point where the priorities of the U.S. president with "no more important relationship than" with the Americas, had a definite turn. But still some issues remain active in the region. The war on drugs is one of them, through the *Plan Colombia* that dates from the Clinton administration years, and some changes in the certification process that eased relationships with some other countries. But the stark confrontation of Venezuelan President Hugo Chávez with the United States, applauded by other newly elected populist South American leaders, could very well have an effect on the concerns of American diplomacy towards the region.

If we look at countries individually, we will find a radically different face from the one they portrayed at the beginning of the 1990s, particularly with respect to the advancement of the left. At the time we write, nine Latin American countries—Argentina, Bolivia, Brazil, Chile, Ecuador, Nicaragua, Peru, Uruguay, and Venezuela—have elected governments from the left. And it is unlikely that the presence of the left will be diminished anytime soon.[1] After all, these leftist governments are scheduled to remain in power at least until 2010.[2] That is, by the end of the decade, half of the countries—and almost two thirds of the population (ECLAC 2006e)—in continental Latin America will be governed by the left. In this context, we are pressed to ask: what has been the role of the left in shaping the current face of Latin America? This book seeks to address this question.

The recent rise of the left

Imagine it is January 1, 1990. If we were to identify countries governed by the left in the hemisphere, we would only be able to locate two: Cuba and Nicaragua. Interestingly enough, neither of these governments was elected, but took power by armed means. With a more lenient definition, we could locate a third candidate for our count: Chile. By late December 1989, Chileans had elected their first post-Pinochet government and had chosen a coalition of parties that included Socialists. Strictly speaking, the Chilean Socialists were not in power as it was the Christian Democrats that held the presidency. Less than two months after this development in Chile, the Nicaraguan Sandinistas would be defeated in the first democratic election held in the country since they took power. It would take nearly eight years to have another government from the left in the continent: that of Hugo Chávez in Venezuela. Since then, seven more leftist governments have been elected.

By the end of 2007, nine countries have elected or reelected parties that identify with the left or the center-left. These parties have been in power in Chile since 1990, Venezuela since 1999, Brazil since 2003, Argentina since 2003, Uruguay since 2005, Bolivia since 2006, Peru since 2006, Nicaragua since 2007, and Ecuador since 2007. Briefly, these are the stories behind these elections:

Venezuela   Hugo Chávez was first elected into office on the 1998 elections with 56 percent of the vote under the label of his recently created Movimiento Quinta República (MVR). After the ratification of the new constitution, he was reelected with 60 percent of the vote. He was reelected for the second time[3] in the 2006 elections with 63 percent of the vote, defeating the Social Democratic candidate Manuel Rosales by a margin of over three million votes (about 25 percent of the vote).[4] The remarkable fact is that Chávez has increased his vote share in every election since he first took office.

Brazil   Luiz Inácio "Lula" da Silva, the Partido dos Trabalhadores (PT) candidate, won the presidency for the first time in the 2002 elections with 61 percent of the vote. He was forced into a runoff with the candidate of the Partido da Social Democracia Brasileira (PSDB) José Serra after failing to obtain 50 percent of the vote in the first round. He was reelected in 2006 with almost 61 percent of the vote after an intense, two-way campaign against PSDB's Gerardo Alckmin that gave him a 20 percent margin of victory. Still, Lula's 48 percent share of the vote in the first round was substantially higher than the 46 percent he obtained in the 2002 first round and much higher than those of his previous, unsuccessful electoral bids— 32 percent in 1998, 27 percent in 1994, and 16 percent in 1989.[5]

Chile   The Concertación coalition was first elected in the 1989 elections. Its first two governments were headed by Christian Democrats: Patricio Aylwin (1990–1994) and Eduardo Frei (1994–2000). It was not until the 2000 election that a Socialist was actually the presidential candidate. Ricardo Lagos won the election in a runoff against the rightist Joaquín Lavín with 51 percent of the vote that produced a bare 2.6 percent advantage. Michelle Bachelet, despite being forced into a runoff election in January 2006 against Lavín, managed to increase Lagos' share of the vote by 2 percent in the runoff that produced a comfortable 7 percent margin of victory, giving her 53 percent of the vote.[6] With this feat, Concertación governments were elected for the fourth consecutive time, with the last two headed by Socialist candidates.

Argentina Cristina Fernández de Kirchner managed to leisurely win the 2007 presidential election under the Frente para la Victoria (FV) label, a spin-off of the Justicialista Party that led her husband into office in 2003. Her 45 percent of the vote[7] made a runoff election unnecessary, and more than doubled her husband's share of the vote four years earlier. Néstor Kirchner was elected president in 2003 with 22 percent of the votes. Since neither candidate obtained 45 percent of the votes, as required by the 1994 constitutional reform, a runoff between him and Menem was inevitable. But foreseeing his defeat, Menem declined, effectively giving the presidency to Kirchner.

Uruguay Tabaré Vázquez was elected in 2004 as the candidate of the leftist coalition Frente Amplio (FA) with 51.7 percent of the vote.[8] Vázquez won the election by increasing his share of votes from his two previous unsuccessful bids in 1999, where he obtained 45.9 percent, and in 1994, where he obtained 30.6 percent.

Bolivia Evo Morales, the *cocalero* leader and founder of the Bolivian Movimiento al Socialismo (MAS), was elected president in 2005 with 53 percent of the votes:[9] a historical achievement considering that his closest competitor trailed him by 25 percent of the votes. In 2005, Morales more than doubled his previous share of votes—the 20 percent he obtained when he ran in the 2002 presidential elections. In just two elections, MAS and Morales became the main fixtures of the left in the country.

Nicaragua Daniel Ortega, the renewed, leftist ex-guerrilla leader of the Frente Sandinista de Liberación Nacional (FSLN), was elected again as president of Nicaragua in 2005, with 38 percent of the vote.[10]After being out of power for sixteen years and suffering defeats in three previous presidential bids, Ortega decided to reinvent himself and his campaign on a more moderate platform: he ceased his opposition to CAFTA–DR, he expressed his willingness to maintain diplomatic relations with the United States, and he definitely shied away from the seizure of private property, which he had implemented in the 1980s. He also took a step to the right by openly declaring his opposition to abortion. Despite winning the election, Ortega suffered a notorious electoral setback and obtained nearly 4 percent less of the vote than in his 2001 bid.

Peru Alan García became president of Peru for the second time as the APRA candidate in an unexpected comeback, defeating the populist Ollanta Humala by a mere 5 percent of the vote in a runoff election.[11] García left office in 1990 amidst severe hyperinflation, economic turbulence, and a surge in violence. A change in his discourse was necessary, and so he openly supported the US–Peru Trade Promotion Agreement and advocated fiscal soundness. However, he also engaged in the inevitable populist promises, such as the death penalty for terrorists and cuts in the wages of ministers and members of Congress. Despite his sixteen years out of office, he managed to increase his vote share by 4.8 percent relative to his last candidacy in 2001.

Ecuador   Rafael Correa, the candidate of Alianza PAIS, became president with 56.67 percent of the vote in a runoff against the rightist candidate, Álvaro Noboa.[12] After a close outcome in the general election, where he ran on a populist and pro-Chávez platform, political pragmatism prodded him to reinvent himself as a moderate candidate for the runoff election. Thus he distanced himself from Chávez, promised to keep the Ecuadorian economy dollarized, and played down Ecuador's debt default.

There are three patterns worth mentioning. First, all governments on the left that have faced an election—Venezuela, Chile, Brazil, and Argentina—have been leisurely reelected. Second, the governments of the left elected since 2000—except for Kirchner and Fernández in Argentina (2003 and 2007), and Ortega (2006) in Nicaragua—have been elected with more than 50 percent of the votes. Finally, voters in the majority of the countries seem to prefer more moderate candidates on the left to the outspokenly populist types, which was confirmed when moderate versions of former populists—Alan García in Peru (2006) and Daniel Ortega in Nicaragua (2006)—or timely moderation of new ones—Rafael Correa in Ecuador (2007)—were elected into office instead of the current populists, Ollanta Humala in Peru (2006) and Andrés Manuel López Obrador in Mexico (2006). That is perhaps the most notorious lesson of the most recent elections.

But there is also a less noted electoral development for the left during these fifteen years: most of these countries have shown a consistent increase in the votes that the left receives election after election. Figure 1.1 clearly shows the increase in vote shares of the left in Latin America *relative to the previous election* for the period 1990–2006. Note that the left grew on these countries by an average half percentage point during the 1990s, but by 12.2 percent between 2000 and 2006. Note also that except for four years—1990, 1995, 1996, and 2000—the left grew consistently throughout the period.

As we are also interested in showing the electoral success of the parties that are currently in power for the same period, Figure 1.2 shows the percentage change *relative to the previous election* for the parties that have prevailed throughout the period in Graph (a)—Brazil's PT, Chile's Concertación, Nicaragua's FSLN, Peru's APRA, and Uruguay's FA—and those of recent creation in Graph (b)—Bolivia's MAS, Venezuela's MVR, Argentina's FV, and Ecuador's Alianza PAIS—starting with their first time at the polls. It becomes clear that, except for Nicaragua and Peru, these parties increased their vote shares throughout the 1990s and the 2000s. Furthermore, except for Nicaragua in 2006, these parties showed positive growth throughout the 2000s.

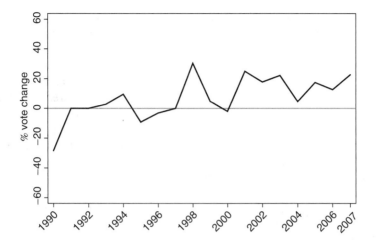

Figure 1.1 Aggregate change in vote shares of the left in Latin America (1990–2007).

How many lefts?

As witnesses to and students of the rise of the left, we have a most relevant question in our hands: why do we find significant differences among the leftists elected to power? Or, phrased differently: are there one, two, or more lefts in Latin America? The last decade and a half saw an increase in the number of elected governments that subscribe to the tradition of the left, and we want to understand this phenomenon. Thus, it is necessary to determine whether our object of study is the same in all cases to avoid drawing incorrect conclusions. Differences between these cases suggest that they do not belong in the same category; there is more than one left. Their origins are

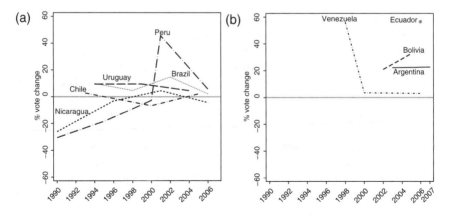

Figure 1.2 Change in vote shares of the left in Latin America by country (1990–2007).

divergent: some spring from a historical left that updated itself to accede to and remain in power, while others appeared with a flamboyant and appealing discourse (Castañeda 2006). Their means of rising to and maintaining power also conflict: some subscribe to the limits of the democratic game and the rule of law, while others tend to tramp over institutions that become inconvenient for their immediate needs. Furthermore, the ultimate long-term goals of their policies are different: some look for immediate results that will cement their support and allow them to remain in power, while others undertake policies that will have longer-lasting effects in the areas that they care about the most—poverty and inequality.

Striking—and convenient—is that overlaps between these distinctions strongly suggest the adequacy of a dichotomous classification for the Latin American left. The labels convey information about the distance between the two leftist poles. Thus, it is irrelevant whether the labels are "good" vs "bad," "right" vs "wrong," or "modern" vs "old"; the point is that the two extremes in this spectrum provide a robust frame for analysis. Are two categories enough, or do we need more (Schamis 2006)? Taxonomies are schematic by definition. They are supposed to capture certain commonalities in a given population. But if a taxonomy has as many categories as there are cases, it simply will not help to improve our understanding of the phenomenon we observe.[13] A dichotomous classification could be subject to another subdivision in order to refine the contours of the differences between groups. Yet parsimony is better appreciated when new schemes fail to improve our understanding. So we will not discard refinements from the outset, but will simply point to the tradeoff involved when adding complexity to models and gaining little explanatory power in return.

Grouping Chávez with Néstor Kirchner of Argentina and Evo Morales of Bolivia as the polar opposites of Lula, Bachelet, and Tabaré Vázquez is not without challenge. The former do belong to a different category, it is argued, because they delivered and fulfilled their promises (Weisbrot 2006) and respond to "long-ignored needs and building much-needed human capital" (Álvarez Herrera 2006). Nevertheless, the core question is *not* whether poverty was reduced by a certain percentage, whether direct transfers to the poorest were implemented, or whether motives agree with discourse. The relevant question has to do with the *sustainability* of these policies. How long can poverty be reduced by direct transfers to the population *without* additional instruments to help people overcome poverty *and* remain out of poverty afterwards? If poverty-reducing policies are based on cash-availability, it is only natural that when the flow of these funds stops, so will the programs and, consequently, poverty might return to its previous levels.[14] Furthermore, it is necessary to ask whether financing these direct cash transfers is the best use of resources to tackle poverty. After all, if there is a better use for these funds, elected leaders have—at the very least—a moral obligation to engage in them.

And making this distinction, as we exemplified above, clarifies—and does not obscure (Cleary 2006)—the actual trend that we are seeing in the region: it is both types of left that have come to power, but it is the moderate versions of the left that are more successful at winning elections. Were Hugo Chávez and Evo Morales anomalies? It is hard to say without better defined counterfactuals, and that is beyond the scope of this text.[15] However, the evidence presented in this volume suggests that the rise of the left is the result of successfully courting a broader mass of voters. If the left wins elections because it can appeal to voters from the left, the right, and the center, then gaining—and retaining—office might just require more moderate policies.

Following the same line of reasoning, we also subscribe to an explanation in which it is not institutions so much as voters that determine the winner in an election.[16] A country might have somewhat stable democratic institutions—such as Mexico in 2006—but if the candidate from the left cannot appeal to a sufficient amount of voters because of a radicalized discourse, then it is highly unlikely that this candidate can win the election.[17] Was it a stable institutional framework or his ability to alienate more centrist voters that kept López Obrador out of office? We tend to think it was the latter.

Analysts might choose to question the basis for a distinction between lefts or, jeopardizing their credibility, impose some value-charged "ulterior motives" in the taxonomy (Borón 2006). The latter adds nothing to our understanding of the rise of the left; the former opens a venue for potentially profitable discussion. By claiming that there is only one left and, therefore, only one surge to be explained, we would necessarily have to assume that the same factors affect all countries in the same manner. And somehow it does not make sense to impose this assumption when explaining the rise of Chávez, Morales, Bachelet, and Lula. Nonetheless, if distinguishing between cases shows—beyond all reasonable doubt—that the factors explaining the political success of some cases are equally applicable to the rest, then we might confidently conclude that distinguishing between cases with certain common features was but an exercise that strengthened our confidence in a single "left wave" in Latin America. For the time being, however, we would not advise throwing out the baby along with the bathwater.

The structure of the book

The debate on the number of categories for the left is hardly one to be settled soon. For this reason, it is more satisfying—and perhaps more illuminating in the long run—to provide a more structured analysis of the Latin American left during the last decade and a half. In essence, we need to go beyond the historical recounts of the processes that led the left to reach power in specific countries. More interesting is to attempt to detect patterns that could more coherently explain the surge and the functioning of the left in Latin America over recent years.

A reasonable starting place is to seek plausible reasons for the surge of the left in Latin America. Are all explanations related to the elites and discontent? Has it all been a matter of presenting better candidates? Or is there anything else to learn from voters? Did voters become more prone to vote for the left in recent years? More importantly, have voters become more leftist in recent times? If so, can we explain the rise of the left as a function on the change in ideological tastes? As it turns out, Latin Americans did change their ideological preferences: we became more identified with the right during the 1990s, but shifted to the left during the 2000s. But these changes were never extreme: the fact is that the majority of individuals do remain identified with the center of the ideological spectrum. Marco Morales provides the empirical evidence to support these shifts, but also identifies a pattern in the data: the countries where the left has been able to win the presidency have been able to enlarge their ideological base of support during the years prior to their ascent to power. Furthermore, it seems to be the case that the election of governments from the left and their consistent reluctance to enact extreme leftist policies may be related: as their ideological base of support widens, they need to cater to voters that do not want extreme policies, and they are forced to remain moderate if they want to be reelected.

Our assessment can also profit from revising whether the left distanced itself from its past preconceptions, and whether we can detect this change in its praxis. In other words, is the contemporary Latin American left different from that of the early 1990s? Has it been able to overcome its reluctance to engage in a globalized world? Has it been able to cope with its nationalistic tendencies and change its discourse? Furthermore, coping with poverty and inequality will hardly leave its agenda anytime soon. Poverty and inequality remain in alarmingly high levels in the hemisphere. Has the left been more effective at coping with poverty and inequality than governments of other "flavors"? Overall, is there anything in a cross-country analysis that can help us detect differences between governments that subscribe to the left?

Diana Tussie and Pablo Heidrich analyze the goals and policy instruments that the governments from the left have implemented as means to detect differences between the current policies and those implemented by their predecessors, as well as the differences among governments from the left. They make a compelling case for analysts to take a broader—and closer—look at domestic economic instruments—especially those linked to fiscal and monetary policies—and trade-related policies to make a broader assessment of economic policy. Looking exclusively into trade stands, for instance, obscures the constraints imposed by other instruments on the final economic outcome, such as exchange policies. Few consistent patterns are detected, other than a tendency by governments from the left to favor state intervention on the economy over the laissez-faire approach that seemed to prevail during the 1990s. What they find is a show of pragmatism in the economic arena, mostly shaped by national opportunities and country-defined constraints. According to their conclusions, it seems to be the case that variables, other than the ideological orientation of these governments, account for economic policy choices.

Social policy remains a staple of the left, and if reducing poverty and inequality is such a pressing concern for the left, some results should be evident on some general indicators. The creative analysis of José Merino looks into this matter, attempting first to determine whether the left is more successful in this task than right-wing governments, but also whether populist governments, both left and right, achieve more concrete results. His conclusions based on a broad range of indicators over time are quite interesting. For a broad range of indicators, the performance of the left seems indistinguishable from that of the right, except for the case of infant nourishment, maternal mortality, and primary education, where the left clearly outperforms the right. Yet the right seems to be more effective at improving health conditions for infants. Furthermore, when looking within the left, populism seems to be consistently related to inferior performance relative to the non-populist variants.

One of the prominent features of the Latin American left has been its tendency to exploit a nationalist rhetoric. Jorge Castañeda, Marco Morales, and Patricio Navia tackle the issue from different perspectives and advance a puzzling finding: even when voters do not seem to be clearly aligned with the typical nationalist discourse that has prevailed in the region, leaders on the left—at least quite clearly in some of its variants—still adhere to an anti-American, anti-trade nationalism when presenting themselves to the public. It seems to be the case that this nonsensical behavior of the left must be the result of using nationalism as a symbolic glue to hold the ideological structure together. The reasons might be various. Perhaps the leaders on the left have not noted the mismatch between discourse and voters' attitudes, or maybe they are simply too constrained by the discursive inertia. Or it might simply be that it is a useful *ex ante* justification for nationalizing natural resources in an attempt to return them "to the people." The fact of the matter is that the Latin American left without nationalism—at least its less modern versions—seems to be unable to conceive itself as a coherent ideological pole.

But the left in Latin America has taken divergent paths to achieve its current face. What is interesting for our purposes is that these differences can be, to a large extent, accounted for by the variations in organizational structures of the parties, the particular context during which the left evolved into a full-fledged party structure, and the presence—or absence—of particular types of leaders willing to be a *primus inter pares* figure within their own party, as opposed to figures that give life to the left.

One of the most emblematic cases for the contemporary Latin American left is Brazil. Lula keeps proving his critics wrong, even after a term and a half in office. He was not the radical socialist that the markets feared, nor has he blindly aligned with Cuba—or Chávez—for that matter. On the contrary, he has followed a more responsible approach regarding the economy, and engaged in the celebrated poverty reduction program to address a traditional programmatic concern of the left using non-traditional approaches for the left. Gianpaolo Baiocchi and Sofia Checa give us a detailed account into the internal dynamics of the Brazilian left: the constant tension between the old and the new that shape the face of PT. The party engaged in a participation-based approach to local government, which would produce a legitimate government that could actually govern well and would allow everyone to participate. As a result of taking a more democratic and participatory approach, PT became more reliant on civil society and other organizations, instead of unions as the traditional organization of the left would dictate. But the recent change that Baiocchi and Checa underscore is that of a PT that relies at the national level in Lula and a broad set of coalitions instead of the participatory tradition of PT. As a result, the party has grown away from its staple and closer to a personality-based party that seems to be the exact opposite from what an innovative party of the left should do. The matter, again, is one of the "acceptable" tradeoffs between an effective party and an ideologically coherent and true-to-itself version of it.

Chile did not share many problems with other countries in the region during the 1970s and 1980s, mostly because of the Pinochet dictatorship. Once it ended, Chile elected a center–left coalition of parties that has been in power for four consecutive terms. Not only that, it has successfully managed to combine economic growth programs with poverty reduction. It could be argued that its free-trade and sound economic fundamentals approach to economic policy is closer to a neoliberal economic program than to one that would be typically favored by the left. Yet it has still managed to address the concerns of the left. So what is peculiar about Chile? Patricio Navia points out that it is a combination of peculiar conditions. On the one hand, a long period of economic growth fostered by early economic reforms helped Concertación to remain in power during four administrations. But also, a coalition of parties that leads to more moderate policy positions has been able to address poverty and inequality as part of its running platform. The outcome of this interaction is a program that maintains economic stability, while addressing postmodern issues such as the reduction of inequality, gender equality, and human rights.

David Altman, Rossana Castiglioni, and Juan Pablo Luna provide us a rich recount of the path followed by FA in Uruguay, and the twenty years it took for the party to become the main opposition party before finally ascending to power. FA is not only a successful case for the left, but a particularly interesting one as well. The administration of Tabaré Vázquez has only been in power for a couple of years. Yet a dissection of his governing style along with the dynamics that have prevailed in his cabinet clearly shows a more complex picture than is typically allowed from political parties, especially those that have been portrayed as role models. Their analysis produces an interesting conclusion: there is more than one left even within FA, and the party has had to cope with this situation during its first years in power, not always producing the most coherent bundle of policies for an administration that subscribes to a modern left.

These cases shed some light on another difference within the left: some do not depend on a particular character for survival, while others rely on a character and its followers to subsist. Navia also points to an issue that is at the core of this matter: it makes little sense to argue for similar outcomes from countries where there is a strong party on the left, and compare them to a country with a weak left where the president—or its candidates—*must* build their own personal support in order to remain in power. That is what makes Chile and Uruguay so interesting: the left in both countries was built without full reliance on a single personality. While Brazil initially had a left that did not depend on personalities, it has somewhat departed from that point, although Lula is not making the irrational populist claims made by other South American leftists, and has remained instead on the responsible end of things.

The Peruvian left presented by Martín Tanaka is one of missed opportunities to consolidate as a national political force, or at least one with a decisive influence in national politics. His revision invites further thought on the benefits and costs related to important figures within a party. It seems to be the case that it was only in times when a public figure appeared that the left was able to establish a degree of coordination, only to collapse at the last minute, right when it was more important to present a unified front: at the time of an election.

The Mexican left, as analyzed by Kathleen Bruhn, has followed a long path that crystallized with the formation of PRD in the 1980s led by the figure of Cuauhtémoc Cárdenas during its first decade of existence. Yet, the lack of institutionalization of the party might have played against Cárdenas and allowed the surge of another important figure in the party since 2000: Andrés Manuel López Obrador. Notwithstanding, the case of PRD could not be categorized as one where a figure fully takes over the party. Early on, PRD chose to select its candidates by democratic means, which has had the effect of institutionalizing internal groups and making it unusually hard for one person to single-handedly control the party. López Obrador might temporarily exert a high degree of influence on the party, but ultimately the ability of the internal groups to coordinate—and not the leader *per se*—will determine the fate of the party.

The risk is always present. The construction of the left may not always follow the institutional and *caudillo*-free approach. Peru, for instance, has struggled endlessly to build a successful left, yet the absence of a uniting figure has kept parties in the Peruvian left from constituting a common front. The opposite is true for Mexico, where Cuauhtémoc Cárdenas has kept the Mexican left from collapsing into powerless groups. But his attempts to maintain the left cohesion have also had an unforeseen effect: making it vulnerable to the threat of new personalities arising.

Venezuela is perhaps the opposite extreme, as Raúl Sánchez Urribarri details. Today, given the prominence of Hugo Chávez, it would seem natural to think of him as *the* Venezuelan left. While Chávez is certainly on the left, it would be hard to argue that he represents *the only* left in Venezuela. The left—a different one—had existed in Venezuela before Chávez. A skillful politician and a pragmatist, he was able to trample over the left, and create an ad hoc organization—first, MBR-200 and then his Fifth Republic Movement (MVR)—to support his attempts to transform Venezuela and put it on the path of the Chávez-centered Twenty-First-Century Socialism. The recent developments in the country, along with the constitutional modifications proposed by Chávez, strongly suggest his desire to become the State, the left, and "the path." An important point to stress is that the fate of the left in Venezuela seems to be inevitably tied to Chávez, and not the other way around.

For a number of reasons, the left is well and alive in Latin America. How did all of this come about? Jorge Castañeda wraps up this volume with, among other things, some interesting observations on the matter. The end of the Cold War was, in the end, good news for the Latin American left. Essentially, there was no longer a reason to prevent the left from being a legitimate political force once the threat of Soviet-style socialism in Latin America had died out after the fall of the Berlin Wall. Full-fledged democracy, especially in a region with high poverty and inequality, would eventually bring to power some parties with a natural propensity to address these issues. And that has been the case, although not always with the success rate that would be desirable. The rise of the left ran parallel to a process that diversified it. Over the last years, it has become evident that the left in many countries can have more than one face. The old traditional left has in some cases gone through a transformation that rendered parties resembling the European social democratic tradition. In others, this renewed left coexists with the more populist versions that seem to surface every so often in the hemisphere. And yet, other countries have had to live with the old lefts that refuse to update according to the needs of the time, but that are forced to re-examine their positions when confronted with real constraints in government.

These different dimensions and perspectives seek to provide a broader, more detailed and empirically driven analysis of the Latin American left since the publication of *Utopia Unarmed*. The multidimensional approach that we advance is certain to give some new evidence that has been suggested, although not proven, before. Sometimes the evidence-based conclusions do not correspond to commonly held views, and sometimes they do, with some caveats. One thing is certain: there is too much diversity across the Latin American left to conceive it as a single entity, and there might be too much variation to conceive a dichotomous classification as means to understand patterns in the behavior of the left. We advance our own views on the matter, although enough room is also left for readers to form their own assessments about taxonomies, and about the current state of the left in Latin America.

Notes

1 Over the next couple of years, six countries are scheduled to hold presidential elections: Paraguay (2008), El Salvador (2009), Panama (2009), Honduras (2009), Chile (2009), and Uruguay (2009). Only if the left loses the presidency in Chile or Uruguay—neither of which seems likely at present—is the left ratio likely to be altered.

2 Uruguay will have presidential elections on October 2009, but whichever government is elected will not take office until March 2010. As for the rest of these countries, Bolivia, Ecuador, and Brazil will hold elections in 2010, Nicaragua and Peru in 2011, and Venezuela in 2012.

3 It would actually be his second full term since the new constitution entered into force in 2000. But he had served for two years as president after being elected in 1998 for the first time.

4 Official results from Venezuela's Consejo Nacional Electoral.

5 Official results from Brazil's Tribunal Superior Eleitoral.

6 Official results from Chile's Servicio Electoral.

7 Official results from Argentina's Dirección Nacional Electoral at the Ministry of the Interior.

8 Official results from Uruguay's Corte Electoral.

9 Official results from Bolivia's Corte Nacional Electoral.

10 Official results from Nicaragua's Consejo Supremo Electoral.

11 Official results from Peru's Oficina Nacional de Procesos Electorales.

12 Official results from Ecuador's Tribunal Supremo Electoral.

13 One of the clearest examples of this preference can be found in Corrales (2006b).

14 This is not a very popular perspective on this debate, where most accounts seem to care only about immediate results. For alternative formulations, see Stiglitz (2006) or Cardoso (2006).

15 Interestingly enough, even those critical of the most moderate versions of the left in Latin America recognize the emergence of a different kind of left—not only in Latin America—even if it is thought to be spearheaded by Chávez's Twenty-First-Century Socialism (Raby 2006).

16 For the opposite view, see the piece by Maílson Da Nóbrega (*Tendencuas Weekly*, June 20, 2006).

17 It could also be argued that López Obrador nearly won the election, but this is more a function of the effective number of candidates in the election. Had there been a runoff between Calderón and López Obrador, we could have seen a reshuffling of votes from the excluded candidates to those in the runoff. However, we need to point out that there were three-party contests as well in 1994 and 2000, yet Cárdenas was never as close as López Obrador to winning an election.

Chapter 2

Have Latin Americans turned left?

Marco A. Morales

The left in Latin America has gained notoriety since the 1990s, either because some newly elected governments subscribe to this ideology or because it has become a strong enough political force to impact policy decisions.[1] It could be the case that political parties that describe themselves as leftist have been able to recruit and field more viable candidates than in the past. Given the limited choice of candidates in each country, voters either support these candidates or simply do not turn out to vote. But it could also be the case that—holding parties' positions constant— voters leaning towards the left have become more numerous relative to those leaning towards the right, thus accounting for the recent electoral success of the left. Any suitable explanation is, most likely, a mixture of both processes.[2]

For the most part, the literature seeking to explain the rise of the left has avoided considering voters individually, focusing instead on contextual conditions: economic explanations, policy failures, and general discontent become "natural" causes for the rise of the left. While it would seem obvious that scholars should look into voters' individual preferences and ideology—as they are the ones who elect governments—available research has failed to do so. By ignoring voters to explain the rise of governments from the left, we are missing important parts of the story. Considering that "natural" causes have been a constant at least over the last two decades, why is it that governments from the left have been elected only in the past few years? There must be, then, some variation that the "natural" causes are failing to address. The aim of this chapter is to provide an empirical assessment of a plausible change in ideological "taste" for the left among Latin Americans, and to gauge the ideological bases of support for successful parties on the left. Hopefully, by bringing voters back into the electoral equation, we can gain a much richer perspective that helps us understand the rise of the left in a more comprehensive manner. I address the public opinion side of the equation using individual-level data for Latin American countries between 1990 and 2005.

The data

The survey data necessary to undertake this task was scarce twenty years ago. Fortunately, the World Values Survey (WVS) and the Latinobarómetro time series provide the necessary individual-level data from representative samples for a variety of countries with consistent phrasing of questions over time. Unfortunately, data availability impedes us from having a full 1990–2005 time series, given the differences between both studies. On the one hand, WVS includes representative samples for six Latin American countries during the 1990s: Argentina, Brazil, Chile, Mexico, Peru, and Venezuela, which comprise roughly three fourths of the total population of the hemisphere (ECLAC 2002). On the other hand, Latinobarómetro collected representative samples of all Latin American countries during the 2000s: Argentina, Bolivia, Brazil, Colombia, Costa Rica, Chile, Ecuador, El Salvador, Guatemala, Honduras, Mexico, Nicaragua, Panama, Paraguay, Peru, Uruguay, and Venezuela. I employ the survey data for 2001 and 2005 for ease of comparison.[3]

Latin Americans' ideological swing (1990–2005)

By now, the surge of the left in Latin America is common wisdom (Panizza 2005b; Castañeda 2006; Weintraub 2006). Headlines pertaining the region are no longer about the prospects for economic growth, or the effects of the recent economic crises. Rather, a growing number of stories are reported about electoral results, specifically the prominent and charismatic leftists that are either ascending to power or very close to doing so. In broad terms, this can be because of better candidates under leftist labels, or a change of tastes of voters that has increased the vote shares of the left. On the candidate side, it is undeniable that the left has been able to nominate candidates that are attractive enough for voters. Candidates are typically not randomly drawn from a country's population: they self-select for the internal party competitions and play by the rules that determine which candidate is chosen by each party. Yet we know next to nothing about voters and whether they now like the left better than they did before. With the available data from 1990 to 2005 I explore the ideological placement of Latin Americans on a left–right dimension. The aim of this text is certainly not to explain why these shifts happened, but rather to detail ideological shifts and the context in which they take place.

Are Latin Americans turning left?

It is hard to understand contemporary politics absent some dimension that "locates" individuals, parties and candidates in an ideological scale (Benoit and Laver 2006). We are now used to defining—and associating—the left and the right with particular sets of policies. By virtue of this association, individuals are able to locate themselves and parties on ideological scales that denote "how much to the left (right)" a party or candidate is relative to other parties or candidates. Similarly, individuals are able to place themselves on the same scale denoting their particular tastes on this dimension.

Graph (a) in Figure 2.1 shows the pooled ideological placement of Latin Americans from 1990 to 2001, grouping data by WVS waves. It is quite remarkable that, contrary to what would be expected given the election of governments from the left, Latin Americans did not show a drastic ideological shift towards the left. On the contrary, if any shift is evident, it is one towards the right which is confirmed by statistical tests.[4] Looking into the details, we see first that the majority of Latin Americans are strictly moderates, and that was true throughout the 1990s. But it is also interesting to note a slight ideological shift of individuals towards the right. By the beginning of the 2000s, there was a roughly similar proportion of individuals on the extreme left as there was in the 1990s, but the proportion of individuals placing themselves on the extreme right had increased. We can also trace a tendency of non-extreme leftists shifting, not necessarily towards the right but towards the center. In sum, Graph (a) suggests that Latin Americans became more oriented towards the right during the 1990s, which is the result of a relative decrease of the center-left and a growth of the center-right and right.

But Graph (b) in Figure 2.1 shows a clearly different story. While the aggregate public opinion in Latin America shifted to the right during the 1990s, it began a shift to the left between 2001 and 2005. This means that the years after 2000 showed a slight shift to the left, resulting from larger shares of Latin Americans identifying with the left relative to the right.

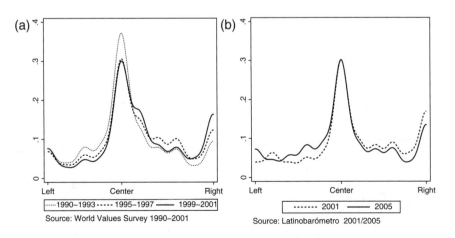

Figure 2.1 Shifts in pooled ideological placement in Latin America.

Interestingly, this coincides with the years in which more governments from the left have been elected into office. It is tempting to claim that recently elected governments from the left are the *result* of a change of ideological "taste" among Latin Americans. With the evidence at hand, it is hard to tell whether individuals became more leftist and then elected governments from the left, or whether they liked the performance of governments from the left and then became more identified with it. The matter is further complicated by the fact that many candidates from the left elected after 2000 had been unsuccessful candidates during the 1990s, but were able to increase their vote shares precisely when we see a shift towards the right.

It could be the case that the aggregate data hides some country dynamics where public opinion might have turned more drastically to the left—or to the right. Note that the sample contains countries where the left has been recently elected (Argentina, Bolivia, Ecuador, Nicaragua, Peru, and Uruguay), reelected (Chile, Brazil, and Venezuela) or where the left has recently gained some traction at the polls (Mexico and Colombia). This variation might help uncover some particularly useful trends to assess the relevance of ideological shifts. Let us take a closer look at these specific country cases.

Countries where the left ascended to power

At the time this chapter is being written, candidates from the left have won office in nine Latin American countries: Hugo Chávez (1998, 2000, 2006) in Venezuela, Ricardo Lagos (2000) and Michelle Bachelet (2006) in Chile, Luiz Inácio da Silva (2002, 2006) in Brazil, Néstor Kirchner (2003) and Cristina Férnandez (2007) in Argentina, Tabaré Vázquez (2004) in Uruguay, Evo Morales (2005) in Bolivia, Daniel Ortega (2006) in Nicaragua, Alan García (2006) in Peru, and Rafael Correa (2006) in Ecuador. If there were any ideological changes in the electorate, particularly to the left, and we suspected them to be causally related to the rise of the left, we should see more pronounced shifts in these countries.[5]

Argentina   The consistent pattern shown by Graph (a) in Figure 2.2 is a diminution of the mass of individuals located on the left and the center-left, while there has been a notorious growth on the moderate right and the right. Yet, the vast majority of Argentines still concentrate on the center-right of the ideological spectrum. But Graph (b) shows virtually no changes in the ideological distribution of Argentines since 2000. In sum, Figure 2.2 shows that Argentines shifted to the right during the 1990s, but have not had any further ideological shifts since 2000.

Bolivia   While no data is available for the 1990s for Bolivia, it is nevertheless interesting to note the ideological distribution of individuals between

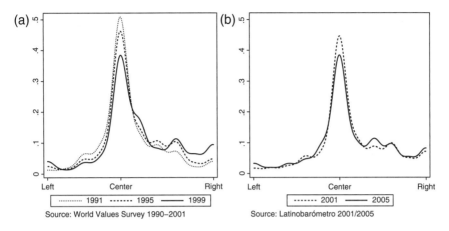

Figure 2.2 Shifts in ideological placement for Argentina (1991–2005).

2001 and 2005. As can be seen in Figure 2.3, Bolivians showed a remarkable shift to the left over these years. While the ideological distribution was concentrated in centrist positions by 2001, more individuals now identify with the left and the center-left in 2005 than they did at the beginning of the decade.

Brazil The swing of Brazilians towards the right shown on Graph (a) in Figure 2.4 seems to be the result of the decrease of moderates and those positioned on the center-left, but also of an increase of those in the moderate right and the center-right. More surprising is the shift that Brazilians show towards the left between 2001 and 2005, mostly as a result of the increase in identification with the center-left as shown in Graph (b). The interesting fact is that Brazilians were quite ideologically polarized by the beginning of the 1990s, and became much more centrist and less polarized fifteen years later.

Chile Figure 2.5 shows interesting patterns for the Chileans. During the first half of the 1990s, they showed a slight shift to the right, but no further movements in this direction happened during the second half of the decade. But more interestingly, while there were no ideological shifts during the second half of the 1990s, Chileans did turn left during the first half of the 2000s. As shown by Graph (b) in Figure 2.5, this shift is due to an increase in Chileans identifying with the center-left. The remarkable fact is that Chileans are mostly centrist, and the ideological swings are minor as they can be mapped down to Chileans pivoting around the center and mildly moving towards the center-right or the center-left.

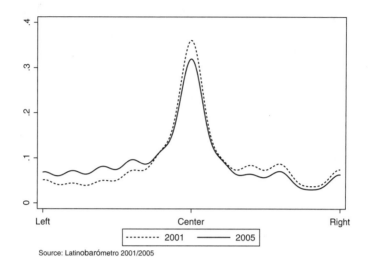

Figure 2.3 Shifts in ideological placement for Bolivia (2001–2005).

Ecuador Like most of the previous cases, Figure 2.6 shows that Ecuadorians shifted to the left between 2001 and 2005. The shift can be traced back to a reduction in the share of Ecuadorians identifying with the extreme right, coupled with an increase in those identifying with the center-left. Aside from this fact, there was a very little degree of ideological polarization in Ecuador by 2005.

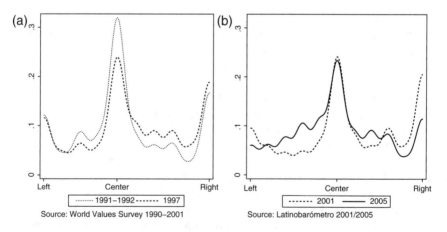

Figure 2.4 Shifts in ideological placement for Brazil (1991–2005).

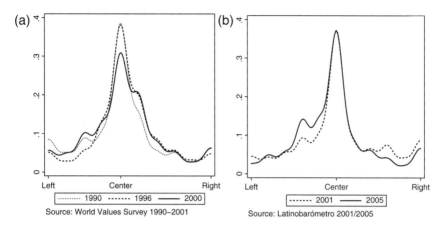

Figure 2.5 Shifts in ideological placement for Chile (1990–2005).

Nicaragua Figure 2.7 shows that Nicaraguans held the same ideological positions throughout the 2001–2005 period. A peculiar characteristic of Nicaragua is the high degree of polarization as well as the relative increase of Nicaraguans identifying with the right by 2005. Yet, statistical tests confirm that, on average, Nicaraguans remain ideologically in similar positions.

Peru Figure 2.8 shows virtually no ideological shifts among Peruvians during the second half of the 1990s. Notoriously, the majority of them

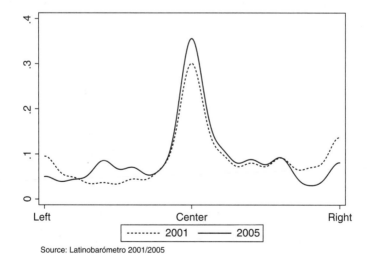

Figure 2.6 Shifts in ideological placement for Ecuador (2001–2005).

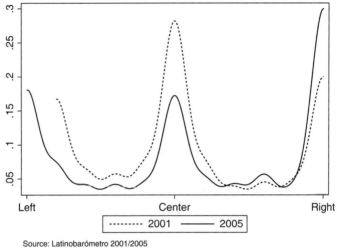

Source: Latinobarómetro 2001/2005

Figure 2.7 Shifts in ideological placement for Nicaragua (2001–2005).

identify with the center. But it also shows that by the first half of the 2000s Peruvians had moved to the left, especially by increasing the proportion of individuals identified with the center-left.

Uruguay   As shown in Figure 2.9, Uruguayans did shift to the left between 2001 and 2005. The shift is the result of a decrease of individuals identifying with the center-right, accompanied by an increase in identification with

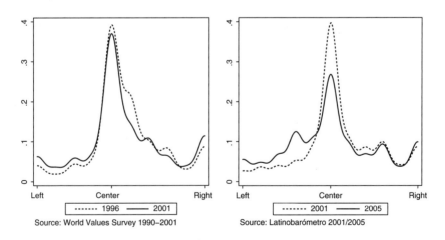

Source: World Values Survey 1990–2001   Source: Latinobarómetro 2001/2005

Figure 2.8 Shifts in ideological placement for Peru (1996–2005).

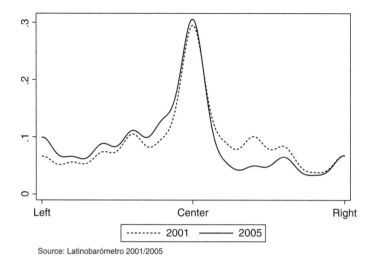

Source: Latinobarómetro 2001/2005

Figure 2.9 Shifts in ideological placement for Uruguay (2001–2005).

the center-left. It is interesting to note that as a result of this shift, the majority of Uruguayans are concentrated in the space delimited by the center and the left.

Venezuela This is a unique case in ideological terms among those countries that elected governments from the left in Latin America. Figure 2.10 shows that Venezuelans shifted to the left during the second half of the 1990s, as a result of an increase in the proportion of them identifying with the center. By the mid-1990s, a large proportion of Venezuelans identified with the right, but the balance had shifted by the second half of the decade with a decrease in rightists coupled with an increase in centrists. Graph (b) confirms the trend for the first half of the 2000s. The difference during this period is that there was an increase in the share of Venezuelans identified with the center *and* the center-left that was accompanied by a further decrease in those identified with the right. It is important to note that the overall shift is not one where everyone became an extreme leftist, but it was mostly the result of a concentration in the center and the center-left, with a mild reduction of extreme positions.

Countries where support for the left has increased

The electoral surge of the left has not only happened where their candidates have won the presidency. There has also been an increase in vote shares for the left in countries where they have not won elections. Perhaps the most notorious cases are Mexico and Colombia, both governed by parties from the right, but where the left has been able to increase its vote shares considerably.

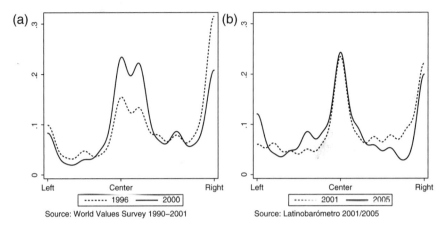

Figure 2.10 Shifts in ideological placement for Venezuela (1996–2005).

Mexico   It is interesting to see the ideological evolution of Mexicans during this period, described in Figure 2.11. Note first that there were no changes in ideological location during the first half of the 1990s. Yet, there was a clear shift to the right during the second half of the decade that can be seen in the stark increase in the share of Mexicans identified with the extreme right and the reduction of centrist positions. By 2000, most Mexicans identified with either the extreme right or the center. This shift to the right became more notorious by 2001, when the majority of Mexicans were located between the center and the right, only to shift back to the center—a shift to the left—by 2005, when most Mexicans had become centrists.

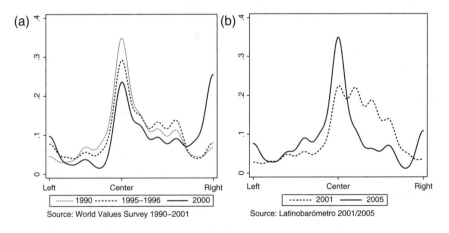

Figure 2.11 Shifts in ideological placement for Mexico (1990–2005).

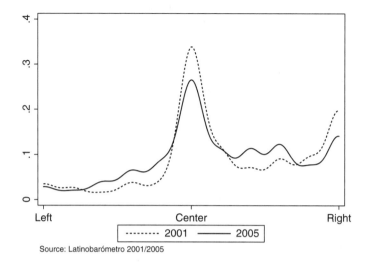

Figure 2.12 Shifts in ideological placement for Colombia (2001–2005).

Colombia Figure 2.12 highlights an overall slight shift to the left between 2001 and 2005 in Colombia. But this shift is accompanied by a mild increase in center-left positions and a much larger increase in center-right positions among Colombians. It is interesting to note that while the majority of Colombians were centrists by 2005, the ideological distribution remains skewed towards the right of the ideological spectrum

A preliminary assessment

The 1990s in Latin America were not times of stability. Most countries in the region were still trying to cope with the difficulties caused by the economic crises of the 1980s, which required taking stringent measures that affected large portions of the population. The 1990s were also times of economic distress inaugurated by the peso crisis in Mexico (1994–1995), followed by the East Asian (1997) and Russian (1998) crises, and their subsequent effects that spread throughout the region. Many countries also suffered from political instability derived from corruption scandals, attempted coups, guerrilla warfare, and the like. It is nonetheless puzzling that Latin Americans should have an ideological shift to the right while enduring these conditions.

Current research in Social Psychology strongly supports the notion that individuals tend to become more conservative—i.e. identify with the right— when facing severe threats or in crisis situations (Bonanno and Jost 2006; Jost 2006; Jost et al. 2007).[6] This, it is argued, is the result of the psychological need of individuals to cope with uncertainty and threat (Jost et al. 2003a, 2003b). Based on this evidence, the conservative tendencies in Latin America observed during the 1990s could be the result of critical economic, social, and political conditions. If that is the case, Latin Americans should become less conservative once these conditions recede. Coincidentally, that is precisely what we observe during the first half of the 2000s. Economic, social, and political conditions have improved in the majority of the countries since 2000, to the point that the threat would have vanished, thus deactivating the push towards conservatism.

We have a plausible explanation for the ideological shifts in the region, but the puzzle still holds. Is the ideological shift related to the election of governments from the left in Latin America? The answer seems to be negative. We know that every country in Latin America—but Venezuela—shifted to the right during the 1990s. In contrast, most countries—except for Argentina, El Salvador, Nicaragua, and Paraguay—showed an overall ideological shift to the left during the 2000s, while no country shifted to the right. But we also know that even the countries that did not shift to the left during the first half of the 2000s—Argentina and Nicaragua—elected governments from the left despite no stacking of the "ideological deck" among voters. Furthermore, the remaining countries that elected governments from the left during the "shift to the left" in the 2000s—Bolivia, Brazil, Chile, Peru, and Uruguay—did so with candidates that had consistently increased their vote shares during the time when ideology was more rightist in their own countries. As a matter of fact, Venezuela and Ecuador are the only two countries that elected governments from the left *while* a swing to the left was effectively taking place: Venezuela in the 1990s and Ecuador in the 2000s. With this evidence at hand, it is hard to present a compelling case for the surge of the left causally linked to an ideological shift to the left among voters in every country.

In sum, there are reasons to believe that the "shift to the left" that we observe during the 2000s is the result of a regression to an "equilibrium" ideological point in every country. That is, it might be the case that Latin Americans are not becoming more leftist, but are simply becoming less conservative. But if the observed shift to the left is a regression to a natural ideological point *and* ideology translates into vote choice, we should have observed governments from the left before the crises began, and we did not. That could be due to a left that presented bad candidates in the 1990s, or to a mechanism—other than pure ideological motivation—at work when electing candidates from the left in Latin America.

Sources of support for leftist parties (1990–2005)

If we have reason to doubt that an ideological shift is behind the election of governments of the left in Latin America, what would other available explanations be? One path to answering this question begins by looking into the sources of support for the left in Latin American countries. If the left is getting more votes, that can only be the result of voters identified with the left that vote for the left, or an increase in the appeal of leftist candidates such that they are able garner the support of a broader ideological range of voters. Given the evidence presented above, it seems more plausible that candidates from the left have been able to attract the sympathy of voters that are not on the left, but may be on the center and even on the right. Again, this matter can only be settled empirically.

To do so, the ideological location of those individuals who claim to be supporters of a given party can be reviewed. I will focus on those countries that have already elected governments from the left, as this can provide more compelling evidence related to their election into office. When possible, I will trace the support for those parties that have existed throughout the last fifteen years. Otherwise, I will present the sources of support for the main parties of the left and contrast them with the support for the parties/coalitions elected into office. In general, data for the 1990s is used to map the ideological distribution of supporters for the left in each country for various years. To provide a better guide as to how far apart is the current support for parties from the left from the general public, data for 2005 is used to show the support for the left and its overlaps with the general distribution of voters.

Argentina   As a point of comparison, Graph (a) in Figure 2.13 details the ideological location of supporters of the dominant parties on the left during the 1990s, namely Unión Cívica Radical (UCR), Frente por un

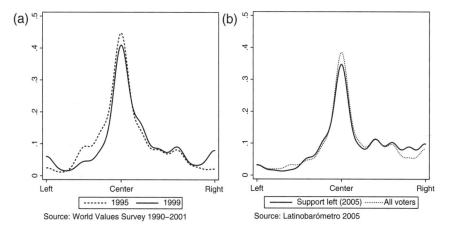

Figure 2.13 Ideological support for the left in Argentina.

País Solidario (FREPASO), and their subsequent alliance in the 1999 elections that made Fernando de la Rúa president. Interestingly enough, most of the UCR and FREPASO supporters identify with the center, and there seems to be more support from the center-right than from the center-left. But more interesting is the comparison with Graph (b) that shows the ideological distribution of the support for the Frente para la Victoria that led Néstor Kirchner into office, despite the lack of ideological changes among the electorate during the 2000s, shown in Figure 2.13. Although it might be odd to think of a spin-off of Partido Justicialista (PJ) in the left, Kirchner has certainly made it clear that he is a president on the left. But the interesting fact here is that, two years after the beginning of his term, the majority of support comes from the center and the center-right, which is not that different from the general ideological distribution on the whole population.

Bolivia   It is interesting to note the case of Bolivia. Given the behavior of Evo Morales, it would not be far-fetched to assume that his base of support— and that for his Movimiento al Socialismo (MAS)—was mostly located in the left of the ideological spectrum. But as Figure 2.14 shows, the ideological base of support for MAS by 2005—almost three months before Morales was elected—spreads almost uniformly across the ideological spectrum in a pattern that distinguishes MAS from other parties of the left in Latin America. Note the contrast with the general population, which is concentrated in the center of the ideological spectrum. This simply shows that Morales has a wide ideological constituency to cater to.

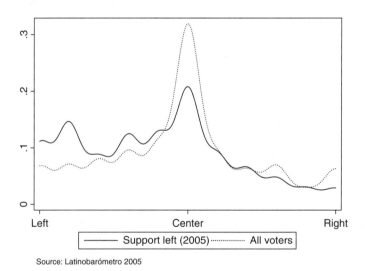

Source: Latinobarómetro 2005

Figure 2.14 Ideological support for MAS in Bolivia.

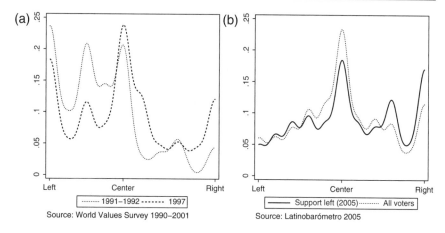

Figure 2.15 Ideological support for PT in Brazil.

Brazil The Brazilian case shows an even clearer story because it is possible to trace the evolution of support for Partido dos Trabalhadores (PT) over fifteen years. Graph (a) in Figure 2.15 shows that by the beginning of the 1990s, it was a party favored almost strictly by the left and the center. But as the decade passed, PT was able to get a much broader base of support that evolved to include more centrist voters and an important share of the center-right. This trend continued throughout the 2000s as can be seen in Graph (b), which shows that the support for PT has widened considerably to garner even more support from the center, but also much more support among those identified with the right. An interesting thing to note in Figure 2.15 is that PT was able to appeal to a broader base of support some years *before* Lula was actually able to win the presidency in 2002.

Chile This is also an interesting case worthy of discussion because we can follow the same coalition of parties—Concertación—over fifteen years, with the Christian Democrats holding the presidency during the 1990s, and the Socialists since 2000. If we trace the support for Concertación during this period (Figure 2.16), it is clear that its main base of support was the center by 1990, but it became more reliant on the left by the end of the decade. Notably, the support for Concertación has swung back to the center during the 2000s with a heavy reliance on the center-left. Note that the ideological distribution is less skewed on the general population. In general terms, Concertación has a wide base of support but this has receded to concentrate in the center and the center-left of the spectrum.

Nicaragua Following the Nicaraguan left equates following the Frente Sandinista de Liberación Nacional (FSLN). The only data available is for

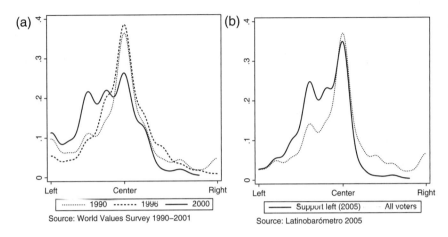

Figure 2.16 Ideological support for Concertación in Chile.

2005, almost a year before the election that took Daniel Ortega back to power. Figure 2.17 shows that the main base of ideological support for FSLN comes from the extreme left, although it also has some appeal to centrist and extreme-right voters. Note that the general distribution of voters, while also polarized, is mainly concentrated on the extreme right, followed by the center and the extreme left. As it stands, it seems that Ortega has much wider support among those identified with the left, but FSLN hasn't attracted much support from the extreme right and the center, which together constitute the majority of Nicaraguans. Interestingly enough, Ortega managed to become president without any ideological shifts to the left among Nicaraguans, as shown in Figure 2.17.

Peru   The peculiar history of the Peruvian left during the 1990s leaves little room to explore its ideological base of support, given its meager performance. But we can track instead the ideological support base for APRA during this period. Note from Graph (a) in Figure 2.18 that it was heavily reliant on the center and the center-right by 1996, but it had shifted to become more appealing to centrist voters by 2000. Graph (b) shows that, by 2005, APRA had become a party mostly supported by the center and the center-left, although still maintaining its supporters on the right. That is, roughly six months before the 2006 election, APRA had managed to construct a wide ideological base of support, to which Alan García must cater.

Uruguay   We only have data available to assess the ideological base of support of the Uruguayan Frente Amplio (FA) in 2005, which corresponds roughly to the first year of Tabaré Vázquez in office. Figure 2.19 reveals an interesting pattern: the support for FA comes almost exclusively from the

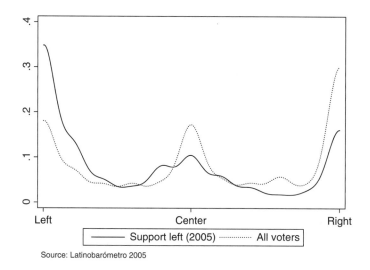

Source: Latinobarómetro 2005

Figure 2.17 Ideological support for FSLN in Nicaragua.

center and the left, and clearly not from the right. Even while the general ideological distribution in the population is also heavily skewed towards the left of the spectrum, the support for FA concentrates markedly in a range limited by the left and the center.

Venezuela The dotted line in Graph (a) of Figure 2.20 corresponds to the bases of ideological support for Causa R and Movimiento al Socialismo (MAS), the main parties from the left prior to the foundation of Hugo

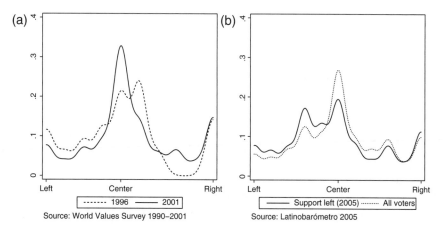

Figure 2.18 Ideological support for APRA in Peru.

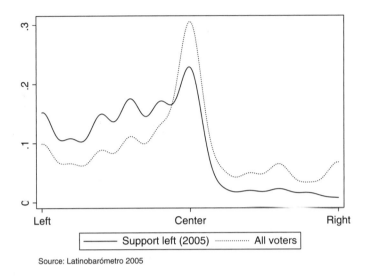

Source: Latinobarómetro 2005

Figure 2.19 Ideological support for FA in Uruguay.

Chávez's Movimiento Quinta República (MVR). Note the wide but skewed to the left ideological distribution of the supporters of both parties. The solid line in the same graph corresponds to the support for MVR in 2000, roughly five months after that year's election. Note that, compared to MAS and Causa R, the ideological base of support for MVR was more skewed to the center and the right than the parties from the left in that year. Graph (b) shows the ideological support for MVR in 2005, almost a year before the 2006 election. Here, we see that the ideological support for MVR comes

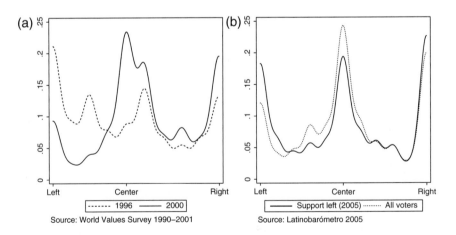

Figure 2.20 Ideological support for the left in Venezuela.

overwhelmingly from the center, but also from the extreme left and right. The ideological distribution for the whole population shows that Venezuela is highly polarized, but also that the ideological distribution of MVR supporters is not so different from that of the general population.

Although Ecuador is also one of the countries where the self-proclaimed left achieved power, the data available for 2005 does not allow assessing the sources of support for Correa, as his Alianza PAIS was created after this time.

A second assessment

It seems to be the case that the surge of the left in the region was not necessarily the result of Latin Americans becoming more leftist. The more plausible story is that the leftist parties that won elections were skilled at broadening their appeal beyond those that identify with the left. It is noteworthy that by 2005 all parties in power from the left, except for Nicaragua, have centrist voters as the core of their constituencies. MAS in Bolivia, PT in Brazil, APRA in Peru, and MVR in Venezuela have been particularly successful in creating wide bases of support. At the other end is FSLN in Nicaragua, which is overwhelmingly supported by the extreme left, although it does not alienate centrist and rightist voters. And in between these poles, we find Chile's Concertación, Uruguay's FA and Peru's APRA, with more concentrated constituencies that nearly exclude the right and center-right. Following the pattern, even candidates that won with less than a strict majority of the votes—Argentina and Nicaragua—were able to form broad ideological coalitions that are not only limited to the voters that identify with the left.

It is hard to establish a clear line of causality. Was it strictly the case that as the parties from the left became more moderate—or included more postmaterialist issues (Inglehart 1997) in their discourse—they were able to attract a large ideological base of support? We couldn't confidently rule out that parties from the left were forced to moderate their discourse or broaden their platforms as more people came to support the parties from the left. Most likely, causality runs in both directions. But leaving the issue of causality aside, the fact that the parties from the left that are now in office have constituencies that include almost all regions of the ideological spectrum does have political consequences, especially if these officials and their parties want to remain in office.

Discussion and conclusion

Many explanations have been advanced for the recent surge of governments from the left in Latin America. The majority of them are related to the existence of poverty and inequality that translates into mass mobilization (Cleary 2006), or to the discontent caused by bad economic performance (Panizza and Yáñez 2005). A troubling fact with these types of explanations is that poverty and inequality have been staples of the Latin American reality for a long time and have not particularly worsened in the last few years. But also, if it is the effects of economic reforms that Latin Americans are trying to minimize, there would be no reason to elect—and reelect—governments from the left that are, for the most part, comfortable with market economics. More traction could be gained from these explanations, but not without first addressing the flawed causality in the arguments and this is certainly not the place to do so.

This chapter, implicitly, advances an additional and more pragmatic perspective: candidates from the left have been elected into office when they have been able to garner broad ideological coalitions of voters that are not only limited to the left and include the center and moderate positions, and sometimes the right. Why? It is hard to point out a single reason. But it is certainly the case that parties from the left have been able to present more appealing candidates, and those who were not so appealing once have learned their lessons and fine-tuned their candidacies to attract more voters, mainly by moderating their discourse.

The evidence presented here also shows that Latin Americans have, for the most part, undergone ideological shifts: to the right during the 1990s and to the left during the 2000s. Even though most governments from the left have been elected during this shift to the left, it is hard to make a credible case for the election of leftists to be causally related to the ideological shift to the left. Such a claim would be especially dubious, as most of the candidates that finally won presidential elections during the 2000s had been recurring candidates during the 1990s, when they built most of their support, and most of this implied widening their base of ideological support. It seems that it is not that Latin Americans have turned left so much as that the left has finally turned to Latin Americans. That is, the left began winning elections once it stopped catering exclusively to leftists and began speaking to the general array of voters.

At the end of the day, why should this be an important matter to look into? One relevant answer is that the ideological distribution of a party's supporters might have a strong influence in the policies a party is willing to implement in order to maintain support *and* remain in office. Thinking in terms of median voter models so popular now in Political Economy (Alesina and Rodrik 1994; Llavador and Oxoby 2005, for example): the more restricted to the left is the support a leftist party maintains, the closer it is to implementing its most preferred policies without constraints, but unless a large enough mass of voters is located in this area, all of its electoral bids will be unsuccessful. In order to win, it needs to create a broader coalition. But the broader the coalition, the less extreme the median—pivotal—voter will be, and the more constraints a party from the left will have on implementing its preferred policies if it is to be reelected. It seems to be the case that the successful parties from the left in Latin America have recognized the need to appeal to a larger base, but this has also constrained them to implement less extreme policies.

What seems clear is that a full account of the surge of the left in Latin America would be incomplete if we were only to look at context and elites. It is true that elites select the rules and thus generate the incentives for candidates to self-select into a presidential race. But it is also true that voters decide which of the available candidates will end up in office. The empirical evidence offered by this chapter aims at providing an additional element towards a more complete understanding of the Latin American left as a result of the interaction between rules, candidates and voters using the lens of ideological orientations.

Appendix

World Values Survey data   European Values Study Group and World Values Survey Association. European and World Values Surveys Four-Wave Integrated Data File, 1981–2004, v.20060423, 2006. Aggregate File Producers: Análisis Sociológicos Económicos y Políticos (ASEP) and JD Systems (JDS), Madrid, Spain/Tilburg University, Tilburg, Netherlands. Data Files Suppliers: Análisis Sociológicos Económicos y Políticos (ASEP) and JD Systems (JDS), Madrid, Spain/Tilburg University, Tilburg, Netherlands/Zentralarchiv für Empirische Sozialforschung (ZA), Cologne, Germany:) Aggregate File Distributors: Análisis Sociológicos Económicos y Políticos (ASEP) and JD Systems (JDS), Madrid, Spain/Tilburg University, Tilburg, Netherlands/Zentralarchiv für Empirische Sozialforschung (ZA) Cologne, Germany.

The exact phrasing of the ideological location and party preference question is as follows:

> [E033] In political matters, people talk of "the left" and "the right." How would you place your views on this scale, generally speaking? (scale 1 for left and 10 for right)
> [E179] If there were a national election tomorrow, for which party on this list would you vote? Just call out the number on this card. If DON'T KNOW: Which party appeals to you most?
>
> (2001)

> [E179] If there was a general election tomorrow, which party would you vote for? COUNTRY SPECIFIC LIST OF POLITICAL PARTIES.
>
> (1999)

> [E179] If there were a [COUNTRY] election tomorrow, for which party on this list would you vote? Just call out the number on this card.
>
> (1995)

Sample sizes and dates for each country and wave are detailed in Table 2.1.

Table 2.1 WVS country sample sizes

Country	W2 (1990–1992)	W3 (1995–1997)	W4 (1999–2001)
Argentina	Feb–Apr 1991 n=1002	Aug 1995 n=1079	Jan–Feb 1999 n=1280
Brazil	Nov 1991–Jan 1992 n=1782	Aug 1997 n=1149	—
Chile	May 1990 n=1500	Spring 1996 n=1000	Nov 2000 n=1200
Mexico	Jun–Jul 1990 n=1531	Sep 1995–Mar 1996 n=1510	Jan–Feb 2000 n=1535
Peru	—	May 1996 n=1211	July 2001 n=1501
Venezuela	—	Mar–April 1996 n=1200	Dec 2000 n=1200

Latinobarómetro data   Datasets for 2001 and 2005 downloaded from organization's website (www.latinobarometro.org) on June 1, 2007. The exact phrasing of the ideological location and party preference question is as follows:

[P34ST] In politics, people normally speak of left and right. On a scale where 0 is left and 10 is right, where would you place yourself?
[P48ST] If an election were held next Sunday, which party would you vote for?

Table 2.2 Latinobarómetro country sample sizes

Country	Sample size (2001)	Sample size (2005)
Argentina	1200	1200
Bolivia	1080	1200
Brazil	1000	1204
Chile	1200	1200
Colombia	1200	1200
Costa Rica	1000	1000
Ecuador	1200	1200
El Salvador	1000	1010
Guatemala	1000	1000
Honduras	1000	1000
Mexico	1253	1200
Nicaragua	1000	1200
Panama	1000	1008
Paraguay	600	1200
Peru	1023	1200
Uruguay	1200	1200
Venezuela	1200	1200

Data for 2001 was collected simultaneously between April 1, 2001, and May 31, 2001. Interviews for 2005 were collected between August 1, 2005, and September 10, 2005. Sample sizes for each country are detailed in Table 2.2.

Notes

1 To avoid the nuisance of defining the left using some "objective" criteria, governments from the left are simply those that claim to be on the left, as suggested by Castañeda and Navia (2007)
2 For a detailed discussion of the effects on electoral outcomes derived from candidates changing positions vis-à-vis the electorate changing position see Fiorina's (2006) suggestive account for the American case.
3 A caveat is in place: WVS data uses ten-point scales, while Latinobarómetro prefers eleven-point scales with slightly different question phrasings. Despite these limitations, this is the best available data that can provide valuable insights regarding trends in the ideological shifts in Latin American public opinion.
4 From this point on, all statements on ideological shifts in the country or regional populations are based on t-tests performed to assess the difference in means at the 0.5 significance levels or higher. That is, all claims of "ideological shifts" are supported by t-tests that reject the null hypothesis of equal means, and the direction of the shift is assessed in the same manner. For brevity of exposition, the actual test results are not shown, but are available from the author.
5 Where available, data will be provided for the period 1990–2005, otherwise data will correspond exclusively to the 2001–2005 period.
6 I thank John Jost for pointing this out to me.

Part II

What has the left done right (or wrong)?

Chapter 3

A tale of ecumenism and diversity

Economic and trade policies of the new left

Diana Tussie and Pablo Heidrich

The leftist tide that appears to be sweeping the Americas south of the Rio Grande has given rise to controversies of old as well as new vintage, ranging from whether the policies are good or bad and for whom, how sustainable they are, and how this tide resembles or differs from the left or the populism of yesteryear. The main objective of this chapter is to analyze these questions and place them in the context of the larger debate which is the overall topic of the book.

After almost two decades of technocratic reforms, and with commodity prices soaring, in one country after another leftist administrations are coming to power. This seems to be a response for a region caught between two sets of closely related challenges: on the one hand rising mass mobilization, and on the other strong public (but not elite) discontent with reform strategies, questioned by their failure to generate high levels of growth, to incorporate disenfranchised groups and to promote more equitable patterns of income distribution.

Is there an economic policy intrinsic to the new tide of left of center governments? If so, what are their goals and policy instruments? Could their analysis contribute to our understanding of the nature of those administrations? We propose to focus on this latter point, while using the dual challenges of rising mass mobilization and social demands as the backdrop to the unsettling tensions that usually undermine economic strategies. We assume that policies require a new balancing act that can address popular dissatisfaction and social equity as fully integrated issues, and in that light, economic and trade policies are central to the very identity of governments in current discussions in the region.

For example, Néstor Kirchner in Argentina came from the Peronist Party, the quintessential populist movement, one that, given its capacity to control both the electorate and organized labor, over a fifty-year time span has been able to go from the historical populist nationalism of Perón to the neoliberal conservative policies of Carlos Menem.[1] Kirchner was, however, to most local and foreign observers today a leftist president by virtue of his economic policies (*The Economist*, November 14, 2006). In contrast, Luiz Inácio "Lula" da Silva in Brazil and Michelle Bachelet in Chile are both presidents elected on leftist and center-left tickets, but both have been systematically accused of holding on to orthodox or neoliberal economic policies by domestic and foreign critics (*La Voz del Interior*, October 31, 2006). Lula founded the Partido dos Trabalhadores (PT), the largest leftist organization in Brazil, and Bachelet is a long-standing political figure of the Chilean Socialist Party, a member of the ruling Concertación there. All these three presidents have their just or unjust labels of leftist pale when compared to other leaders, such as Chávez from Venezuela and Morales from Bolivia, who claim for themselves the role of modernizing and boosting up "true Socialism to the Twentieth Century in the region" (Touraine 2006). They have both introduced important reforms in their economies and display very radical discourses, announcing even more changes to come.

We confront, then, a double paradox. Leaders who were not envisaged as leftists are seen nowadays as such, and others who were supposed to be leftists are in fact perceived as not being so. Meanwhile, others claim to be the true leftists in every speech and take high-profile measures in order to prove it, seemingly in countercurrent with the evident dismissal of socialism worldwide since the 1990s as a strategy of economic development. For those living in Latin America today as well as those observing it close up from outside, the discussion of what is to be leftist while in office is then in great part due to the content of economic policies. But is there a discernible trend in the economic policy of the present left? Have specific leftist practices been adapted to the advent of globalized capitalism? If so, how? Can the contours of policies be defined or do they resist definition? Can detected particularities be condensed into a unity of sorts to characterize the present trend? The objective is to revise the contemporary discussion in a manner which understands differences both over time and between countries to account for the wide array of down-to-earth economic policies that are now practiced.

A conceptual framework: a left-looking window or looking left from a window?

Historically, the political left in Latin America has identified with goals of social justice, economic development, national emancipation, and socio-economic equality (Castañeda 1993). In terms of policies, it advocated redistribution of wealth through progressive taxation, structural reforms (such as agrarian reform), the expansion of welfare services, the protection and expansion of workers' rights, a strong participation of the state in the process of industrialization, and hostility to foreign capital (Panizza 2005a). The left has had, however, very few chances to be in office in the past, with Arbenz in Guatemala in the 1950s, Allende in Chile in the 1970s, the Sandinistas in Nicaragua, and Alan García in Peru in the 1980s.[2] All tried to implement some or all of the above policies with these goals in mind, but were victims of their own financial mismanagement and political destabilization that ended in the meltdown of their governments with high costs for those very populations to which they had meant to bring improvement. Judging by past experience one might have thought, then, that leftist economic policies were a dead end and that their proponents would most likely never be returned to office.

In fact, from the ashes these parties (and on occasion the same leaders) have been voted back into office, but in a transformed manner. Their ultimate goals may remain nominally the same but their old policies to attain those goals have been jettisoned. Not only are the new leftist governments taking account of the interplay over time of the collapse of socialism and broad structural economic changes. There has also been a sizeable learning process. The origins of learning and adaptation started in the late 1980s, through two watershed experiences. One was the advent of a pro-market set of reforms under the Washington Consensus with neoliberal or centrist technocratic governments in the 1990s, which fundamentally changed the political economy of the region, specifically the relations between states and markets, as well as capital and labor, profoundly opening these countries to international trade and financial flows. The second is that the political left (except in Chile and Costa Rica) was only able to gain local government postings during that same period, managing states or provinces such as Rio Grande do Sul in Brazil and large metropolises such as Buenos Aires, Rosario, Montevideo, Bogotá, Mexico City, and São Paulo. The combination of both experiences implied an adjustment of perceptions to the new reality, where the policies to achieve those objectives of social justice and economic development would have to be necessarily adapted (Panizza 2005b).[3]

The structural adjustment of the 1990s drastically reduced (but did not eliminate) state ownership in the economy, liberalized prices for essential goods and services and, most importantly, opened up the economies to external competition. In addition, the leftist parties' experiences at local government during that decade of reforms provided lessons on what an effective agenda for social policy could be, although extrapolation to a national administration could still be tricky.

The resultant, then, was not "the end of history" but the translation of lessons learnt into new economic conditions and a new climate of opinion composed, on one hand, of a positive consensus born of the experiences in local government (i.e. the need to step up public investment in health and education, to bring the state back in to coordinate the provision of physical infrastructure and energy, and other measures assisting the overall competitiveness of the economy) and, on the other, of a negative consensus derived from the critique of neoliberalism (i.e. a moratorium on privatizations, stricter regulation of private monopolies, and a halt to further unilateral trade liberalization).

But the learning from the neoliberal experiences of the 1990s has been much more impressive and far reaching than that. In fact, it transcends the repetitive chorus of leftist politicians criticizing those reforms now and it informs the most substantial debates on macroeconomic policy in today's Latin America. The main lesson is that massive fiscal deficits—just as current and trade deficits—are unsustainable over time. No amount of continuous pro-market reforms can feed the expectations of future gains of foreign and local investors for ever. Eventually, even the most neoliberal governments can lose favor if they do not balance the fiscal and monetary books. That is the lesson learnt from Menem's Argentina, Battle's Uruguay, Cardoso's Brazil, Frei's Chile, Salinas' Mexico and several others. In all those cases, financial crises provoked by these governments' systematic lack of concern for deficits, or contagion from crises in countries with similar vulnerabilities, brought them political disfavor. And that is precisely the juncture where the political left has come to power in most Latin American countries. In a period of less than two years after each financial crisis, leftist parties or candidates won the following presidential election. In a world of integrated trade and capital markets, floating currencies, and volatile financial markets, the limits of the possible sting are in everyone's mind, and even more so for governments either on a leftist ticket or attempting to follow leftist policies.

The alternative, then, has been to construct a government that can uphold an agenda with a leftist heart, with policies that emphasize local responses to cover social deficits, but remain fiscally conservative, not merely because of the primacy of previous lessons from the left of the 1970s and 1980s, but to adequately compete with the party that was previously in office, showing the electorate that in fact a left-of-center administration can be *more* socially sensitive *and more* economically responsible. Both components, a social heart and a responsible pocket, play at once, and have key electoral importance. These must be made compatible with walking on the tightrope of the day-to-day running of economic affairs once in office.

The dividing line between the left and populism is often blurred in the region, and more so in an era of mediatized and globalized politics. For some influential authors, populism is "the very essence of the political" (Laclau 2005, p. 222), "the mirror of democracy" (Panizza 2005a, p. 99). Furthermore, the construction of a people is "the political operation *par excellence*" (Laclau 2005, p. 153). Even with this positive view of populism as an almost necessarily recurrent development, there is no a priori guarantee that the people as a historical actor will be constructed around a progressive identity. Paradoxically, the fact that populism can represent "the people" as an oppressed whole in a society also contributes to blur the extreme income inequalities, poverty, and political polarization that characterize every society in the continent.

Populism—and to a certain extent even more than the left—in Latin America has a long and ample history allied to charismatic leaderships. Nonetheless, the background conditions favoring the birth of populist options have not been wiped out. They revive with relative ease in contexts where social and economic demands remain unsatisfied, political parties suffer from recurrent discredit and there is a general lack of trust in equal treatment before the law. The gap between what democracy ought to mean and what it actually means remains extremely wide. Such realities applied equally to mainstream parties unable to conduct urgent economic reforms in the late 1980s and early 1990s, and also overwhelmed by populist newcomers, such as Fujimori in Peru or Collor de Melo in Brazil.

One could say that populist manners are never really put aside in some leftist governments thanks to their assessment that status quo institutional arrangements ought to take a back seat to other urgencies, such as redistribution of wealth in Bolivia and Venezuela and jump-starting economic growth in Argentina. That assessment is grounded on the recent experiences of severe institutional crises in these democracies, with revolts in these three countries and lack of voters' turnout in Venezuela and Argentina. This analysis also implies that a populist detour from democracy "in order to save it" is, however, temporary because once these grievances or lacks are addressed and there is a certainty that they will continue to be addressed by non-populist political alternatives, the populists can be defeated in elections. This is, however, a slippery road, as electoral competition is highly sensitive to the consequences of economic policies and, especially, to the disregard for institutions.

For the purpose of analyzing the economic policies of the new leftist administrations in Latin America, we only consider populism as a style of government that regards economic policies as tools with specific *political* goals in mind, and not necessarily to take stock of economic realities. For such populism, these political goals are, in order of importance, to mobilize support within organized labor and lower middle-class groups, to obtain complementary backing from domestically oriented (largely small and medium-sized) businesses, and to isolate politically the landed oligarchy, foreign enterprises, and big business. The corresponding economic policies are, also in order of importance, neo-Keynesian budget deficits to stimulate domestic demand, nominal wage increases plus price controls to affect income redistribution, and exchange-rate controls and appreciation of the currency to control inflation and to raise wages and profits in non-tradable goods sectors (Dornbusch and Edwards 1991). In trade policy, populist policies would go along lines such as the increase of real rates of protection via non-tariff barriers, or outright raising of tariffs to consolidated levels, grandstanding and nay-saying posturing in trade negotiations to derail multilateral and regional trade talks, arbitrary controls on sources of hard currency, affecting trade volume and flows, plus conflating trade negotiations with declarations of standing up to or caving in to American interests, or other sources of foreign capital present in the domestic economy. This account is based on the historical record of past populist experiences, usually recalled when suggesting that some of the current left-of-center governments are just reborn populists.

Having defined what we mean by leftist economic policies, their stated goals and learning process while out of office, as well as the persistent populist traditions of Latin America, we focus now on two complementary exercises. We analyze first the external face of these leftist governments, namely their foreign trade policies, as a way to observe their relationship patterns with the global economy. Such reading allows us to see them as a whole, expressing their similarities and differences towards each other at once. We will analyze then their national economic policies, country after country, to see in a comparative form what their similarities and differences are grounded on domestically.

Trade policy: that wild side of the Latin American left

In Latin America, as in anywhere else, trade policy processes have unique distributional features which we need to take into account when thinking about the conformation of political regimes. Under import-substitution in this region, for example, it was politically easier to turn to high tariffs to protect mobilized working- and middle-class constituencies from international market shocks than to instrument efficient systems of social welfare in times of crises (Kaufman and Stallings 1991). The emphasis on the domestic market justified measures then destined for all types of wage support. Business and labor were able to fix a price structure which favored that Keynesian social compact, drawing together domestic producers and workers. The international distributional effects of trade were at that time undercover; if and when they emerged, business and labor met on the same side in favor of retaining protection, sustaining high wages and domestic consumption. But when layer after layer of trade protection was finally shed, as in the 1990s reforms in Latin America, the international price structure became internalized and the international negotiations that followed had an evident and immediate impact on prices and incomes.

Once the phase of unilateral trade opening was completed in the 1990s, gains in efficiency were absorbed and productivity for those sectors that survived the opening was impressive. Latin America changed from a region with low exports concentrated in just a few primary goods to one where a widening range of manufactures and processed commodities drives foreign trade growth. Such strong development has come short, however, in at least three important dimensions: exports have grown less than those of other developing regions, especially East Asia and Eastern Europe, resulting in less global importance for Latin America; exports have remained very sensible to external protectionism in North America and the European Union; and finally, but most important, the growth in exports of Latin American countries has not been able to finance the even stronger growth in imports, product of the unilateral opening of the 1990s, making debt financing an essential support for these policies.

Such triple challenge was taken on aggressively by private actors, pushing governments to improve their trade policymaking. The conditions were ripe when Latin America was overridden by a series of financial and economic crises in the 1998–2002 period, and trade deficits contributed greatly to marking countries as economically vulnerable. This showed that the previous policy of just opening unilaterally and making "open regionalism" with neighbors was insufficient to generate balanced trade accounts.

Therefore, and in order to sustain present levels of openness to trade, governments have focused instead on signing preferential and reciprocal trade agreements at the bilateral and subregional levels. The main drivers of this are the new "heroes" of trade policy: the exporting firms, which lobby governments on which preferences to seek and what markets to target. In Latin America, this may mean often—but not always—the traditional "export oligarchies" of yesteryear linked to the exports of commodities, and new ones such as those linked to metallurgy and telecoms.

Beyond that symbolism, there is an undiluted requirement on governments to seek reciprocity in all negotiations, bringing new teeth to Latin American negotiators, and that should not be confused with political (leftist) militancy. But on the other side, the incidence of reciprocity means that the gains obtained abroad for a given export require a "concession" in the domestic market. Hence, this process leads to heightened import competition and increased domestic sensitivity to the adjustment process, a combination that in a democratic setting cannot be wished away (Gilligan 1997).

As most tariffs have already been reduced drastically in the region, trade negotiations are no longer just about trade but about exchanging concessions, including other areas related to it such as investors' rights, intellectual property rights, and government procurement. That is particularly the case in the Free Trade Area of the Americas (FTAA) and in the bilateral deals bargained with the United States, but also in those between Mercosur and the European Union. To the extent that Latin American countries still have a willingness and capacity to employ those policy instruments, they are relevant bargaining chips to obtain market access in the markets their exporters desire.

Trade has, after the crises, acquired an unprecedented salience in domestic politics. The emergence of articulate international coalitions and domestic pressure groups now constrain government action and require intense efforts of interest articulation. The common tendency to view trade negotiations as straight liberalization, with cheating taking place on all sides, fails to capture the complexity of the reciprocal bargaining game in place. The weaving of negotiating positions has thus become not merely a technical task but, moreover, a touchy political one in a game that pits export-oriented winners against import-competing losers.

The current governments of Brazil and Argentina, in particular, have often been portrayed as reluctant participants in trade negotiations, and especially in the American project to create the FTAA. Several reasons lie behind this image. In the first place, both are sizeable economies with dense domestic markets; both are the least open economies of the region with the highest average regional tariff (14.3 percent) and with exports accounting for less than 20 percent of GDP. Local business interest in the hemispheric initiative has been lukewarm and, according to public opinion polls, mostly indifferent. A referendum organized in Brazil in 2002 by more than sixty civil society organizations with the support of the National Confederation of Catholic Bishops revealed that more than 90 percent of the people that cast a vote were opposed to the FTAA and in favor of quitting negotiations altogether.

Brazil stands apart in other respects too. Brazil's main exports to the United States—which range from relatively high-tech goods such as aircraft, tractor-parts, explosion engines, and telecommunications equipment to low-skilled labor-intensive goods such as footwear, and semi-processed natural resources like sugar, orange juice, and iron ore—have often been the target of the wide gamut of U.S. protectionist instruments (tariff peaks, antidumping and countervailing duties, to name a few). That has been the case, for instance, with orange juice, footwear, apparel, and sugar exports.

The demand for attention to these issues is not necessarily anti-liberalization altogether. While the export gains may be embraced, they are not done at all costs, but with a demand to obtain access to markets which could conceivably generate some economic growth, perhaps in exchange for limited openings of some segments of the market. At the core is a developmentalist reaction to repackage trade adjustment, a concern with distribution which accepts inevitability but seeks to manage potentially destructive aspects with continuous counterproposals, as often expressed by Brazil and the other Mercosur countries in the Doha Round of the World Trade Organization (WTO). Ultimately the aim is an attempt at consensus-building with the new players capable of holding the balance, an attempt to bring together the external face of the government together with the concern with development and social justice at home.

The Brazilian posture towards the United States throughout the negotiation process has been critical but knowledgeable and never as confrontational as Venezuela's. The distinction is important. Economic isolation is not on the cards. The aim is to preserve the domestic market while at the same time opening access for business abroad. The direction is evident in the Brazilian efforts to build the South American Community of Nations, bringing together the countries of the Andean Pact with those of Mercosur, through initiatives of energy integration and development of physical infrastructure (Giacalone 2006). While it might constitute a direct challenge to U.S. desires of hemispheric free trade, it is seen in Brazil as the simple projection of national exporters' interests in regional markets. Such initiative does have the support of Argentina, also interested in expanding its exports to the region, while it waits out U.S. agricultural protectionism, a search for balance that is long-standing in Brazil and therefore pre-dates the present administration. No doubt some of Lula's achievements in this regard owe much to his predecessor, Fernando Henrique Cardoso.

The fact that these initiatives were put together by right-of-center governments in Brazil (Cardoso) and Argentina (De la Rúa) does not stop new leftist administrations from following up on them, to strong public support. Indeed, such continuity shows the increase in export lobbying as the engine of policy, a general trend at the heart of our argument. With disparate degrees of intensity it has acquired force in all countries, even directing some to making alliances with the United States. But in all cases, the incidence of these agreements on inequality and income distribution has become the issue of first-order priority in polarized political campaigns.

Moving away from regional integration, Chile, Peru and Uruguay have strong exporting interests that see themselves as able to enter the U.S. market in spite of American protectionism. Their production mix, anchored on fresh produce—as opposed to traditional agricultural exports—and small size, in the case of Uruguay, are the basis for such understanding. Chile was an early mover in this regard, signing a free trade agreement with the United States in 2003; Peru negotiated from 2004 onwards, and the new leftist government of Alan García—elected in 2006—voted it through congressional approval. Uruguay had tried negotiating with the United States as well since 2003, and again, the new government of Tabaré Vázquez has continued that policy, in spite of strong domestic and Mercosur opposition. As a consequence of such resistance, Tabaré Vázquez recently re-shuffled the initiative to signing a trade and investment framework agreement.

The turn to open economies, in sum, is seen as a good thing in the long run by almost all leftist governments in Latin America. But their different directions, towards a regionalist or a bilateralist posture in trade negotiations, are to be read in function of their objective exporting interests, much beyond the current political sign of their governments. What remain intrinsically political are the ways to deal with the transitional costs and the collective action problem derived from trade negotiations. In highly unequal societies with an impaired tax base, such as these in Latin America, these costs place a major limit on the capacity of governments to deal with the distributive pressures that stem from sudden income loss, when economies open up to trade.

As a way of comparison, in the small open Scandinavian economies, the expansion of welfare transfers has been part and parcel of liberal trade policies, being applied especially to even out the differential gains and losses associated with international market shocks and trade shifts (Gourevitch 1986). Since such welfare state models and the taxation policies they require are difficult, if not impossible, to implant in Latin America, the new left-leaning governments must seek to redress the social imbalances with a patchwork quilt of policies, some social transfers, some provision of social goods, and some political limits to the free rein of market forces. Governments there juggle with the two competing forces typified by Karl Polanyi's classic volume as a "double movement" in which two organizing principles interact one with the other. Each principle sets specific institutional aims, has the support of discernible social forces, and uses its own distinctive methods:

> The one was the principle of economic liberalism, aiming at the establishment of a self-regulating market, relying on the support of the trading classes, and using largely laissez faire and free trade as its method; the other was the principle of social protection aiming at the conservation of man and nature as well as productive organization, relying on the varying support of those most immediately affected by the deleterious action of the market.
>
> (Polanyi 1944, p. 132)

This double movement may be the hallmark of the post-reform age in this region. In the next section we look at how governments now deal with the pincer movement unleashed by trade shifts in an era of rocket-high export prices and heightened social demands.

Looking at the colors and sizes of leftist administrations

This section compares the national experiences of leftist governments in Latin America, starting with those perceived as leftist, such as Kirchner's in Argentina, continuing with those self-defined as leftist, such as Lagos' and Bachelet's Chile, Lula's Brazil, and Tabaré Vázquez's Uruguay, and ending with those claiming to be leftist, such Chávez's Venezuela and Morales' Bolivia. In all cases, there is a marked difference made between intending to carry out a leftist agenda of social justice and self-determination at the micro level and the macro policies employed to manage the economy at large. The resultant is that while the first provides improvement in social indicators, those can also be achieved by across-the-board macro policies; and the results of the latter ones could be much strengthened by having an accompanying social policy. These reflections are not alien to a liberal approach to politics, central to Western thought, as summarized by John Rawls (1971): "The principle of efficiency cannot serve alone as conception of justice" (p. 71).

With this reflection as a backdrop, we now propose to depict the different trajectories of these governments and their specific economic policies. We start with Argentina, where Néstor Kirchner took office in May 2003 with an economy just beginning to recover from its deepest crisis in history, and the consequent levels of poverty and unemployment it brought.[4] His macroeconomic administration has focused on pumping up fiscal surpluses, even after accounting for debt payments, keeping the currency undervalued to help the recovery of local industry and maintain a trade surplus, and controlling the inflationary adjustments of the devaluation done by the previous administration of Eduardo Duhalde. These three policies account for the dramatic upswing of the economy, growing at 8.5 percent yearly until 2007. Such accumulated growth more than recoups the losses accrued in the recession that marked the last years of the Carlos Menem and Fernando De la Rúa administrations and the final meltdown of the Convertibility scheme.

The achievement of the fiscal surplus included a very hard renegotiation of the foreign debt, in default since 2002. Kirchner managed in 2005 to get over 76 percent of the bondholders of the $100 billion debt to accept a reduction of 65 percent in the value of their bonds, thus reducing the weight of the total debt of Argentina to less than 60 percent of the GDP (EIU Argentina Country Report 2007). This allowed the government to expand its budget for public investment in infrastructure and subsidies for transportation and energy services, while restarting to pay its reduced debts, all while keeping a fiscal surplus. Notoriously, the fiscal largesse of Kirchner has not reached public sector employees and the pension system, where salaries are still 40 percent below their 2001 levels, after adjusting for inflation. Public employment has expanded less than 5 percent since 2003, also underlying the emphasis on putting monies on public works to promote the private level of economic activity (EIU Argentina Country Report 2007).

Investments in public infrastructure have accompanied increases of private investment in manufacturing and services, eventually reducing unemployment from 20.4 percent in 2003 to 9.7 percent in 2007. The ensuing policy reaction has been a dramatic reduction in welfare expenses, especially in the plan designed by the previous administration of Eduardo Duhalde, of minimum income for the unemployed, from 2.5 million beneficiaries to just 600,000. Besides, all beneficiaries are now to be moved to a World Bank-designed program that provides checks only to those doing retraining or proving to be actively looking for employment. Such trust in the benefits of a private-led recovery is partially confirmed in a reduction of poverty from 57 percent in 2003 to 27 percent today, a level considered still too high for historical standards in Argentina (ECLAC 2006b).

As the economy is visibly overheating from such speed of growth, the government since the end of 2005 has applied price controls to those goods measured in the state's inflation index. It has also created certain export controls, to reduce the translation of exports' international prices, measured in dollars, to local prices for similar goods, measured in devalued pesos. Those sectors are beef, corn, and wheat, accounting for over 10 percent of the total exports. His fiscal tightness has stopped any reductions in taxes, increased during the last efforts to prop up the Convertibility in 2001 and to manage the aftermath of its demise in 2002. Most visible among those are taxes on exports of primary goods, such as soybeans and petroleum.

Such macroeconomic conventionalism—strong fiscal accounts, competitive currency, and emphasis on physical infrastructure—moves on without going into any neoliberal measures, such as further privatizations of state banks or nuclear plants, as demanded by the International Monetary Fund (IMF) since 2002 but patently also, without going into large-scale nationalizations, currency controls or large real wage increases (Ramírez Gallegos 2006). In fact, his populist rhetoric criticizing the IMF role in Argentina's crisis and the complicity of international banks against his debt negotiations are in the strongest possible contrast with his mainstream macroeconomic policies and his visible disregard for social policy, as an instrument to reduce poverty. He seems to believe that markets indeed are the answer to accelerate economic growth in Argentina, of course under his rather severe "guidance," in the guise of selective price controls and some export taxes.

Lula provides the starkest possible contrast to Kirchner, which shows the uneasy relationship between the two presidents, visibly affecting the lack of progress in Mercosur, for example. Since Lula took office in Brazil in 2003, his promotion of socially conscious policies has radically changed the role of the state there, now providing minimum income levels to some 44 million people, or 25 percent of the population, through the *Bolsa Família* program (Hall 2006). His government has also made very systematic efforts to direct the little fiscal investment monies available at the federal level to installing running water and schools in the most impoverished areas of the Northeast of the country. Such efforts have paid out in reducing poverty nationally from over 30 percent to less than 25 percent in the last three years, a remarkable achievement when one considers that unemployment has increased from 8 percent to 10 percent in that same period, according to official figures (ECLAC 2006a).

These efforts to carry out a leftist agenda have, however, been accompanied by economic policies that have benefited the richest segments of society, especially those related to the financial sector. Lula has maintained extremely high interest rates in an effort to reduce inflation levels, which were at 17 percent when he took office, down to barely 3 percent today.

The price for that is the sky-high real interest rates that have boosted profits on the financial sector to record levels, while manufacturing and agricultural businesses suffer increasing costs just to borrow operating funds, and turns them away from further productive investment (EIU Brazil Country Report 2007). In fact, the Brazilian economy, long known for its vitality, has grown at 2.3 percent per year in the presidency of Lula, the second lowest rate in the whole of Latin America, better only than Haiti, immersed in civil strife.[5] While the economy barely expands at the rate of population growth and cannot possibly generate enough jobs for its new workers, short-term financial flows have moved to the country at breathtaking speed, now accounting for over 50 percent of the financing of the Brazilian state domestic debt, and whose profits were made tax-free by Lula in 2006, a benefit not even local investors receive (*Bloomberg*, November 14, 2006).

To finance such debt, now totaling over 65 percent of the GDP, between domestic and foreign, his government has had to issue more and more bonds, eventually paving the road to a large crisis in the next years. The only way out would be a reduction of fiscal expenditures in other items beyond debt payments, such as state wages and pensions, but Lula has emphasized that such changes will not happen under his clock (*The Economist*, October 10, 2006). In fact, during his presidency, state employment has grown at 2 percent per year, especially in state enterprises, such as Petrobras (17,000 new jobs, or 25 percent of the firm's workforce), Banco do Brasil, and others. Brazil, with one of the youngest populations in Latin America, already has a large retirement pension deficit, equivalent to 2 percent of the GDP. Still, Lula, after initially limiting pension benefits in 2003, has increased them by over 17 percent, more than compensating total inflation rates since 2003 (*Bloomberg*, July 21, 2006).

In sum, Lula's government has followed a leftist agenda to deal with social problems, especially aid to the poorest sectors of the population, generating state jobs and increasing pensions. In macroeconomic policy, his fiscal largesse has, however, contributed to an increasing debt, whose interest payments now consume over 8 percent of the GDP or 20 percent of total fiscal expenditures (IMF 2006). To sustain that, he has increased the size of the state in the economy to 40 percent of the GDP, but without investing much in public infrastructure or in production-friendly measures, such as softer credits (*Valor*, October 26, 2006). His monetary policy, with high real interest rates, has attracted foreign investors ready to finance him in return for high, quick profits, at the cost of an overvalued Brazilian currency. That in turn has lowered employment, brought in lots of imported manufactures, and reduced Brazilian competitiveness. Only high export prices for Brazilian primary goods, such as soybeans, sugar, iron ore, and coffee, have reduced the impact of these policies on the overall sustainability of Brazil (EIU Brazil Country Report 2006).

His government seems to believe that repeating some of the irresponsible management of previous centrist administrations of the 1990s can be electorally forgiven if social policies are put in place, and on a scale unseen before in Brazil. Such vision was certainly confirmed in his reelection in 2006, when the Northeast voted for the first time massively for his party, after decades of supporting conservative clientelist parties, while the industrialized South and the agricultural exporter Center voted strongly against him (Reuters, October 23, 2006). Only the fear Lula awoke of the supposedly privatizing tendencies of his neoliberal opponent allowed him to win in a second round, however. This was the political dictum on his policies, and as such it is very valuable insight on the electoral value of economic and social policies of such important left-of-center administration. It remains to be seen whether he will keep the markets' favor or, as has happened to other neoliberal and centrist governments before, they will turn on him when they decide he cannot really continue to afford favoring the poorest and the richest at once, and in such a radical manner.

Ricardo Lagos and Michelle Bachelet's administrations offer a rather moderate lesson on what being leftist might be like. Lagos had a much more difficult time than Bachelet, as the Chilean miracle appeared to be gone or suspended in 1998, when its economy went into recession. After fifteen years growing at the East Asian speed of 7 percent, GDP fell in 1998 and has grown at only 3.2 percent on average, way below the rate for all developing countries and just as good as mediocre performers in Latin America, such as Ecuador or El Salvador. The response of Lagos to that crisis was to reduce capital controls for financial flows, allow the currency to devalue, and argue strongly against the monetarist approach of his central bankers, bent on increasing interest rates to contain inflation (Weintraub 2002). He held a strong preference for higher inflation if that reduced the effect of the recession on unemployment, in the classic Keynesian sense. He also argued for fiscal deficits to finance public investments, a luxury no other Latin American country could afford, thanks to the small amount of public debt.

Lagos was not able to advance more of a true leftist agenda, such as a modernization of labor laws (enacted by Pinochet's dictatorship) and large increases in the budget for education and public health due to the weakness of his Concertación alliance. His partners in the alliance systematically vetoed those initiatives, just as much as the rightist opposition parties, afraid that more rights for workers and more state expenditures could stifle the hand of the market in Chile (*The Economist*, May 3, 2001). The strong reaction from the business community against those measures, and Lagos' critical rebukes to them, affected the investment climate in the country, contributing to its slow recovery from the 1998–1999 crisis, finally completed in 2003.

The good fortune of high commodity prices, which has also helped other Latin American countries, has assisted Chile more than any other.[6] Its main export, copper, accounting for over 60 percent of total exports in 2006, has skyrocketed, with its price growing by 310 percent since the lows of 2001. Bachelet arrived in that rapidly improving context but has not continued on her predecessor's lines, focusing instead on cosmetic measures to improve the efficiency of social expenditures. She has adamantly refused to provide any substantial increases in public education and health expenditures, producing the largest demonstrations in Chile's history this year, when over half a million students protested her education policy (*The Economist*, June 22, 2006). She remained focused instead on keeping the newfound government surpluses abroad for the use of future generations. In contrast to Lagos, she has not objected to the appreciation of the currency, to the detriment of non-copper exporters (of wines, fruits, and textiles), or to the very high real interest rates that favor financial over productive sectors (*Financial Times*, May 9, 2006). As in Brazil, the economy is growing timidly, and while poverty is low in Chile by regional standards, around 20 percent, there have been no improvements since 2001, more than six years ago, a break in the tendency of previous Concertación governments that eventually brought it down from over 40 percent in 1990 (ECLAC 2006b).

It was therefore no coincidence that in the 2005 elections her opposition mounted a very serious challenge with a populist billionaire, Sebastián Piñeira, who campaigned credibly on the failures of the Concertación to reduce poverty and, especially, to deal with increasing social inequality (COHA 2005). Interestingly, Piñeira made the argument that slowness in the reduction of poverty and inequality were relevant causes for the slower economic growth of the country in the last years, an idea that belongs to the most traditional critiques of the Latin American left-to-neoliberal governments.

Tabaré Vázquez in Uruguay illustrates an interesting mix of features already seen in the previously described leftist administrations. As with Lula and Bachelet, he follows a careful line in welcoming foreign investment and promoting the benefits of a careful management of fiscal and trade accounts. This is reflected in the strong flows of financial capital back to Montevideo since he took over, appreciating the currency, just as in Brazil and Chile, against the U.S. dollar. Building on the measures taken by the previous centrist government, Vázquez has overseen a recovery of the economy and important reductions in unemployment. That, combined with strong investments in social services and subsidies in the range of $100 million, has contributed to a reduction in poverty from 22 percent to 17 percent (ECLAC 2006b). But just as with Kirchner, the main thrusts of his government are in the provision of public infrastructure to accelerate economic growth, such as optic fiber for telecommunications, seaport improvements, and roads to assist the development of the new surging sector, cellulose plants.

Just as with Lula and Bachelet, Vázquez must carry the weight of having been chosen on an officially "leftist" ticket and thus be expected to follow leftist policies. He therefore shares the fate of being strongly criticized domestically by sectors of his electorate and his own party for following policies that do too little to reduce social inequality, favor foreign financial capital, and in trade, as explained before, seem too close to the United States (COHA 2006). Ironically, it is Kirchner who, chosen on a typically populist ticket of Peronism, surprised his country with policies soon branded as leftist, a label he never admitted to, preferring to be called, just like his "officially" leftist colleagues, a "pragmatist."

These nuances are impossible to apply to the rambunctious administrations of Hugo Chávez, the most senior of this new left, and Evo Morales, one of the newest comers to this club. Both claim to be socialist nowadays, and engage in deep institutional changes of their countries' politics and economics, harboring desires for radical change. Their speeches point to achieving strong changes in the distribution of wealth as well as of income, setting strict limits to the influence of foreign capital, and repeat their perception of a threatening United States. However, their deeds, in economic policy, provide a more interesting window to assert their claim to be the "true" leftists of this era in the region.

Chávez had already taken office over eight years ago, in a context of deep recession induced by very low oil prices ($12 per barrel in 1999, compared to $70 in June 2007), and of popular dissatisfaction with the political and economic establishment that had ruled the country since the 1950s. While in his first years he made radical reforms in the politics of the country with a new constitution; he filled the judiciary with his supporters and attempted to organize unions close to his party, but left the economy rather untouched. In fact, he maintained the policies of the previous administration, gradually reducing trade tariffs, keeping the Bolivar convertible and real interest rates very high to curb inflation via orthodox measures. He continued to receive foreign investment, at a pace of $3 billion per year from 1999 until 2001, largely thanks to the oil industry, and did not tighten up regulation in any important economic sector (*Business Week*, September 20, 1999). His approach to poverty reduction was, however, from the beginning very decisive, hiking expenditures in public education and health, establishing a system of transportation subsidies and, most importantly, a system of state-owned and worker-operated food markets and drug stores to cheapen basic goods for the poorest sectors of the population. In contrast, he slashed public funding for physical infrastructure, such as roads, ports, and energy transportation, all projects historically privileged by Venezuelan governments to buy support among the wealthiest elite, mostly dedicated to serving public contracts (Ellner and Hellinger 2003).

These socio-economic policies, plus his verbal sparring and aggressive rhetoric against the establishment of Venezuela, soon brought in the open support of Fidel Castro, who offered to exchange doctors and teachers, for the poorest sectors in Venezuela, for oil for Cuba. They also brought a radicalization of Chávez's opposition, which in 2002 attempted a coup d'état, headed by the main business leaders. When that failed, the opposition soon after promoted a strike in PDVSA, the state oil company, against Chávez's insatiable desire to control it. Even though that coup and the following strike did not succeed, the conflicts have continued as Chávez's main response since has been to radicalize his economic plans (Fletcher 2003).

And what he has followed since 2002 is a three-pronged strategy, clearly along the broad lines of Latin American historical populism: one initiative is to redefine the contracts with foreign oil companies to isolate PDVSA internationally, a second is to foster the growth of cooperative-state industrial and agricultural firms, and the third is to "migrate" Venezuela from the Andean Common Market to Mercosur. All measures are accompanied by a policy of keeping the currency overvalued to maximize private consumption (of imported goods, ironically) of salaried workers, currency controls to impede capital flight, and very lax fiscal and monetary policies to accelerate the economic recovery from the depression caused by the 2002 strike and coup attempt. This cocktail has produced a dramatic recovery in the GDP, growing at 8 percent per year from 2004 until the time of writing. High oil prices have certainly helped, mostly to expand the budgets allocated to social policies and the funding for the new cooperative sector (*The Economist*, July 30, 2005).

As often happens to such populist experiments, the results are in the short term very impressive: unemployment has fallen from 25 percent in 2003 to just 11 percent today, poverty from over 60 percent in 2002 (it was 52 percent in 1998) to less than 35 percent now, and there is an unprecedented consumption and construction boom driving the economy to clear overheating, expressed in an inflation rate of over 15 percent for 2006, under much stricter controls than Kirchner would ever dream of having, down in Argentina (ECLAC 2006b). The apparent success of this policy is most evident in the fact that in December 2006, for the first time, Chávez faced a serious challenger to the presidency, Manuel Rosales, who is an avowed populist, promising to expand social expenditures even more and to convert the increased funds for public education and health into cash vouchers to be given directly to the poorest sectors of the population, thus fueling the consumption boom even more. That would be a rather "privatized" but equally populist ending to the supposedly socialist Bolivarian Revolution of Chávez.

A more recent but often similar populist experiment is that of Evo Morales in Bolivia. After a year in power, changes in economic policy have been very few, and several of them in a rather counterintuitive direction. For example, he decreed the nationalization of the oil and gas industry, but called on foreign investors in this sector to accept new contracts that would turn them from owners of hydrocarbon reserves into providers of services for exploitation. After months of heavy bargaining, Morales eventually achieved his goal, with all foreign companies signing up to the new rules. This, plus a rise in taxes on that industry, which he had promoted while in opposition in 2005, has finally moved the Bolivian state from a deficit situation of 2.3 percent of the GDP in 2004 to a surplus of 5 percent in 2006 (ECLAC 2006a).

The big surprise is that such a massive increase in fiscal income has not been accompanied by a corresponding *populist* increase in expenditures, as in Venezuela. Morales has voiced his preference for following Bachelet's example, setting up a stabilization account abroad with the surplus funds (*The Economist*, December 13, 2006). The second surprise is that the Bolivian state, after decades of depending on foreign aid from European NGOs and the U.S. government, no longer needs either, and these agencies have lost their influence in Bolivian policymaking, as well as withdrawing their essential policy capacities from Bolivian ministries. Therefore, Morales' government has lost the capacity to channel those extra funds to social policy because his own bureaucracy is unable to do it. In that context, Morales' policy is to redistribute wealth proceedings—not income—with plans to nationalize mining, and redistribute agricultural land in the eastern provinces. Whether his administration has the capacity to instrument those changes, as opposed to implementing policies for gradual social improvement, remains an open question.

Table 3.1 summarizes these points, spelling out the ample diversity of specific policies being applied by current leftist administrations. It underscores the considerable pragmatic blending that goes on, and hence the difficulty of conceptualizing the phenomena of the new left in a dichotomous fashion as far as economic and trade policies are concerned.

Conclusions

The picture we present here shows the emergence of a fresh disposition and, in contrast with the agenda of the 1990s, a clear turnaround from the confidence in the cure-all ability of markets. There are also very stark differences with the old left associated with import-substitution, state capitalism, and over-expansionary macroeconomic policies. Considerable social learning shows the extent up to which specific leftist inclinations have been pragmatically adapted to new structural conditions. And economic policies show a strong awareness that volatile world markets can be ignored only at their own peril.

Two readings can be done from this progression. One is of a tidy order, commending some good leftist administrations for their apparent acceptance of globalized market forces, while deriding some others that intend to put some limit to those same forces. This understanding overstates political

Table 3.1 Summary of economic and trade policies implemented by governments of the left

	Monetary policy	Exchange policy (currency value)	Fiscal position (after debt payments)	Debt administration	Social expenditures	Support for FTA with the US	Support for regional integration
Lula	Tight	Overvalued	Deficit	High, increasing	High	No	Yes
Lagos	Loose	Devalued	Deficit	Very low	High	Yes	No
Bachelet	Tight	Overvalued	Surplus	Nil	Low	Yes	No
Vázquez	Tight	Overvalued	Deficit	High, but decreasing	High	Yes*	No
Chávez	Loose	Overvalued	Deficit	Low, and decreasing	Very high	No	Yes
Morales	Tight	Overvalued	Surplus	High, but decreasing	Low	Yes*	Yes
Kirchner	Loose	Devalued	Surplus	High, but decreasing	Low	No	Yes

*Vázquez has expressed opposition to the FTAA as its project stands today, but is inclined to sign a Trade and Investment Framework Agreement (TIFA) with the United States. Morales has asked for the continuation of the current level of trade preferences the United States grants to Andean countries as part of its drug eradication policy in that region.

measures of economic nature supposedly favoring global markets, such as trade agreements with the United States or privatizations, and those limiting them, such as selective price controls or contract renegotiations with foreign investors. We have argued that in the realm of economic policies this categorization does not provide an accurate picture. To take the example of Morales: while bent on renegotiating state contracts with foreign firms, his administration shows no distaste for a bilateral trade agreement with the United Sates; moreover, he has not caved in to pressures to follow in Chávez's footsteps and withdraw from the Andean Common Market, or commit massive amounts of fiscal revenues to social policies.

A more accurate picture requires standing clear of over-dichotomization, still taking the search for a new balance between states and markets into account. Thus leftist administrations must be ordered across the more realistic analysis of their central economic policies, including the whole array of trade policy options and constraints and, especially, the resultant from fiscal and monetary policies, these last two being the genuine and most objective indicators of these administrations' leanings and structural constraints, more relevant today than ideological likes and dislikes. In light of the arguments made earlier, this experience should not be altogether surprising. Pragmatic policies are those that package sound economic principles around national constraints and opportunities. Since these national circumstances vary, so do the policies that work. True, the shadow of Chávez, not quite a pragmatic figure, looms large in the Americas today. But Chávez's Venezuela (or oil-rich Venezuela, for that matter) is in a league of its own and not a safe benchmark from which to draw generalizations elsewhere in Latin America.

The many examples provided here, of qualitative and quantitative nature, imply that the left today in Latin America incorporates such a diversity of policies and leanings that the whole concept of *left* is rather narrow to account for all of them in a conclusive manner. National characteristics and the timing of these countries' recoveries from previous neoliberal experiments in the 1990s could provide an interesting alternative explanation. For example, those countries most negatively affected, such as Bolivia and Venezuela, are moving towards radicalized experiments of a populist tone; others less affected, such as Argentina, are moving to milder expressions of leftist policymaking (and verbal populism); and the least affected, such as Uruguay and Brazil, remain with similar economic and trade policies, as in the 1990s, plus much stronger social policy components. Only Chile seems to be backsliding under Bachelet, in its road to creating a government that is as socially sensible as it is macroeconomically sound.

All told, if we are to point out the single coincidence in this diversity, there is a very significant one: the emergence of a pragmatic belief in a role for state management. Such belief is not an unhealthy development for democracy, and even for the markets, as it injects in politics a sense that hope is not vain for confronting the enormous social demands in Latin America. It is also positive for market economics, as social expectations are no longer overplayed on them, and business can concentrate on doing business: produce and compete with each other. This points to a road where, within the context of a continued market liberal regional order and a mostly market liberal global economy, the scope for real clashes of interest and of values will remain wide, and it is in fact here that we will continue to see the deepest changes. Politics may now be allowed to come into its own, either on the left or on some other current: as such, we now urgently need nuanced concepts to take account of this interplay over time, and across countries and their particular circumstances.

Notes

1 Weyland (1999) and others have advanced the argument that Menem's administration as well as Salinas' in Mexico and Fujimori's in Peru were in fact populist governments with neoliberal agendas. While in this chapter, we look at the inclination of some new left governments in Latin America to follow populist trajectories, the possibility of an amicable relationship between populism and neoliberal agendas is not denied in terms of economic and trade policy.

2 Cuba is the exception, as Fidel Castro has ruled with a socialist agenda uninterruptedly since 1959. Such experience was influential on Latin American leftists in the 1960s and 1970s, but its influence has dramatically receded with the democratization of most Latin American countries since the 1980s. However, Castro's social and economic policies have been brought back as examples lately, but then only by Chávez in Venezuela and, to a lesser extent, by Morales in Bolivia.

3 At a more global level, the Latin American left has also had to cope with the dismissal of the Soviet Union and its "real" socialism. In terms of demonstrable effect, Soviet economic policies were eventually shown to have produced much less development than had been believed before, with much higher side-effects such as environmental degradation and inefficient use of resources. In terms of possible alliances, it definitely canceled the remote possibility of integrating to an alternative system to the one dominated by the United States.

4 GDP fell between 1998 and 2002 by a total of 20.7 percent, unemployment reached 24 percent, and poverty 60 percent (ECLAC 2006a).

5 According to the *Financial Times* (September 13, 2006), Brazil can no longer be considered part of the BRIC economies, the group pooling together the largest and most dynamic of the developing world, such as China, India, and Russia, because of its low rate of growth and continuous fiscal deficits.

6 According to the ECLAC annual trade report, for the 2003–2006 period high commodity prices explain over 70 percent of the growth in Chilean exports, 60 percent of Venezuela's, 50 percent of Brazil's, and close to 20 percent for Uruguay and Argentina (ECLAC 2006c).

Chapter 4

No such thing as a social advantage for the left?

José Merino

It is now a commonplace that Latin America has turned to the left as parties (or candidates) with this orientation have won elections in Chile, Nicaragua, Bolivia, Ecuador, Venezuela, Argentina, Uruguay, Peru, and Brazil. These developments have opened a door to a debate about the character of these administrations, both in terms of their performance and, in some cases, of their democratic credentials.

There is a central question and a prominent suspicion that this chapter seeks to address. The question is whether or not governments on the left have done better than those on the right in what can be seen as the centerpiece of their public agenda: social policy. Intuition suggests that, even in terms of social policy, there are two lefts in Latin America. One is based on solid party platforms, is not afraid of the market, and behaves acceptably in terms of social policy. The other is anchored on populist leaders, preaches against the market and free trade, and carries controversial and inefficient public policies.

The empirical evidence offered in this chapter shows that there is no obvious superiority of leftist governments over those on the right regarding social policy indicators. However, the same evidence leads us to conclude that non-populist leftist governments systematically outperform populist leftist governments. But a surprising conclusion arises as well: rightist populist cases did—for the most part—fare better than the left when assessing their performance in social policy.

The chapter is organized as follows. Section I provides a brief review of the arguments that relate ideology to public policy performance. Section II summarizes the arguments that distinguish between "good" and "bad" leftist governments in Latin America. Section III assesses the relative performance of left/right and populist/non-populist governments in terms of social policy by analyzing changes in social expenditure, social well-being indicators and the relationship between both. Finally, Section IV offers some concluding remarks.

Getting to the point: ideology and public policy

Left and right are categories used by political scientists to signal a particular ideological direction on a given policy dimension. Furthermore, left and right signal a direction that is relative to the status quo. Norberto Bobbio (1997) has argued that when it comes to equality, the key distinction between left and right is that the right prioritizes individual freedom to the expense of social equality, while the left promotes social equality to be achieved through some sort of redistribution of abilities, opportunities, or even wealth.

The question remains: do these different attitudes towards equality translate into identifiable differences in public policy and/or government performance? Analyzing economic policy, Carles Boix (1998) notes that "many political economists have concluded that, due to towering institutional and economic constraints, parties fail to affect economic policies and aggregates permanently" (p. 2). Boix debates this conclusion by stating— and proving empirically for OECD countries—that even though all parties prefer to engage in growth-maximizing policies, policies diverge according to their redistributive effects. Thus, ideology determines the policies that are preferred by each government. Governments in the left attempt to raise productivity (of both capital and labor) through public sector intervention (i.e. expenditure in infrastructure), while governments on the right conceive their role as providers of private economic incentives, such that market competition maximizes individual and social rates of return (p. 11). Thus, both types of government have distinctive preferences on the paths that lead to economic growth. Of course, Boix is careful enough to delimit the policy leverage of governments on the productivity incentives of capital and labor. That would mean, for a left-wing government, that the extent of taxing and redistribution is bounded by the investment incentives of private actors. In short, as Adam Przeworski and Michael Wallerstein (1988) phrased it: "vote-seeking politicians are dependent on owners of capital because voters are" (p. 12).

Puzzling as it is, there are far fewer works devoted to analyzing empirically whether or not there is a difference in terms of social policy between left and right governments (e.g. Huber and Stephens 2001; Iversen 2005; Rodrik 1998). Even more intriguing is finding that, in some cases, the ideological orientation of a government does not affect the level of social expenditure, at least in the case of OECD countries (López-Moctezuma 2007).

Getting even closer: Latin America

Let me narrow the question even more: what does it mean to be a government on the left in Latin America after the end of the Cold War?

Specifically, has ideology shaped public policy in Latin America? These are very much open questions in the hemisphere, and the time seems ripe to answer them. The last decade has been characterized by the democratization of all countries in the region (with the clear exception of Cuba), but also by the emergence of governments labeled as populist usually identified with the left.

The main debates have tried to identify the elements of populist governments and distinguishing them from non-populist ones. However, there has not been an empirical effort to identify the elements that separate governments on the left from those on the right in terms of public policy and performance; much less between populist and non-populist governments, particularly on the left but also on the right. That is the void that this chapter aims to fill.

For some analysts the only relevant distinction is between old and new Latin American leftist governments, where the old was formed by national populist governments devoted to vast reform and development projects, and the contemporary leftist governments are oriented to find the tools to improve the well-being of the population (i.e. reduce poverty and inequality) all within the bounds of democracy (Vilas 2005).

Conversely, most analysts have come to identify the co-existence of two lefts in Latin America. As Jorge Castañeda (2006, p. 29) describes it,

> there is not one Latin American left today; there are two. One is modern, open-minded, reformist, and internationalist, and it springs, paradoxically, from the hard-core left of the past. The other, born of the great tradition of Latin American populism, is nationalist, strident, and close-minded.

Castañeda's description contains the central elements that define a populist government: party origin and discourse. Both are closely related, but imply different paths when it comes to classifying a government as populist or not.

From the first element—origin—we can identify populist governments as those based on the supremacy of a national leader who relates directly to "the people," the origin of moral and political legitimacy. In some sense, this approach conceives populism as a type of discourse instead of an actual kind of governmental functioning.

The second element—discourse—takes this attribute a bit further and identifies a common feature in populist governments: distaste for institutionalized representation (Savarino 2006; Paramio 2006). By vindicating "true democracy," populist governments place themselves as a salvation from the vices of party politics and, as such, gain power as independent candidates or as candidates from political parties created merely around their presidential candidacy. This is what Bovero (2006) has labeled "anti-politics."

However, the relationship between party politics and populism is complex. Many governments originating in traditional parties have been often classified as populist, such as those of Carlos Saúl Menem and Néstor Kirchner in Argentina. Yet some other governments that did not spring from parties—and sometimes developed in opposition to them—have never been identified as populist, such as Álvaro Uribe's in Colombia or Alberto Fujimori's in Peru.

Castañeda (2006) is then justified in identifying the governments in Chile, Uruguay, and Brazil as part of the modern left, originated from traditional, albeit formerly radical, left parties, but also when he places the leftist governments in Venezuela and Bolivia as part of the populist left, since both Hugo Chávez and Evo Morales trace their origins not to parties but to movements against parties.

Ideology, populism, and social policy in Latin America (1990–2006)

With countries classified by their ideological orientation and their populist tendencies (see Appendix I for details on classifications), the obvious question is whether these categories have any effect on social policy. That is, do leftist governments do better in terms of social variables than right-wing governments? What about the populist cases?

I should establish first that this chapter does not attempt to determine causal relationships; there is no statistical analysis here that allows me to make any conclusive statement on the causality between ideology and/or populism and social government performance. What this chapter provides is a description of the patterns that arise when social indicators are conditioned on ideological attributes of governments. This allows me to identify some basic patterns where they exist, but nothing else. But in order to detect changes in these variables, it is important to look not only at recent years, when the rise of the left became notorious. I have chosen 1990 to 2006 as a period of analysis to get some baseline years as point of reference. But also, in order to fully understand the relative performance of the left and the populist left, an assessment of their comparative performance is required. Doing otherwise would decrease comparability and variance, and would eliminate observations in time that provide a solid base for inter-temporal comparison.

This section also provides summaries of variables for the whole of the period. Given that not all data is available for all countries and all social variables, I have chosen to use a baseline year and all available recent data to feed into the comparison. In some cases, we have data contrasting 1990 to 2005. However, it is often the case that periods are much narrower, which implies that some variation is lost because of data availability. Whenever a country is excluded through lack of information on a given variable, it is always explicitly stated. That being said, and to the best of my knowledge, this is the first effort to provide empirical evidence on the differences in the social policy performance of Latin American governments looking at their ideology and populist traits.

This chapter is not about the existence and attributes of specific social programs in the region, although some are mentioned and briefly described when necessary. I aim at providing a general picture of the effects of social policy based on empirical data. I thus consider two possible ways to evaluate the performance of governments regarding social policy: (1) how much they spend in social areas, and (2) how much better off their populations are in terms of social indicators. The interaction between these two will help us get a handle on how effective has social expenditure been to improve the welfare of the population.

Social expenditure

There are three possible measures of social expenditure that account for the relative size of the economies, governments, and populations: as percentage of GDP, as percentage of total government expenditure, and per capita.[2] Figure 4.1 shows changes in social expenditure as percentage of GDP between 1990 and 2003, classifying countries by ideology and populism. In terms of social expenditure, all countries in the region—but Ecuador—have increased it as a proportion of GDP, yet it becomes apparent that left-dominated governments have not outdone their right-wing counterparts. With the exception of Bolivia and Costa Rica, which had both types of governments,

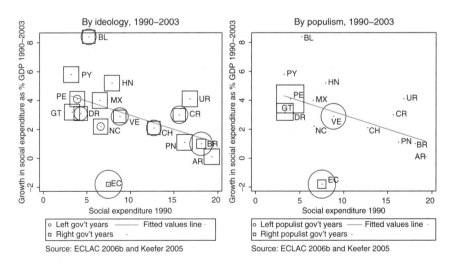

Figure 4.1 Social expenditure as percentage of GDP.

it has been rightist governments that have increased social expenditure above the regional average.

The graph shows changes in expenditures relative to 1990. As is usually the case, countries that already had high spending levels show smaller increments, which explain the negative slope in the fitted line. We can think of countries above the line as "over-achievers" and those below the line as "under-achievers" in a very descriptive way, since we are not performing any causal statistical analysis controlling by other relevant variables. Thus, with the exception of Ecuador, left-dominated countries had an average increment in social expenditure; while at least four right-dominated countries (Paraguay, Mexico, Honduras, and Uruguay) had above-average increments. What is clear, as shown on the right side of Figure 4.1, is that all countries with any populist years are under-achievers, although only Ecuador is way off the fitted line.

To further understand the differences between governments on the left and the right regarding social expenditure, we can look at expenditures in some specific social areas. Figure 4.2 shows the percentage change in per capita education expenditure between 1990 and 2003. Once again, left-dominated governments do not do better than right-dominated governments; in fact, countries with left-government years show a higher dispersion than right-wing cases. While some countries governed by the left are below the fitted line and close to increases of 0 dollars per capita in the period (Ecuador, Venezuela, and Brazil), some countries which have had a similar distribution of left and right governments are clearly above the average performance in the region, such as the Dominican Republic, Bolivia,

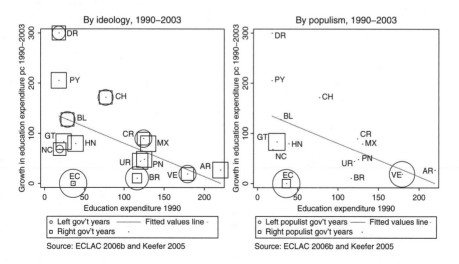

Figure 4.2 Per capita expenditure on education.

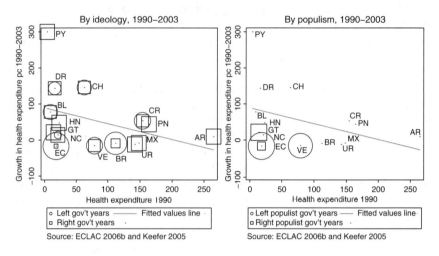

Figure 4.3 Per capita expenditure on health.

Chile, and Costa Rica. In any case, it is worth mentioning that rightist governments do not surpass leftist cases either (only Paraguay, Argentina, and Mexico can be seen as over-achievers), but do have similar behavior among themselves and are just off the fitted line. Once again, all populist cases are under-achievers, with very small increments even in cases with a low starting expenditure, such as Guatemala and Ecuador.

Figure 4.3 shows percentage changes in health expenditure for the same period. The patterns closely resemble those seen in education expenditure in terms of the ideological profile of over-achievers, composed of countries with government years of both ideologies (the Dominican Republic, Bolivia, Chile, and Costa Rica) and countries with only right-wing governments (Paraguay, Panama, and Argentina). Once again, Venezuela, Ecuador, and Brazil, which are the countries with the highest number of left years, show some of the lowest changes, along with two completely right-wing countries (Uruguay and Mexico). In contrast with education expenditure, where only Ecuador had a decrement in per capita dollars, those five countries actually reduced expenditure in health.

Thus, in terms of health spending, there is no clear ideological trend among countries; although it looks as though "mixed" cases did better (with the clear exceptions of Brazil and Venezuela). As happened before, the three countries with populist governments for which there is information are below the fitted line of expenditure in the region, which in this case is particularly problematic since they were already among the countries with the lowest per capita spending in 1990. For instance, Guatemala had a per capita expenditure of $14 in 1990, which increased by only 21 percent in

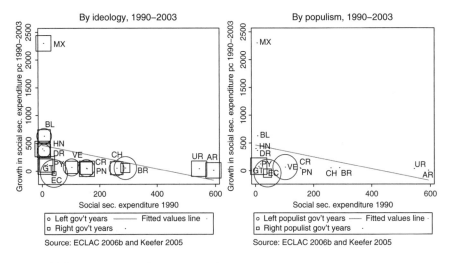

Figure 4.4 Per capita expenditure on social security.

the fourteen-year period; in Ecuador the value in 1990 was $18 and decreased by 16 percent, while countries in a similar situation in 1990, such as Paraguay with $4, Bolivia with $9, and the Dominican Republic with $16, had increments of 300 percent, 78 percent, and 144 percent respectively. The same applies to Venezuela, which in 1990 had a health per capita spending of $79, above the $63 reported in Chile; by 2003 Chile's spending had grown by 146 percent and Venezuela's had decreased by 15 percent.

When it comes to social security expenditure (Figure 4.4), right-wing governments do seem to have a lead.[3] The four countries above the fitted line (over-achievers) had a clear right-wing profile: Mexico, Argentina, and Uruguay had only right governments in the fourteen-year period, while Bolivia had ten right-government years in the period. Also, other right-wing dominated countries show notorious increases below the line (due mostly to Mexico being such an outlier), such as Honduras (400 percent) and the Dominican Republic (367 percent, with eleven right-government years). Even when only Ecuador had a decrement in social security spending in the period (-44 percent), the other two countries with populist governments are also in the bottom of spending growth (Venezuela 67 percent and Guatemala 82 percent).[4]

Social expenditure on housing (Figure 4.5) is the only area in which countries with populist governments performed above average.[5] Guatemala had the highest growth among all countries, with 1,350 percent (from $2 in 1990); Venezuela actually had a decrement of 55 percent, but it was already spending $86 in 1990. Note also that the remaining two countries above

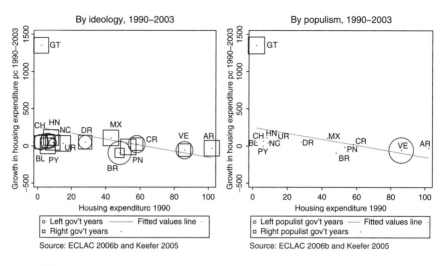

Figure 4.5 Per capita expenditure on housing.

the fitted line are both right-wing cases: Mexico (107 percent from $43 in 1990) and Argentina (29 percent from $102 in 1990).

Thus, if there is a pattern in housing expenditure, it is not defined by the ideological profile of countries. The top three cases of increases come from countries with only right governments (Guatemala, Honduras, and Mexico), but also three countries with the same ideological profile had decrements (Paraguay, Panama, and Argentina). While countries with some left-government years had important increments (Chile 67 percent, the Dominican Republic 50 percent, and Bolivia 50 percent), two countries with an even bigger number of left years had the largest decrements (Brazil -94 percent and Venezuela -55 percent). Clearly, the problem here is that the period from 1990 to 2003 does not include some recent left-wing governments, which impedes a richer assessment. In any case, the average growth for countries with only right-wing governments was 38 percent (excluding Guatemala for comparability purposes), while the average for countries with some left-government years was -7.93 percent.

In sum, in terms of expenditure in social areas we must conclude that countries with some left-government years have not outperformed countries with no left-government years; in fact, in some cases they seemed to actually do worse (i.e. social security and housing). However, there seems to be a distinction among countries with some left experiences, particularly when we disaggregate social expenditure in the areas of education and health. While Costa Rica, Chile, the Dominican Republic, and Bolivia have performed above—or close to—average, Brazil, Venezuela, and Ecuador showed changes below the regional average, and even decrements (i.e. health spending). Also, with the exception of housing expenditure, countries with some populist experiences are always under-achievers.

These findings are merely descriptive, but provide clues to identify some differences in performance related to ideology. Of course, we cannot conclude that left governments do worse; but we can affirm that they do not better, either. Indeed, contrary to common expectations, right-dominated countries have shown positive results in terms of social expenditure; as shown by the examples of Mexico, Honduras, Paraguay, Panama, Argentina, and Uruguay.

Social well-being

Another way to evaluate social policy performance for countries in Latin America is to look at changes in the well-being of their population in terms of poverty, inequality, education, health, and housing conditions. This would reflect relative improvements in social indicators, regardless of how much governments have actually spent. In the previous section we concluded that there was no patent left advantage in terms of social expenditure; and in fact both left and right had pretty similar changes after 1990 in the absence of any populist experience. We also concluded that non-populist cases from the left systematically did better than their populist counterparts, which in fact also did worse than right populist cases (where enough information existed to make such a comparison). In terms of social well-being the patterns are strikingly similar.

Countries with a significant number of non-populist left years do not clearly outperform the equivalent right cases. Either they perform similarly (i.e. poverty and inequality), or they have a very small advantage over right-wing cases, usually driven by a few successful countries. The only case where there seemed to be an obvious left advantage is maternal mortality. Also, non-populist left cases do steadily better than countries with some left populist experiences for almost all measures of social well-being, acutely in terms of poverty and inequality reduction, as well as education improvement. Finally, a more surprising—but repeated—result is to find that within countries with some populist years, right-wing cases do better than left cases.[6]

Poverty and inequality

Probably no other indicator is as closely related to the goals of social policy as a redistributive tool as is poverty. The struggle against poverty has been a constant element in the government agendas in the region, particularly among left-wing governments, and for good reasons. By 1990, 48.3 percent of Latin Americans were below national poverty lines. This happens in the developing region of the world with the highest levels of per capita income and development.

When it comes to poverty and inequality, countries with leftist governments do not have a noticeable advantage over countries with mostly right-wing government years. Poverty has been reduced identically among non-populist governments, regardless of their ideological experiences. The only indicator where left-government years had a clear positive effect is undernourishment, where non-populist left experiences reduced hunger at a visibly higher rate than their right counterparts. More unexpectedly, countries with some left-wing populist government years in the period did not show a superior performance than their right-wing counterparts.

Thus, in general the left does not seem to have leverage on poverty and inequality reduction. This is due to the fact that some right-wing countries have been undoubtedly successful at reducing both aspects; but also to the fact that left experiences have been quite contrasting. While Chile and Brazil show positive results for all measures, other leftist cases systematically are under-achievers, in particular Venezuela and Bolivia.

As shown in Figure 4.6, most countries in the region actually reduced the proportion of the population living below national poverty line between 1990 and 2005.[7] The only two cases where poverty increased are Argentina (1.8 percent) and Venezuela (4.3 percent). Since we are accounting for the proportion of the population living in poverty in 1990, we should expect higher decrements for countries with higher poverty rates in 1990 (as shown by the negative slope in the fitted line). Thus, the countries above the line are in this case the under-achievers while those below are the over-achievers.

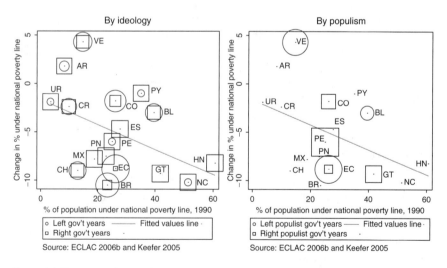

Figure 4.6 Poverty reduction by national poverty line 1990–2005.

Astoundingly enough, there is no clear pattern in terms of ideology for average poverty reduction, although once again countries with significant left years are more dispersed than right-year cases. The most successful stories come from countries with both ideological profiles; from the left Ecuador and Brazil, from the right Nicaragua, Guatemala, Mexico, Uruguay, and Panama, and the mixed cases of Costa Rica and Chile. On the contrary, poor performance cases seem to be evenly distributed between ideologies. On average, governments with at least fourteen years of right-wing governments reduced the poverty rate by 5.7 percent (-6.48 if we exclude Argentina), while countries with at least five years of left governments averaged -4.9 percent (-6.7 percent if we exclude Venezuela).

Leftist governments have not shown a substantially better performance than right-wing governments. In fact, when we only consider cases without any populist experience, the average poverty reduction is identical across ideologies (-5.9 percent), although the populist experiences are located both above and below the fitted line. On average, countries with some populist government years decreased poverty by 4.1 percent, while countries with no such years averaged a 5.6 percent reduction.

What is notable are the contrasting results for left populist cases, where Venezuela increased poverty rates by 4.3 percent, while Bolivia decreased them by 3 percent and Ecuador by 8.8 percent. On average, populist governments did worse than non-populist ones, and this is particularly true for left populist cases. Countries with left populist governments decreased poverty by 2.3 percent (in contrast with the 5.9 percent reduction for non-populist left cases); while countries with any right populist years decreased poverty by 5.7 percent (thanks to the cases of Peru, -6 percent, and Guatemala, -9.3 percent). Thus, if there is any ideological gap in performance it comes from populist experiences, and here Venezuela takes all the credit.

A more tangible (and painful) measure for poverty is the proportion of the population that do not attain the minimal caloric daily intake: hunger. As shown in Figure 4.7, when it comes to undernourishment reduction, countries with a high number of leftist governments seemed to do better that their right-wing counterparts for the 1990–2002 period. The clear exception is Peru. Indeed, if we average reduction by ideology, countries with leftist government years reduced the indicator by 2.6 percent and their right-wing counterparts by 2.4 percent. However, if we only consider cases with no populist experiences, the left cases averaged -4 percent and the right cases -1.2 percent. In both cases the dispersion of the values is relatively small.

Intriguingly, populist cases are far more dispersed: for both cases they contain the most and least successful cases. On the left, while Venezuela increased the undernourished proportion of the population by 6 percent, Ecuador reduced it by 4 percent. On the right, while Guatemala increased

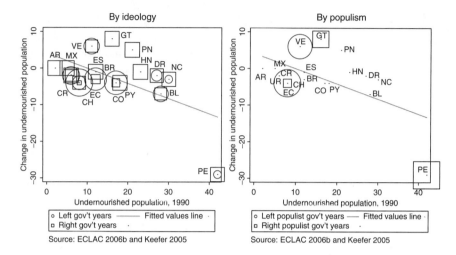

Figure 4.7 Undernourishment reduction 1990–2002.

it by 8 percent, Peru reduced it by 29 percent. Thus, on average, countries with left populist years increased undernourishment by 1 percent, while their right counterparts decreased it by 10.5 percent.

If there is one area where we would expect ideology to play a key role, it is inequality. Latin America has been the most unequal region in the world for a long time now, and this situation has been at the center of the agenda of the left in the region. Figure 4.8 presents two measures of inequality, the commonly used Gini index and the ratio of incomes of the tenth decile over the first decile. Given data availability, we lack the measure for the starting year (1990) to account for relative changes; for that reason, the graphs measure change in inequality measures vis-à-vis the number of years of left governments. In that sense, it comes as a surprise that the slope is positive: that is, that the higher the number of left-government years, the more unequal the country has become.

This unexpected result is driven entirely by Bolivia, which has drastic increments in both measures.[8] In any case, even if we excluded Bolivia, the fitted line would be flat: that is, more left-government years did not imply a reduction on inequality.[9] It is surprising how little inequality has been reduced in the region, regardless of the ideological profile of government years.

Only five countries out of the twelve with information on the Gini index have actually reduced inequality in the period, three of them without a single left-government year (Honduras -0.7, Panama -0.3, and Mexico -5), and two with some left-government years (Chile -0.8 and Brazil -1.4).

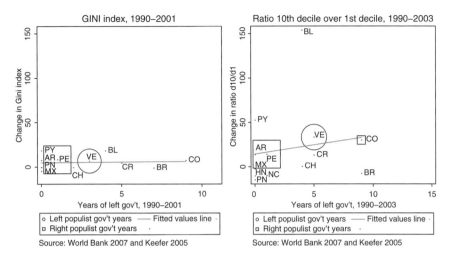

Figure 4.8 Inequality, ideology, and populism.

In contrast, three countries with mostly right governments increased inequality (Argentina 7.4, Peru 8.2, and Paraguay 18.2), as well as four countries with left-government years (Bolivia 18, Colombia 7.3, Venezuela 6.5, and Costa Rica 4.3). Indeed, the average growth in the Gini index is smaller for countries with mostly right governments (4.6) than for governments with some left years (5.6); this result is visibly driven by the Mexican case. Also note that Venezuela and Peru, the two countries with populist experiences, are under-achievers.

Education

Social policy, as a redistributive instrument of opportunities (not income or consumption), has two key areas of investment: education and health. In that sense, social policy finds a fundamental long-run instrument to improve the well-being of the disadvantaged segments of the population in the relative generation of human capital. In order to identify changes in education for the poorest segments of the Latin American population, which would reveal distinctive patterns on the distributive goals of education provision, Figures 4.9, 4.10 and 4.11 show relative changes on school attendance for the poorest 20 percent for twelve of the eighteen Latin American countries between 1990 and 2002.[10]

For ages seven to twelve (primary school), no clear ideological pattern emerges, which is evident in the clustering of countries. Although not shown in the graph, leftist governments did have more than proportional

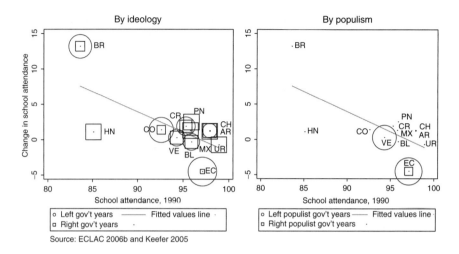

Figure 4.9 School attendance ages seven to twelve (poorest 20 percent) 1990–2002.

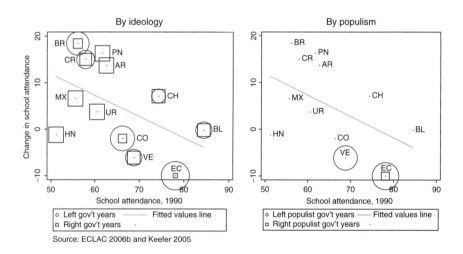

Figure 4.10 School attendance ages thirteen to nineteen (poorest 20 per cent) 1990–2002.

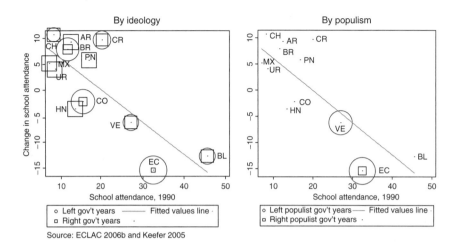

Figure 4.11 School attendance ages twenty to twenty-four (poorest 20 per cent) 1990–2002.

increments for the poorest population vis-à-vis the total population averages (even if we exclude the Brazilian case). The non-populist left actually did better in terms of devoting efforts to the poorest segments of the population, while the populist left actually harmed this segment even more than the total population.

When we look at the next age group (thirteen to nineteen) it is clear that the distinction between left cases becomes even clearer, while the average left advantage over right cases dilutes. Two conclusions arise. First, countries with mostly right governments achieved better results than left cases, but left governments did devote more attention to poorer segments. Second, left populist cases not only did much worse than non-populist left countries, but they actually harmed the poorer segments of the population more than proportionally. Note also that no clear ideological trend appears in the age group between twenty and twenty-four years old (potentially reflecting post-high school education). As shown in Figure 4.11, there is no clear ideological trend. What is more interesting for this age group is that the non-populist left bias in favor of the poorer population disappears; the right cases did better in total and with the poorest 20 percent populations, and left governments had a much smaller increment for the poorer than for the total population.

When it comes to education, Latin American leftist governments seem to have had a slightly better performance than their right-wing counterparts, especially when looking at the poorest population segments. This result is driven by some extremely successful cases, particularly Brazil, and to a lesser degree Chile and Costa Rica, while countries with left governments characterized by a populist profile did systematically worse for all measures. Interestingly, as we move up in the education levels the advantage of non-populist governments over their right counterparts decreases (or even reverses); the left bias in favor of poor segments vanishes; and the relative under-performance of left populist governments becomes even more dramatic.

Health

Health policies, along with education, are fundamental to improve the long-run well-being of the population. Both generate human capital and contribute to the future improvement of income and consumption opportunities for disadvantaged groups. Within health attention two areas are exceptionally critical: maternal and child health.

Figure 4.12 shows relative changes in the region related to maternal mortality.[11] It is notable that eight out of the eighteen countries have actually seen an increment in their maternal mortality rates, while the highest decrements belong to countries which had huge mortality rates in 1990. Also, while countries with some left years are located close to the fitted line, right-wing countries show a much higher dispersion and contain the most and the least successful cases. This shows that, on average, the non-populist left has an advantage over their non-populist right counterparts. If we look at the average reduction for countries with at least four left years in the period— this immediately excludes Chile and Venezuela given the years contained in

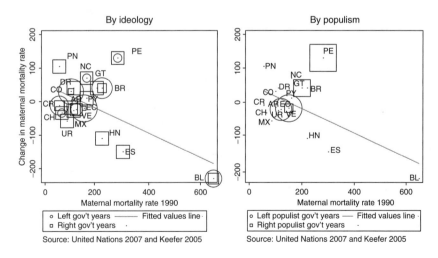

Figure 4.12 Maternal mortality rate, 1990–2000.

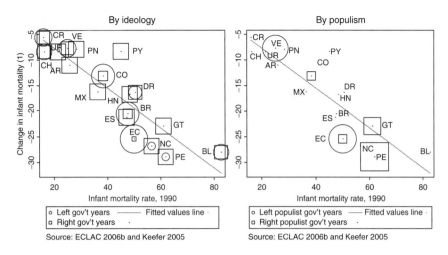

Figure 4.13 Infant mortality rate (under one year old per 1,000 live births, 1990–2003).

the period—they reduced the mortality rate by 43 points. In contrast, the reduction for right-wing countries was an average of 17.8. Also, if we look at the populist cases, for both ideologies their performance is below the performance of non-populist cases. Contrary to what happens on education measures, left populists clearly outperform their right-wing counterparts (a decrement of 20 versus an increment of 85).[12]

Do these findings for maternal mortality also apply for child health measures? The answer is no. Figures 4.13 and 4.14 show changes in the region for two variables related to child health: infant mortality rate (under one year old by 1,000 live births) between 1990 and 2003, and child underweight prevalence between 1992 and 2002.[13]

The first thing to notice with regard to infant mortality in the region, as shown in Figure 4.13, is that this indicator was reduced by all Latin American nations, in obvious contrast with maternal mortality rates. There is no clear ideological trend (once more). While Paraguay, Honduras, Panama, and Guatemala are clear under-achievers and had been right-wing countries in the period, Costa Rica, Venezuela, and Colombia are also performing below average (given their rates in 1990) and have had significant left-government years. On the other hand, Brazil and Ecuador are patent over-achievers from the left, but so are Nicaragua, Peru, and Mexico from the right.

In fact, if we take a look only at non-populist cases, the average for the right is slightly superior to that for the left (-16.8 versus -15.1).[14] What is truly intriguing for this measure is that countries with some populist

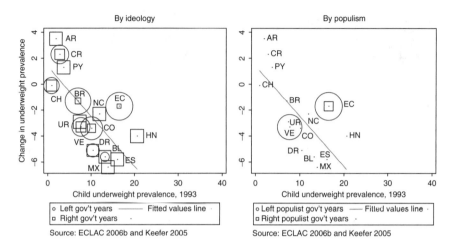

Figure 4.14 Infant health (child underweight prevalence, 1993–2002).

years did substantially better than their non-populist counterparts (-21.2 versus -14.9). Of course, part of the story is that, with the exception of Venezuela, all populist cases had quite large infant mortality rates by 1990, but that is not enough to explain the difference, since some non-populist cases had similar initial rates (Brazil, El Salvador, Honduras, the Dominican Republic, and Bolivia). Not only did countries with populist cases do better than non-populist, but within populist cases those with a right ideological bias did much better than left ones (-25 versus -16.5).[15] Thus, the contrast between maternal and infant mortality rates is sharp. Not only did the non-populist left lose its leverage, but it was the group with the smallest average decrements in infant mortality, with a performance below the left populist, the right non-populist and, particularly, the right populist.

The data on child underweight prevalence prevents us from doing a similar comparison because of the absence of populist cases from the right. However, the results in Figure 4.14 resemble those for infant mortality with respect to the average superior performance of the non-populist right (-3 reduction) vis-à-vis the countries with non-populist left years (-0.6 reduction), although their dispersion is larger, as shown by the Mexican and Salvadorian cases, on the one hand, and the Honduran, Nicaraguan, Paraguayan, and Argentinean cases, on the other hand.[16]

In sum, health measures trends resemble the conclusions from the education indicators, insofar as the non-populist left seemed to have a slight advantage over non-populist right cases and left populist cases—that is, at least with regard to maternal mortality and life expectancy. However, when it comes to child health measures, this completely reverts. Non-populist left cases actually did worse than their right counterparts, and even than populist left cases. Also, resembling the education conclusions, the populist right cases did better than the left ones in relation to child health and life expectancy. In fact, left populist cases outperformed right ones only in maternal mortality reduction.

Housing

The closing issue to evaluate social well-being of Latin Americans after 1990 is their housing situation. It is no secret that Latin America has become prominently an urban region, and that the growth in urban areas in the region implied dramatic increases in the proportion of people living in slums, with no access to basic services such as running water and sanitation facilities.

Figure 4.15 shows changes on the proportion of people living in urban slums between 1990 and 2001.[17] Notably, for five out of seventeen countries there was an increment in this measure (Peru 7.7, Chile 4.6, Argentina 2.6, Costa Rica 0.9, and Nicaragua 0.2), and in two cases there was no change in the period (Venezuela and Nicaragua).[18] Now, in terms of ideology both types seem to perform similarly, although right-wing dominated countries are perceptively more disperse. Indeed, the average decrement for non-populist left cases was -5.1, with -4.6 for non-populist right cases, so that the left had a minor advantage. However, the most prominent

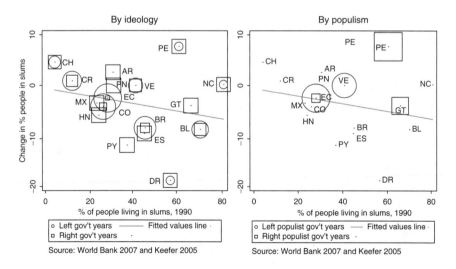

Figure 4.15 Proportion of people living in slums (urban), 1990–2001.

difference was between populist and non-populist cases (.3 versus -4.8); as seen in the graph, all cases with some populist governments were under-achievers. This is particularly true for right-wing populist cases, which increased the proportion of people living in urban slums by 1.85, mostly because of the Peruvian case; left populist cases reduced this indicator by 1.25.

Conclusions

This enterprise began with a question and an intuition. I wondered whether left-wing governments in the region outperformed the right-wing ones with respect to social policy indicators, and suspected that there was a distinction between "good" left governments and "bad" populist left governments. The answer to the question is a surprising no, while the response to the suspicion is an expected yes.

In the two areas analyzed in this chapter related to social policy—expenditure and well-being—the performance of countries with leftist-government years and countries with right-government years was unexpectedly similar. The only exceptions were population undernourishment, maternal mortality, and education inequality (ages seven to nineteen), where the left showed a patently better performance than the right, and the indicators related to child health, where the opposite occurred, with right cases outperforming left cases.[19]

A constant finding throughout this chapter was the superior performance of non-populist left cases vis-à-vis populist left cases. This is particularly true in the Venezuelan case, which steadily performed poorly on all measures.[20] The finding comes to confirm what was already suspected: in Latin America there is a well-behaved non-populist left and an utterly misbehaved populist left.[21]

What was not suspected is that, within populist cases, those with a right-wing profile would perform better in terms of social policy than their leftist counterparts. With the sole exception of the infant mortality rate reduction, right populist cases outperformed left populist instances for all measures, although for most measures countries with no populist episodes of either ideology visibly did better than countries with any populist episode of either ideology. Thus, populist governments are undoubtedly bad news for social policy (and of course, democracy). Yet, if only in terms of social policy, evidence suggests that Alberto Fujimori did better than Hugo Chávez, an embarrassing result for Chávez.

It is important to point out an apparent similarity among some successful stories from both ideological backgrounds. Brazil, Chile, Mexico, Honduras and, to a lesser extent, Nicaragua all have something in common: broad family-based social programs. These programs are characterized by conditioned transfers to impoverished families, subject to the attendance of family members to education and health services. Based on the performance of these countries, programs seem to be working in the right direction: *Bolsa Família* in Brazil (since 1995), *Chile Solidario* (since 2002), *Programa de Asignación Familiar* in Honduras (since 1990), and of course *Progresa*, now *Oportunidades*, in Mexico (since 1997). These programs can be an alternative to countries showing inefficiencies between expenditure increments and indicators improvements, in particular Bolivia and Paraguay.

On a final note, and leaving aside ideological distinctions, we have to acknowledge the positive regional trends in terms of expenditure and some social indicators, particularly poverty reduction, basic education enrollment, and infant mortality. However, we cannot end this chapter without casting warnings on some other indicators where Latin American governments have done what can only be described as a poor job; among them: inequality, education access for the most impoverished segments, postsecondary education access, maternal mortality, and the proportion of people living in urban slums.

Appendix I: Classification of country years by ideology

To classify Latin American governments by ideology and for comparability purposes, I use Philip Keefer's (2005) classification,[22] which produces

Table 4.1 Reclassification of cases from Keefer's data

Keefer's	Reclassified to	Total GY	Cases
Left	Right	0	
Right	Left	12	Argentina (2004–2006), Chile (2000–2006), Paraguay (2005–2006)
Center	Right	29	Argentina (2000–2001), Bolivia (1994–1997, 2003), Dominican Republic (1997–2000, 2005–2006), Mexico (1990–2000), Peru (2002–2006)
	Left	11	Bolivia (2004–2005), Colombia (1990–1998)
No information	Right	43	Colombia (2003–2006), Ecuador (1997), Guatemala (1992–1995), Nicaragua (1991–1996, 2002–2006), Panama (1995–1999, 2005–2006), Peru (1991–2001), Venezuela (1994–1998)
	Left	10	Ecuador (2003–2004), Venezuela (1999–2006)
No executive	Right	0	
	Left	2	Ecuador (2005–2006)

Table 4.2 Final government years

Country	Left	Right
Costa Rica	1990, 1995–1998	1991–1994, 1999–2006
Dominican Republic	2001–2004	1990–2000, 2005–2006
El Salvador	—	1990–2006
Guatemala	—	1990–2006
Honduras	—	1990–2006
Mexico	—	1990–2006
Nicaragua	1990	1991–2006
Panama	—	1990–2006
Argentina	1990–2003	2004–2006
Bolivia	1990–1993, 2004–2006	1994–2003
Brazil	1990–1994	1995–2006
Chile	1990–1999	2000–2006
Colombia	1990–1998	1999–2006
Ecuador	1990–1996, 1998–2006	1997
Paraguay	2005–2006	1990–2004
Peru	1990, 2005–2006	1991–2004
Uruguay	2005–2006	1990–2004
Venezuela	1999–2006	1990–1998

five categories (i.e. left, right, center, no information, and no executive) covering in this case all Latin American countries from 1990 to 2005. I revisited all categories to place them in a binary left/right classification, based on the self-stated orientation of the party and/or the policy orientation of the executive in ambiguous cases (i.e. center parties and cases reported with no information or no executive). This revision of Keefer's classification produced a total of 107 changes out of a total of 306 government years (GY).[23]

I consider populist governments to have one main attribute: they originate from outside the party system. The label "populist" in this chapter reflects governments formed outside the party system or in open confrontation to it. In relation to other analyses, all cases traditionally identified as populist are also classified as such here (with the clear exception of Kirchner's government in Argentina), while some cases usually not considered to be populist are rendered as such here because of their non-party origin. This criteria produces a total of forty "populist" government years in the region between 1990 and 2006 out of 306 (13 per cent): twenty from the right and twenty from the left.[24] (See Tables 4.1 and 4.2.)

Appendix II: Variables, description, and sources

Table 4.3 Variables, description, and sources

Variable	Source	Description
Education expenditure	ECLAC	Government's education expenditure per capita (current dollars)
GDP	IMF	Gross domestic product based on purchasing-power-parity (PPP) valuation of country GDP
GDP per capita	IMF	Gross domestic product based on purchasing-power-parity (PPP) per capita GDP
Gini	WB	GINI index
Health expenditure	ECLAC	Government's health expenditure per capita (current dollars)
High school enrollment	WB	School enrollment, tertiary (% gross)
Housing expenditure	ECLAC	Government's housing expenditure per capita (current dollars)
Ideology	KEEFER	Modified and corrected. Ideology of government, left and right.
Ideology opposition	KEEFER	Ideology of largest opposition party: right; left; center or no party
Income ratio	WB	Income share held by highest 10% over income share held by lowest 10%
Infant mortality	ECLAC	Mortality rate for children below one year old by each 1,000 live births
Legislative control	KEEFER	Whether or not party of executive control all relevant houses
Life expectancy	WB	Life expectancy at birth, total (years)
Maternal mortality	UN	Maternal mortality ratio per 100,000 live births
Party	KEEFER	Name of party in power, if any
Populist	KEEFER	Party origin of president
Poverty	ECLAC	Population living under extreme poverty measured by nationally defined poverty lines
Primary enrollment	WB	School enrollment, primary (% gross)
School attendance	ECLAC	School attendance for total population, for age groups 7–12, 13–19 and 20–24
School attendance poor	ECLAC	School attendance for total population, for age groups 7–12, 13–19 and 20–24, within the poorest 20% of the population
Secondary enrollment	WB	School enrollment, secondary (% gross)
Slum	UN	Slum population as percentage of urban population
Social expenditure	ECLAC	Social expenditure as percentage of GDP, as percentage of government total expenditure or per capita
Social security expenditure	ECLAC	Government's social security expenditure per capita (current dollars)
Taxes	WB	Tax revenue (% of GDP)
Undernourishment	ECLAC	Proportion of the population unable to consume the daily minimum caloric requirement
Underweight	UN	Prevalence of low weight in children below five years old

Notes

1 Data was gathered from four different sources: the International Monetary Fund (IMF); the Economic Commission for Latin America and the Caribbean (ECLAC); the World Bank's World Development Indicators (WB); and the United Nations (UN). For a complete description of variables and sources please see Appendix 2 at the end of the chapter.

2 All data obtained from ECLAC comes from: ECLAC 2006b. The measures for social expenditure as percentage of GDP and per capita exclude El Salvador and Colombia, where no data was available for the period; the measure as percentage of total government expenditure also excludes Costa Rica.

3 Social security and assistance includes public spending on education, science, technology, culture, religion, and recreation, depending on the availability of information from individual countries.

4 This figure excluded El Salvador, Peru, Colombia, and Nicaragua, for which there was no complete information.

5 Note, however, that there is no information for Ecuador.

6 By exploring the interaction between expenditure and performance related to social policy (efficiency on spending) we confirm most of our previous conclusions. First, there is no clear advantage by countries with left-government years over countries with mostly right-government years. Second, the most significant distance is between left populist cases and left non-populist cases, where the first always perform below the second; with the exception of the unusual improvements showed by Ecuador on poverty and infant mortality. Third, where such a comparison is possible, right populist cases tend to perform better than left populist cases (with the already mentioned exceptions).

7 This figure excludes the Dominican Republic, which had no information for the period.

8 Unfortunately, because of data availability, the periods are narrower; this of course excludes some variability on ideological and populism cases. Note also that in the case of the income ratio we have no data for the Dominican Republic, El Salvador, Guatemala, Ecuador, and Uruguay; for the Gini index we lack information for those countries plus Nicaragua.

9 Unless, of course, we assumed that the Liberal Party in Colombia is not a left party; which we had already previously justified.

10 This data was gathered from: ECLAC 2006b. All age groups exclude information from the Dominican Republic, El Salvador, Guatemala, Nicaragua, Paraguay, and Peru. We replicated this analysis for school enrollment in elementary, secondary and high school education; they resemble the results for the poorest 20 percent. Although the left seemed to have an advantage over the right, this was driven entirely by the enormous increments reported by Brazil. In all cases, if we exclude the Brazilian case the average for right and left cases becomes practically the same. The most notable difference was between countries with no populist years and countries with some populist years; where the first systematically did better than the second; especially when contrasting both types within the left. Because of data availability the period reaches only up to 2002, and this of course excludes many governments from the recent 'left and populist wave' in the region. Note as well that since this data is based on information reported by the countries, some cases look suspicious with respect to their reported level in 1990 (i.e. Ecuador and Bolivia).

11 The data contained in the graph comes from United Nations measures related to the achievement of the Millennium Development Goals, and shows the death rate by 100,000 live births.

12 We did a similar comparison using life expectancy, and the results closely resemble those from maternal mortality. Having information for all countries and years, the average increments for non-populist cases are very similar for both ideological groups: 4.5 years for right cases and 4.9 for countries with at least four years of left governments in the period. Comparing populist cases is rather more complicated in this case, given their trends in initial life expectancy, such that even if right cases outperformed left (6.7 versus 4.5), this might be due to the fact that they already had a relatively low life expectancy to begin with (and of course, Venezuela had the lowest increment out of all countries in the region).

13 Once again, the periods are defined by data availability. The data for infant mortality includes all countries in the region, while the data for underweight prevalence excludes Nicaragua, Guatemala, Panama, and Peru, because of the absence of comparable information for those countries.

14 As in all the previous cases, comparing averages between ideological groups assumes that the distribution of initial rates is similar across ideological clusters; and indeed for most measures this is the case.

15 In these cases, relative rates by 1990 might have played a bigger role.

16 Note that for this indicator three countries actually had increments in the period (Argentina 3.5, Costa Rica 2.3, and Paraguay 1.3).

17 This data excludes Uruguay, for which there was no information.

18 Note that, by 2001, Chile only had two left-government years; for that reason, in the average calculations Chile was included in the right-wing cases, as well as Peru, Nicaragua, and the Dominican Republic, which had only one left year in the period.

19 Most comparisons in this chapter were based on period summaries, such that for cases with a similar distribution of right and left governments it is not straightforward to place indubitable responsibility on either; unfortunately data availability prevented us from reducing the length of periods or even to perform a more sophisticated statistical analysis based on year data. However, contrasting results between countries with a clear majority of right-government years and countries with a relatively large number of left-government years potentially reveal some potential trends (or lack of trends).

20 The Ecuadorian case is not far behind, since it showed superior performances in just a few indicators related to poverty and health care.

21 The only measures in which populist cases outperformed non-populist left cases were those related to child health, a result that was clearly driven solely by the Ecuadorian case.

22 Keefer (2005) classifies government following five steps: (1) using the party name; (2) complementing the information with the site http://www.agora.stm.it/elections/parties, which classifies parties' orientations using one-word labels; (3) spot-checking with the Longman Current Affairs series; (4) recording the executive's orientation where there is evidence that the executive deviates considerably from his or her party; and (5) comparing his coding to Huber and Inglehart (1995), based on party platforms, to revisit and if necessary correct.

23 See Table 4.1 for classification of cases, and those cases reclassified from Keefer's data.

24 The right-wing cases are: Guatemala (1992–1995); Colombia (2003–2006); Ecuador (1997); and Peru (1991–2001). The left-wing cases are: Bolivia (2004–2006); Ecuador (1998–2006); and Venezuela (1999–2006).

Chapter 5

Resilient nationalism in the Latin American left

Jorge G. Castañeda, Marco A. Morales, and Patricio Navia

It had become clear by the early 1990s that the left in Latin America needed to catch up with the times and go through a much needed *aggiornamento* to redefine its general discourse and positions on many issues. Absent this process, the left seemed bound to face electorates without a coherent discourse, or at least one that could respond to the most pressing needs of the time (Castañeda 1993). One of these outdated topics was nationalism. The left had become highly nationalistic in response to the need for nation-building in most Latin American countries and the perceived loss of sovereignty resulting from U.S. intervention in Latin American domestic affairs. This created an undeniable tension with the need of the left to maintain its raison d'être: address poverty and inequality in a sustainable manner. Paradoxically, the most direct way to tackle poverty and inequality depends on economic growth, and the quickest way to achieve it is by focusing on international trade and economic integration. For Latin America, this road runs through the United States, which is by far the largest market in the world.

The prognosis in those early years of the decade was straightforward (Castañeda 1993): the left needed to embrace a "new nationalism," which most likely implied redirecting the open rejection of the United States as an entity and instead opposing the specific policies it advocates. This, in turn, would set limits to American intervention in non-economic domestic affairs. Similarly, it could foster the creation of ad hoc types of regional economic integration, and allow supranational structures to enhance monitoring of elections, protection of human rights or the environment, to name a few. A left that adopted this "package" should be able to enhance the consolidation of nationhood, be better able to address issues related to poverty and inequality, become a weighty player in the international arena, and set a coherent alternative to laissez-faire economics and politics.

More than fifteen years have gone by, and half the Latin American governments identify with the left today. What happened with nationalism in the Latin American left during this time? There are, at least, two interesting ways to look for answers to this question. The first one—deductive in nature—would look into public opinion in an attempt to find overlaps between the preferences of individuals that associate themselves with the left and the nationalist discourse of the left. That is, was anyone listening to the left when it advanced its arcane views on nationalism? The second venue—descriptive in nature—would revise the public discourse of politicians associated with the left seeking to identify whether their rhetoric has changed over the last years, or whether nationalism has taken a different shape once the left ascends to power. We undertake both endeavors, seeking to gain a wider understanding of the dynamics of nationalism for the left in Latin America.

Nationalism as an electoral tool

Be they democratic or authoritarian, political leaders often use nationalism as a rallying cry to shore up support for their domestic agendas. Politicians tend to associate their platforms and agendas with the common good, often equating their road maps with the good of the nation and their ideological objectives with those of the fatherland. As a result, politicians from the entire ideological spectrum resort to nationalism.

Yet, nationalism can only exist when there is an "other." During the independence period in the nineteenth century, the "other" was colonial Spain or Portugal. Since it emerged as the sole political and economic power in the hemisphere after the 1898 Spanish American War, the United States has been a favorite "other." True, nationalism in Latin America has also been defined against direct neighbors. A handful of territorial wars in the nineteenth and early twentieth centuries were readily used to shore up political support waving the nationalist flag. Yet, using neighboring Latin American countries as the "other" has been more common among rightwing leaders. The left has found it more difficult to articulate a nationalist discourse using neighbors as "the other" precisely because of its internationalist approach. In the old Marxist left, the "workers of the world, unite" cry made it natural to articulate a nationalist discourse using the United States as "the other" rather than neighboring Latin American countries.

Perhaps the most classic example of nationalist use of the United States as "the other" for domestic purposes was General Juan Perón's famous phrase "Braden or Perón" in the 1946 election in Argentina. Rather than campaigning against his opponents, the Argentine populist leader successfully campaigned against the U.S. ambassador in that election. Perón won, and that strategy has been widely used in Latin America by many other leaders. Most recently, Hugo Chávez campaigned in Venezuela against George W. Bush. Chávez found it convenient to define nationalism as opposition to U.S. imperialism and label his challengers as a puppet of the United States. Sixty years after Perón inaugurated the populist use of nationalism in elections, Chávez showed that campaigning against the "empire" continues to attract votes.

Rightwing leaders have also occasionally used the United States as "the other" in their nationalist discourse. General Pinochet in Chile denounced the intervention by the Carter administration (1977–1981) against his government. More recently, then President Alberto Fujimori in Peru bitterly complained against what he defined as U.S. intervention in domestic affairs after the Clinton administration pressured Peru to annul a rigged election in 2000 that gave Fujimori a questionable third term in office. The use of a nationalist discourse aimed at the U.S. as "the other" proved insufficient to rally support in favor of Fujimori, who was eventually forced to resign and flee to Japan. Yet, whereas the right can choose between associating "the other" with a neighboring country or with the United States, the left in Latin America has no other option but to define nationalism in direct opposition to the United States.

Naturally, the lasting legacies of the Cold War—when the United States actively sought to undermine the surge of the revolutionary left in the region—further complicate relations between Washington and Latin American governments. But, as we discuss in the next section, precisely because the United States has such an important role in economic and political developments in Latin America, the very definition and evolution of nationalism in the region are directly tied to the perceptions and realities of U.S.–Latin American relations.

Nationalism: is it in the attitudes?

Another question we need to address is the following: is there any clear rooting of nationalism in the ideological spectrum? That is, do individuals who identify with the left have clear attitudes that favor nationalism? This is one very relevant question in need of empirical verification. After all, the left could have spent decades advocating a discourse that was not at the core of the concerns of its own constituency.

One way to address this question is by looking into the dimensions of party competition in Latin America. That is, how do voters' views interact with party positions to define areas where parties compete in Latin America? Using individual-level data, it is possible to measure attitudes and party affinities and use them to identify the relevant dimensions of conflict that are captured by the interaction between voters and political parties. Unfortunately this type of comprehensive analysis was last generated for the 1990s. Despite this fact, some valuable insights can be gained to improve our understanding of the dynamics defined by voters and parties in Latin America during this period.

According to Moreno (1999), it was possible by the beginning of the 1990s to identify two dimensions that were dominant in defining the meaning of left and right in Latin America: a democratic–authoritarian one, and an economic dimension. The first dimension is defined by a general set of attitudes towards democracy and nationalism, while the second is defined by attitudes towards societal change and income inequality. A remarkable finding is that nationalism was related *not* to the left but to the right in Latin America. By the second half of the 1990s, a third liberal–fundamentalist dimension—defined mostly by attitudes towards religiosity and abortion—gained relevance. Again, the analysis reveals that nationalism was related to conservative attitudes. Furthermore, on average, the "less educated, blue-collar workers" were representative of the right in Latin America during the 1990s (p. 121). In light of this, it would make sense that the left—speaking to the masses and the oppressed—would endorse nationalism since these very voters were interested in this topic, yet it was doomed to be an ineffectual strategy as this rhetoric appealed to the voters on the right of the ideological spectrum. It seems to be the case that the left was actually mistaken during the 1990s in endorsing the old versions of nationalism on its discourse. The Latin American left spent years preaching at the wrong church.

Nationalism may have various dimensions, although the most common are those that define nationalism as a reaction to the United States, and also relative to the integration of Latin America (Lomnitz 2006). Fortunately for us, some assessments of these attitudes are available for the last decade and a half in regional surveys, such as the World Values Survey (WVS) and Latinobarómetro series. While some of the questions do not measure attitudes in ways that would be ideal for our purposes, they nonetheless tap into the attitudes that we seek to measure and provide some valuable insights based on individual-level survey data.

The early 1990s waves of the WVS inquired about trust in Americans around the world. We infer that trust in Americans might be related to the assessments of the United States as a country. Not surprisingly, 48 percent of Latin Americans did *not* trust Americans, while 23 percent did trust Americans, and the remaining 29 percent were indifferent. So, it seems to be the case that Americans—and the United States by inference—were not the cup of tea of at least half of Latin Americans. Does this mean that the left was correct in advocating an anti-American discourse? It might if individuals on the left were disproportionately prone to dislike the United States. In this way, the left could differentiate itself and engage its natural constituency. But Figure 5.1 tells precisely the opposite story. It is not a characteristic of the left to show more distrust of Americans. As a matter of fact, ideology does not seem to be a useful filter to distill trust in Americans. The distribution of individuals in the ideological spectrum does not vary much depending on whether they trust, distrust or are indifferent to Americans. Unfortunately, this question was not asked again in posterior WVS waves, which would have given us some points of comparison, and allowed us to track this attitude over time.

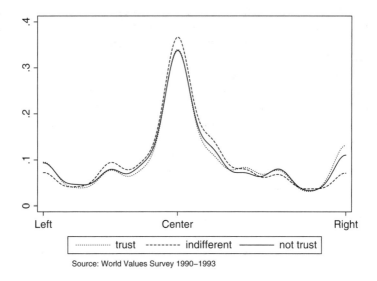

Figure 5.1 Ideological orientation by trust in Americans.

As the bulk of the governments from the left have been elected since 2003, it becomes interesting to ask whether the attitudes of Latin Americans regarding the United States and economic integration have changed lately. The most recent publicly available measurement of these traits corresponds to the 2005 Latinobarómetro survey. To our advantage, it queries directly on opinions about the United States and economic integration.

When asked about their opinion of the United States, 67 percent of Latin Americans reported having a good opinion. Are these opinions distributed equally across countries governed by the left and the rest of the countries? The answer is no. Among the countries governed by the left, only 59 percent said they have a good opinion of the United States, with Argentina having a low 35 percent of approval and Nicaragua with 78 percent. This slightly contrasts with the 75 percent of inhabitants of countries *not* governed by the left that had a good opinion of the United States, with Mexico setting the lower bound of 54 percent approval and Honduras setting the high bound with 90 percent approval. At least on this specific matter there seems to be some congruence between the discourse of the left and the opinions prevailing in countries governed by the left, although it is still surprising to find that more than 70 percent of Ecuadorians, Nicaraguans, and Peruvians had a good opinion of the United States.

Taking a different approach, we can see whether ideological orientations show the patterns that would be expected by individuals identifying with the left. After all, if many leaders on the left have advocated strong

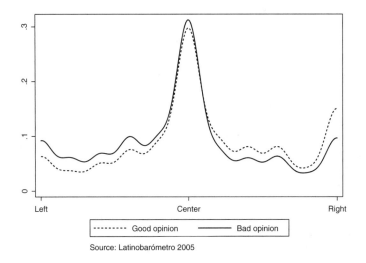

Source: Latinobarómetro 2005

Figure 5.2 Ideological orientation by opinion of the United States.

anti-American positions, we should expect that individuals identified with the left share this same preference. Latin Americans identified with the left were slightly more prone to have a bad opinion of the United States, but not in the overwhelming numbers that the fierce anti-American rhetoric employed by some leftist leaders might make us think. Similarly, people identified with the right were slightly more prone to have a better opinion of the United States, but again the differences were marginal. Figure 5.2 shows that once ideology is taken into account, the differences in opinion about the United States were not as divergent as would be expected.

Nationalism and United States' (lack of) activism in Latin America

The incoming administration of George W. Bush proclaimed its sensitivity towards Latin America and promptly dubbed the renewed ties with many Latin American countries as the "most important" relationships for the Bush White House. That quickly changed after 9/11. And today, the commonplace view is that the United States has neglected its ties with Latin America (Shifter 2005; Valenzuela 2005; Hakim 2006), thus permitting— or at least not obstructing—the rise of governments identified with the left in the continent. It seems naïve to think that this shift in the focus in the Bush administration might be responsible for the surge of Chávez, Morales or Kirchner, especially as evidence suggests that other processes were at work from the beginning of the 1990s (see, for instance, Morales in this volume). But as a counterfactual exercise, had the status of Latin America been upgraded in the White House as seemed bound to happen before 9/11, it is likely that two different effects might have occurred: the nationalist and anti-imperialist discourse of the left could have been fueled as the United States became more active in the region, or sentiments towards the United States could have changes as the renewed interest translated into policies with palpable results. The fact is we will never know.

In the post 9/11 world, and given the low profile of Latin America in U.S. foreign policy, it is relevant to ask if any of the anti-American sentiment that was seen in the hemisphere up to the 1990s changed at all. Zogby International released information on the attitudes of Latin American elites towards the United States, which give us a fuller perspective on the perceptions of the United States in Latin America.

Zogby's 2005 and 2006 Latin America Elite Surveys reveal that 81 percent of opinion leaders interviewed in Mexico, Colombia, Chile, Venezuela, Brazil, and Argentina rate George W. Bush's handling of relations with Latin America as negative. But, in general, the United States continues to be considered the most important country for Latin America. Looking more closely, opinion leaders identified with the left consider China the most important country for Latin America, while those identified with the right think of the United States as the most important country. This can be due to the fact that two thirds of the countries included in the survey are governed by the left, or to the fact that many countries in Latin America have already forged commercial ties with China. Or it could simply be that the United States is losing standing in the eyes of Latin American elites in the left.

The natural question to ask next is whether the attitudes expressed by the elites resemble the attitudes reflected in Latin American public opinion. This is clearly a relevant question since the nationalist discourse is directed at all potential voters on each country. Furthermore, the answers to this question might also illustrate why some governments that are identified with the left do not fully endorse a nationalist discourse, while some others do. In general terms, both Latin American elites and public opinion share positive attitudes towards the United States, although average attitudes become less positive among countries governed by the left. Once the ideological dimension is introduced, most of the differences that would be expected between the attitudes of individuals identified with the left and the right simply vanish. That is, people who identify with the left are not overwhelmingly more likely to have a negative opinion of the United States, nor are they more likely to oppose economic integration.

The nationalist praxis of the left

Surprisingly—and despite what public opinion data reveals—governments from the left keep on adhering to an implicit or explicit nationalist discourse aimed primarily at the United States. So who is the audience for the nation-alists in the left? Interestingly enough, it seems that nationalist leaders are speaking to individuals all over the ideological spectrum, and not only to those on the left. In other words, the use of a nationalistic anti-American discourse is not placing the ideological limits that we would have expected. That is, when leftists speak against the United States, they are being listened to by individuals both on the left and on the right.

It was not hard at the beginning of the 1990s to argue the difficulties of redefining nationalism. Without the hard evidence we provide, it would have been easy to argue that changing the anti-American discourse would alienate leftist voters. Furthermore, it would also have been easy to elabo-rate on the difficulties of convincing elites that the left would endorse the policies that it had previously rejected. Today, it seems that the situation is radically different. The obstacles that the left would have once faced to rede-fine nationalism seem to have been minimized. Latin American elites still place the United States at the top of their list of important countries, and the public generally holds a good opinion about the United States. This is per-haps a good scenario for trying to substitute opposition to the United States, and redirect it to some specific policies (Castañeda 1993).

Of course, this added leeway imposes fewer constraints on the left to change its nationalistic rhetoric, but it also reduces the urgency to change the discourse. This might be one reason that explains leftist presidents throughout Latin America making use of both types of rhetoric: some explicitly anti-American and some tacitly pro-American, some explicitly anti-integration, some explicitly pro-integration. That could help explain why Chile, Brazil, Peru—and Uruguay to an extent—advocate ties with the United States and exchange state visits with the White House, while Venezuela, Argentina, Nicaragua, Ecuador, and Bolivia chastise the United States and even organize protests against George W. Bush when he is in the region.

It is nonetheless puzzling to observe nationalist outbreaks in countries where we would not expect them. Not too long ago—on October 7, 2007—a referendum took place in Costa Rica to determine whether the country should enact the Dominican Republic–Central America–United States Free Trade Agreement (CAFTA–DR) that had earlier been approved by its Legislative Assembly. CAFTA–DR was enacted as a result of a razor-thin margin of votes, as only 51.3 percent of voters favored it. This case is unex-pected because it arose in one of the most stable and consolidated democ-racies in Latin America where, we would think, this fashion of nationalism would not take root. But despite what would otherwise seem adequate expectations, nearly half the Costa Rican voters turned out to explicitly reject free trade with the United States.

Back to the question of interest: if Latin Americans are not necessarily anti-American and nationalism does not particularly resonate with leftist voters, then why do political parties in the left insist on using this rhetoric? Perhaps it is simply that nationalism is written on the left's DNA. That is, the Latin American left cannot imagine itself without relying on a nationalist discourse. Whatever the left in Latin America is, it *must* be based on defending the idea of a nation from foreign powers, namely the United States. As a result of this view, any self-respecting left must abide by a nationalist and anti-American creed. Take away this feature, and the Latin American left is stripped away from a defining characteristic.

But this might be signaling an even deeper problem. It could be the case that the leaders of parties in the left have not grasped the fact that nationalism is an element that resonates not only with voters on the left, but with some voters on the right as well, which might end up simply producing a bad targeting of voters. Alternatively, and perhaps in a much simpler explanation, the leaders of the Latin American left are too constrained by inertia to simply modify their discourse. That is, after years of resorting to nationalism as a key element of the discourse of the left, they might be reluctant to eliminate it from rhetoric as it is uncertain what would happen to their constituencies were this element absent. In other words, given the uncertainty associated with the effects of dropping nationalism altogether, the cost of doing so might simply be too high. But it might simply be a pragmatic decision. To the extent that the left keeps a nationalist discourse in place *before* taking office, it can have a justification to engage in nationalizations—as was the case in Venezuela and Bolivia, for instance—that would serve to "give back to the people" what was rightfully theirs in the first place.

In any case, all of this has been coupled with the inability of the left to generate an alternative element on its discourse to replace nationalism. If that is the case, then it should not come as a surprise that the left in some countries is taking a step back and redirecting its discourse away from nationalism. Sometimes wholeheartedly and sometimes more timidly, the left in these countries seems to be pulling away somewhat from the old-school nationalism. Take, for example, Chile and its open desire to engage in free trade with the United States, or Brazil's Lula taking heat from his own party for photo ops with George W. Bush when promoting ethanol technology in the United States, or Uruguay's Tabaré Vázquez taking some steps against free trade with the United States, yet hosting President Bush during his recent Latin American tour in 2007.

Despite all these changes, the situation seems to resemble in many ways that prevailing at the beginning of the 1990s. Extrapolating from discourse and praxis, we can only conclude that the Latin American left still "knows better what it opposes than what it favors" (Lomnitz 2006). In essence, this underscores a problem that the Latin American left still faces today: it has not been able to define its agenda clearly, nor generate sets of consistent policy preferences that may be coordinated among administrations on the left.

The contrast with the European left has been made time and time again, yet we still have a Latin American left that changes its features depending on its latitude and longitude, but also depending on the leader-in-turn. Not only has the Latin American left not taken the road of coherent unification of goals, but it seems to lack any drive to move away from nationalism.

Tangentially, this brings us back to the issue that has been discussed when attempting to make sense of the recent surge of the left in Latin America, and trying to define its contours. If there were only one relatively homogenous left, it shouldn't be hard to identify what the left stands for, what it opposes, or how it defines itself before the new issues that have forcefully arisen in the last decade—discrimination, minority rights, abortion, environment, and the like. But there seems to be too much diversity among leftists to consider it a single species. If there is more than one left, we might not be able to find a shared agenda or even discourse that unifies the left across countries. And speaking only in terms of nationalism, the features on each country—as we suggested above—seem to be too divergent to confidently state that there is one prevailing view with some minor deviations among the left in Latin America.

Part III

Case studies

Chapter 6

The New and the Old in Brazil's PT

Gianpaolo Baiocchi and Sofia Checa

In June of 2005, the first allegations of a rogue politician in a rightwing party in coalition with the ruling Workers' Party (Partido dos Trabalhadores, PT) seemed spurious enough. The politician himself, Roberto Jefferson, had a long history of allegations of corruption, and of narrowly escaping indictment in Brazil's last national corruption crisis in 1993. According to celebrity magazines, he had had a makeover, including plastic surgery, before coming forward with the allegations of a "payment for votes" scheme in which the ruling PT doled out a monthly allowance for sympathetic politicians in Congress. The allegations seemed so absurd and at odds with the image of the Workers' Party as a party of ethical political outsiders that the first reaction by many inside and outside the PT was to denounce Jefferson and the media as organizing a conspiracy and attempting a coup against Lula, the people's president.

What developed over the next six months strained credulity. Fact after fact appeared to corroborate some of the allegations, and the crisis grew to embroil many important players in the PT. Allegations extended to malfeasance in the running of the national oil company, national telecommunications, the post office, as well as claims about the existence of secret accounting mechanisms that the Workers' Party had used to circumvent election campaign laws. The political theater that followed included hours of live televised debate of the Congressional Inquiry Commission. Streets emptied the way they do when the national soccer team plays and memorable catchphrases were discussed the next day at work like the best soap operas.

It was the worst crisis of the Lula administration, and the low point of the history of the PT. The evaluation of the administration in public opinion polls sank, and the media began to tout the beginning of the end of the party, sounding the death knell for Lula's "adventuresome" years in office and his meteoric career from dissident labor organizer in the late 1970s to president of the world's ninth largest economy. The crisis compounded the party's humiliating defeat at the 2004 municipal elections, which threw out of office several important PT administrations. And that followed the crisis leading to the expulsion of four parliamentarians in 2003 as result of an internal fight over the direction of the country's economy.

A debate has ensued in Brazil about whether the "dream was over"; whether the PT, which for so many years had appeared to do the impossible, balancing social justice, good governance, and electoral results, had finally succumbed to the seductions of power. Or perhaps, that the party that at one point seemed to draw praise from "anti-globalization" activists in the North and the South alike, now revealed itself to be little more than another conventional and corrupt political party in Brazil, driven by electoral calculations and guided by marketing gurus. Or even more sadly, whether the party that originally declared itself a party where movements could speak, turned out to have been authoritarian and opaque all along, with more than a little of the old bad habits of the old left. Books and magazine articles flooded Brazilian bookstores, alleging to show the Michelsian and irrevocable growing authoritarianism in the party evident since its start. Pent-up resentment from conservative sectors of the country's intelligentsia has poured out, with not a little measure of open class prejudice about the fourth-grade educated president. These feelings, which could not find expression during all the years during which the PT might have seemed naïve but also pure and unassailable, had become ubiquitous, coming to drive the editorial line of newspapers and magazines.

The truth is that, despite recent events, the PT can lay claim to inventing, or perhaps discovering, something new for the left in Latin America in the 1980s and 1990s. If the left all over the continent was going local and going social, as Jorge Castañeda presciently wrote in 1993, the PT's innovations in that context were not just its organic relationships with social movements. It discovered, at the local levels, a way to *govern* with all of those movements and with unorganized citizens besides. It found a way to mediate various movements and platforms *through* government, while managing to stay *in* government. This new kind of socialist practice, once perfected, transformed the party as well as the Brazilian political landscape. At the local level the PT managed to build a solid electoral base by being a social justice party that could deliver good governance. Parties from all ends of the spectrum now emulate and invoke participatory schemes originally championed by the PT.

Much of the discussion in Brazil about the PT, however, today revolves around Lula's own "about-face" and the seductions of power, and about the impossibility of doing much in the current global moment. It is true that the PT's platforms have in recent years steadily moved away from mentions of socialism, and it is true that the threat of capital flight is real. But if rather than comparing the national administration to the militant rhetoric of Lula or the PT's founders in 1979 we consider the practices of the PT in executive power in national and local power in recent years, a different contrast emerges. What is distinctive about the national administration is not so much economic pragmatism, but the abandonment of one of the hallmarks of the PT in power: its creative forms of empowered popular participation that accompanied an admittedly growing economic pragmatism. A careful look at the PT in the last few years shows it shifting, not so much to the ideological center, but toward a new model of relationships between state–party–civil society that combined broad-based participation, redistribution, and good governance, a "participatory road" to social change (Baiocchi 2003b, 2003c; Goldfrank and Schneider 2003; Macaulay and Burton 2003). The centerpiece of this participatory strategy has been creative experimentation with forms of progressive governance anchored in broad and empowered participation. These in turn have had the effect for administrators of offering electoral legitimacy, increasing governmental effectiveness, while empowering the disadvantaged to have a voice in state decision-making.

We discuss these facets of the PT in terms of the New and the Old in a political party that reinvented practically everything about itself, but retained some elements of traditional politics in Brazil. Here we will chart the trajectory of the party since its founding, addressing both the party's relationships with movements, its novel local administrations (two examples of the new left within the party), as well as the rudderless coalition politics and personalism that characterized the national administration (examples of the Old that remain within it), before concluding with some thoughts about what has remained of the New after the scandals. To foreshadow our conclusion, we remain cautiously optimistic about the PT as it continues to be a party built by social movement and civil society activists far beyond the organized labor movement over two and a half decades, with many novel governmental experiments to its credit in that time. The Old, which had little expression during the 1980s and 1990s, became apparent again in the following decade. When the PT won Brazil's national elections in 2002, the style of administration was based on a mix of parliamentary alliances with parties of the right (and doling out government positions to those parties), and very much anchored in the popular appeal of Lula himself instead of the governmental participation that characterized the party's earlier administrations.

The party where movements could speak: the 1980s

The years immediately prior to Brazil's transition to the democracy were marked by the burgeoning of mass-based movements around the country, and it is among these movements that the PT was born. Central to the story is the "new unionism" of the late 1970s that challenged both state control of unions and the instrumental use of unions by traditional leftist parties, demanding full union freedom (Branford and Kucinski 1995, pp. 9–10). The successful labor strikes of 1978–1979, in particular, in which Lula was a leader, propelled the discussion about the formation of a Workers' Party. Original disagreements among founders revolved around whether the new party should be class-oriented or have a broader platform, and on who the leadership should be. Lula and other union leaders wanted a party where workers could represent themselves rather than be represented by others. Many intellectuals, including those from the left and center-left, did not believe that the workers had "the knowledge needed to run a party, far less govern the country" (p. 47).

The PT was founded officially in 1980, and from its inception the party's ideology embraced sometimes contradictory elements like workerism and class-consciousness, a participatory democratic ethos, a commitment to social movement autonomy, and a "vocation to govern"—social movement demands for better access to government services. The leaders of the new unionism

> mistrusted the middle class radicals whose vanguardist communist parties of varying stripes regarded Brazilian labor as unprepared for political action; in many ways the New Union leaders felt Brazil's traditional left to be as stifling, manipulative and co-opting as populist and clientelist politicians.
>
> (Guidry 2003, p. 90)

The PT's first party manifesto states that:

> We do not want to own the PT, all the more so because we sincerely believe that among the workers there are activists who are more prepared and more devoted than us; it will be for them to build and lead our party.
>
> (Branford and Kucinsky 1995, p. 48)

The transition to democracy in Brazil allowed some municipal elections in 1982, and in 1985 full municipal elections were held. The PT did not fare too well in the 1982 elections but soon rebounded from its electoral defeat to start a nationwide campaign in 1983 demanding direct elections for the presidency in the 1985 elections, instead of elections through electoral colleges that the military allowed. By the end of 1984 the campaign had turned into a national campaign calling for an end to military rule. In spite of other opposition parties joining in the campaign, the alliance failed to receive the two-thirds majority vote needed in Congress to reinstate direct presidential elections by a few votes. Nonetheless the opposition parties beat "the government at its own game," convincing a majority in the Electoral College, through behind-the-scenes negotiations, to vote for the opposition candidate Tancredo Neves. The PT decided to stay away from this Electoral College vote, criticizing the political elite for returning "to its old practice of resolving everything behind closed doors." Even though the PT was bitterly criticized for this decision, it slowly emerged as the only party that would not compromise its principles as people grew weary of the civilian government.

The PT, since its inception, has had highly decentralized internal structures that were consciously designed to maximize internal democracy and participation. One of the mechanisms established to achieve this goal was the institutionalization of a two-step convention process. The PT holds local (municipal and state-level) pre-conventions that involve a large proportion of the party membership, followed by an Annual National Meeting that basically serves to ratify these earlier decisions at the local levels. Another feature is that the basic organizational structure of the party is the nucleus. These nuclei are organized mostly on the basis of neighborhoods but they can also be organized by workplace, occupational categories, or social movements. The nuclei, which were intended to be "the primary site of political action by party members, reinforcing the party's links with social movements," were meant to guarantee internal democracy and informed participation in decision-making within the party (Keck 1992, pp. 104–105).

Another feature is the party's structure of internal tendencies, basically smaller ideologically based groups that contest power in the party's internal elections but that act as part of the larger Workers' Party at election time. Some of the tendencies that originally joined the PT at its founding were remnants of underground organizations that had resisted the dictatorship, and in the early years operated as "parties within parties." Since the mid-1980s the issue of tendencies has been regularized, with a requirement that tendencies have to adhere to the party's program in order to be part of the PT.

While the party's commitment to internal democracy allowed for a wide array of opinions and factions to co-exist within the party, it also made the PT different from most other political parties in that it did not have a set "political identity" save for some broad agreements on the goals of social justice, social change, internal democracy, and a commitment to social movements. The PT thus had a varied composition and ideological make-up throughout the country, depending on the strength of particular movements at various locales. Since the beginning, it has had close relationships with popular movements, unions, human rights groups, farmers' organizations, the progressive Catholic Church and the like. It is no wonder that the PT has been referred to as a "conglomeration of movements—women's groups, organisations of indigenous peoples, Afro-Brazilian groups, environmentalists, Catholic communities subscribing to liberation theology—who retained their group identity while working within the party, which prided itself for its diffuse, decentralised, associationist character" (Ahmad 2006). The Landless Workers' Movement (Movimento dos Sem Terra) or MST was integral to the formation of the PT. A few years after its birth, the PT also helped form the CUT (Central Unica dos Trabalhadores) or United Workers' Central, one of the biggest labor federations in Brazil (Guidry 2003, p. 91). Both movements "became the principal means through which the PT spread its influence in the country at large and especially among the urban workers, landless rural workers and the allied strata" while still remaining autonomous of the party (Ahmad 2006, p. 129).

Even though the PT has its roots in the labor unions, it has never maintained formal institutional relations with unions and is not controlled or funded by the unions either (Branford and Kucinski 1995, p. 7). Lula's "lack of connection with traditional unions and parties on the left," according to Desai (2002), offered "a fresh (albeit unwitting) tactical advantage that galvanized and mobilized previously unmobilized workers." She argues that the party's "movementist character" has been instrumental "to its gains in credibility and its creation of a mass base" (p. 650). The Workers' Party "brings together the interests of both organized labor and the broader social bases on which both the party and labor movement rely for support" (Guidry 2003, pp. 83–84). In the early years, the PT had as its base social movements in particular settings where urban movements or the new unionism were strong. São Paulo's industrial belt (the so-called ABC region) and São Paulo itself, for example, were sites of early PT activity.

Despite the troubles that the PT faced in its initial term in local governance in the late 1980s (see next section), overall the 1980s were a time of increasing popularity for the PT. It drew a lot of attention and support as the only political party in Brazilian politics which refused to compromise its principles, highly valued internal democracy and did not seek to dominate social movements.

Consolidation of participatory mechanisms and the "PT way": the 1990s

If what drew attention to the PT in the 1980s was its novelty in the Brazilian political scene, what called attention in the 1990s was its model of local governance.[1] This model, enshrined as the "Democratic Thesis" in the 1999 party congress, allowed local-level PT administrations to carry out successful tenures in power without having to succumb to excessively broad legislative alliances or to excessive infighting among its bases of support. The PT administrators crafted in the 1990s a model of participatory governance that managed to harness the creativity of civil society while continually expanding the party's bases of support and its arenas of concern.

In the 1988 elections the PT earned particularly significant results at the municipal level. A number of notable mayors belonging to Brazil's left-of-center parties with ties to civil society were elected in Brazilian capitals in 1985 and 1988, including Porto Alegre. Most PT administrations, though, had a rather rough first term in office, the main predicament being the inability of various administrations to effectively negotiate different societal demands. The PT administration in São Paulo, of 1989–1992, for instance, at various times came under attack for giving "special privileges" to social movements sympathetic to the party without considering "the whole city's interests," resulting in charges of "left patronage" (Kowarick and Singer 1994, pp. 240–247). But when the administration did attend to some of those interests, it was accused of "class treason" by some sectors within the party (p. 249).

Other administrations, particularly in areas where the PT was strong within local movements and public sector unions, faced similar problems of administrations being unable to distance themselves from the demands made by sympathetic social movements. Both the Diadema (1982–1985) and Fortaleza (1986–1988) experiences showed that in addition to having to offer effective service provision to all in the city, new PT administrations would also likely be flooded with demands from their bases of support upon their election to office (Simões 1992). Both also showed that good social programs by themselves would not guarantee the party's office.

To avoid similar problems, the party created the National Department for the Discussion of Institutional Action in 1988 to coordinate plans of action for local-level victories (Bittar 1992). Four principles made up the PT vision for municipal government; these included popular participation, transparent governance, state democratization, and the creation of a new political culture. Still, most PT administrations had difficulties in the 1989–1992 period. Of the thirty-six PT administrations in power during this period, twelve mayors left the PT under factional disputes before the end of their terms, and only twelve of the remaining twenty-four won reelection. Different factions within the PT clashed over how to govern, specifically on whether the PT was "an administration for workers, [or a] leftist administration that governs for the whole city, on the basis of a commitment to popular sectors?" (Utzig 1996, p. 210). Another challenge that the PT faced emerged out of the uncertainty of the goals of a progressive administration. There were disagreements over whether local administrations should merely be considered tactical outposts in the larger struggle for a socialist transformation or whether they should be, first and foremost, used to actively carry out effective socioeconomic programs (Vacarezza et al. 1989). The inability of various administrations to effectively negotiate different demands did not just create internal problems, but also led to external pressures, especially in areas where the PT was strong within local movements and public sector unions. Despite their good intentions, most of the PT administrations in its "home state" of São Paulo were voted out of office after only one term in 1992. Still other administrations near industrial centers, like those in the state of Minas Gerais, had similar difficulties. In almost all these administrations, the failures were attributed to breakdowns in the relationships between the administration, party, and civil society (Machado 1993).

The debacle of the Luiza Erundina administration in São Paulo was emblematic of the challenges that faced the party. Having come into power with support of the "left" tendencies of the party, she quickly ran into difficulties with segments of the party that accused her of being too moderate and administratively minded. Despite impressive accomplishments by the end of her first year in office (such as the rationalization of debt payments, cancellation of dubious large-scale projects from the previous administration, and several social programs), Erundina's administration was besieged by its former bases of support, having to face off throughout her tenure with PT-controlled municipal unions. Caught between its attempts to placate its bases of support, whose demands were much higher than its ability to meet them, the administration found itself increasingly isolated from its support base and from the populace at large as it tried to carry out a platform that, in principle, was beneficial to the city's less privileged majority (Couto 1996).

In contrast to the politically costly failures in São Paulo, some PT administrations such as in the city of Santos or Porto Alegre were able to carry out various ambitious reforms such as the implementation of land-use taxes targeted at wealthier citizens in Porto Alegre, which helped fund many urban improvement projects in the city's poorer periphery, as well as the implementation of participatory programs as a strategy for negotiation of demands and legitimation of platforms with the population at large in ways that helped avert some of the conflicts. Successful programs like Participatory Budgeting (PB) in Porto Alegre drew large numbers of participants as empowered decision-makers into matters of governance, here specifically deciding on new forms of local investment.

Since its inception in 1989, PB has evolved into a complex structure of city-wide fora where elected delegates from civic groups meet regularly to discuss, prioritize, and monitor investments needed in each district, ranging from street pavements, sewage, social services, housing, education, and any other projects within the scope of municipal government. Of the hundreds of projects approved over the years, investment in the poorer residential regions of the city has far exceeded investment in wealthier areas, and as a result of these public policies, the city has much broader coverage in terms of services, from running water to sewage and education. It created settings where claimants themselves could be part of the negotiation of demands; in terms of governance, this generated legitimacy for strategies of governance, if not improving governance directly. By bringing conflict to be resolved into participatory settings, administrators found ways to generate consensus around redistributive platforms, and helped prevent conflict against the administration. Participatory Budgeting in time became a widely applied form of the "PT way of governing." The contrast with São Paulo is striking because in Porto Alegre, unlike in São Paulo, the PT originally had a much weaker base of support among unions and neighborhood associations.

Thus, the party continued to grow in the 1990s. During its 1993–1996 tenure, and especially in the 1997–2000 period, PB became a trademark of the party, helping propel its hundreds of municipal electoral victories in the period. In 1998, the party registered gubernatorial victories in the state of Rio Grande do Sul and in the Amazonian state of Acre and the central state of Mato Grosso do Sul, while the left-coalition victory in Rio de Janeiro brought the black PT activist Benedita da Silva to a vice-governor's seat. That year it won seven senatorial seats and fifty-nine seats in Congress. In the year 2000, 187 PT mayors won contests, bringing the PT back to power in São Paulo and reelecting the PT in Porto Alegre for the fourth time. By the late 1990s, the kinds of difficulties faced by early administrations were essentially unheard of. Innovations and accumulated experience were shared across municipalities and new administrators could count on the accumulated knowledge of almost two decades. While in no two municipalities is Participatory Budgeting exactly alike, lessons and best practices were widely disseminated in the 1990s.

"The PT way" seemed to be a successful recipe for the party, as it became known for innovative municipal institutions that were redistributive, transparent, and efficient. One element of the recipe was that the party actually delivered good governance. For many voters, trash collection or an effective transportation system was decisive at election time, and party administrators in time learned to respect the importance of such seemingly prosaic concerns. Another element of the recipe is that broad-scale participation under a clear system of rules has the potential of generating legitimacy for redistributive governmental projects. Having thousands of citizens publicly decide on the redistribution of government resources (be it schools or infrastructure to poor areas) makes it difficult for opponents in the media or in the legislative to derail these projects. No less important is the fact that participatory institutions that were successful drew on large-scale participation of the poor, generally much beyond organized sectors. This was crucial for the legitimacy of participation, lest it be seen as a partisan or special interest project (helping avoid the charge of "clientelism of the left" that befell some early administrations[2]). Going beyond organized sectors also helped moderate the demands of organized sectors that sometimes put administrators in a corner, not able to meet the demands of individual movements, let alone adjudicate between them. The very structure of participatory institutions was designed to *not* privilege the organized. Most Participatory Budgeting institutions, for example, allow citizens to participate individually, and as representatives of their streets or boroughs, but not as representatives of social movements.[3]

Even cities known for high levels of civic organization, like Porto Alegre, have drawn on large numbers of unorganized participants, who in time became a reliable base of support for the party. In the early years of the PT administration the majority of participants in the Participatory Budget might have been tied to neighborhood associations, but as the process matured it came to draw on more and more participants who had no other form of civic engagement. Many of those participants stay with the process and "rise through the ranks," becoming increasingly engaged in it. Many of them go on to start associations in their neighborhoods. These unorganized or formerly unorganized poor urban residents formed a base of support and sympathy for the party-as-government without necessarily joining it. In the case of Porto Alegre, there are districts of loyal PT voters that do not have a PT nucleus, a once unthinkable combination. In those areas the majority of the existing civic infrastructure essentially came to be because of Participatory Budgeting, and participation in Participatory Budgeting is as feverish as its results are tangible. Descriptions of Participatory Budgeting programs in other places with low pre-existing social movement activity are similar.[4]

One of the results of this way of governing was a tectonic shift in the party's relationship to the organized and the unorganized over the decade. Preoccupations and heady debates about the party's relationship to social movements—i.e. a Leninist relationship? a Gramscian approach?—became less important than the discussion of the relationship of the party to a party-led government, and eventually about the relationship of the party-led government to the governed—i.e. a government for all? a government for workers? In many cities with PT administrations that worked, the municipal government became the face of the party, the party-as-municipal government engaged organized and unorganized alike, and the party's relationship to social movements outside questions of governance became more circumspect.

The PT also continued to transform itself through the broadening of alliances as well as the range of issues it took up in local elections and through the continued ideological evolution and refinement of its doctrines throughout the 1990s. During that period its base of support grew across states, spreading out from its traditional stronghold of São Paulo to include central, northern, and northeastern states; it also started winning votes in medium and small-sized cities, inching away from its origins as a large-city based party (Magalhães et al. 1999). The nature of the party leadership also changed, with fewer union leaders and more activists from other social movements, and principally from public administrators who were becoming more central to the party's public face (Gaglietti 1999; Novaes 1993; Singer 2001).

It might be argued that the centrality of governance to the PT and the PT's direct relationship to the unorganized via its administrations has a component of old-style Latin American populism, as do the visible redistributive urban projects it engaged in once in power. This did not escape critics from the right, who at times accused the PT of becoming a party of public works for the poor. For a party founded as an *alternative* to populist models, this was no doubt also of concern to activists within it. But there were two crucial differences with a populist stance: first was a decided *lack* of emphasis on individual politicians and mayors, and a real emphasis on platforms and government programs; and second, there was a real concern with voice for participants, and internal democracy within participatory programs. As documented by many scholarly accounts, such participatory programs were driven by a genuine concern with participation, inclusion, and transparency.[5] Where PT programs were successful they resulted in a transformation of local politics, with the inclusion of many previously excluded voices into the running of government. In some instances, this also resulted in a "fragile equation" in which local politics became a dialogue between a local PT-led state that dialogued with legions of unorganized citizens who participated in its participatory arrangements (Silva et al. 2006).

The decade of the 1990s also saw an evolution of the party's programmatic orientation. In 1993, the party approved the plan for a two-stage "social revolution" moving toward socialism. A few years later, in 1999 at a national party congress, the party defined its platform as "democratic socialism"—a mixed-market model reliant on broad popular participation, income redistribution, rule of law, and heavy investment in the country's internal market (Singer 2001). More and more, the party made "good governance through participation" an integral part of its platforms and administrations. The program laid out in 1999 is an ambitious strategy for an eventual national government that would take the best lessons from local governments under the PT. In addition to connecting with different social struggles using strategies as wide as land occupations, strikes, and other mobilizations, and extending party affiliations, the program calls for an extension of the experience of local-level administrations to the national government. The Program of the Democratic Revolution, a programmatic thesis accepted in 1999, states that

> The PT has been a pioneer in this political experimentalism that permits combining representative with direct democracy. The Participatory Budgets, diffused at the local level, are now being implemented at the state level and must be part of a future national project. The participation of workers, users, and representatives of society will allow the democratization of public policies, of public enterprises, and of private activities essential to the population ... A democratic state—controlled by society—will be called to perform a decisive role in the new political economy.
>
> (Partido dos Trabalhadores 1999, p. 13)

The PT of the late 1990s had much that was new about it. The "political experimentalism" of the decade had paid off; the party "where social movements could speak" had found a way to also be the "party that creatively ran local governments." It had devised a way of doing so by connecting with populations through forms of direct participation, and found ways to dialogue with its traditional base of support in movements, but also, increasingly with the unorganized. Looking across Brazil in the late 1990s it was possible to find a virtual rainbow of issues and causes that were directly supported through local PT administrations. The party also managed to garner middle-class legitimacy and support in many settings. For the Latin American left, it was a story full of positive lessons and examples about the potential for something really new within the left.

The third decade's "about-face"? Little participation, many coalitions and much conflict

It is not surprising that Lula's victory in October of 2002 was met with much anticipation. The election of a militant labor leader and political prisoner of humble origins was unprecedented in the country, and for *petistas* it marked the end of a long quest for national power that had eluded them in 1989, 1994, and 1998, and included years of grass-roots organizing and two decades of managing local administrations of all sizes. For many observers, Lula's victory held the potential for the translation of some of the principles, if not the actual institutions, of participation that had been the hallmark of PT governance in the 1990s.

Early on, there were signs that the administration would embark on the participatory platforms that were part of the party program. Though only subject of a single paragraph in the government plan, national Participatory Budgeting, or something like it, was expected of the administration in many quarters. Lula marked the beginning of his term with the formation of the Council for Economic and Social Development modeled after the Spanish experience of Concertación and inspired by Scandinavian corporatist arrangement. In principle, it was to be a body for state–civil society dialogue, thus enshrining popular voice in the national administration. Veteran PT administrators with participatory experience were placed in prominent posts in the administration. National conferences on topics like Health and AIDS were announced to take place in Brasilia, with the participation of organized civil society.

However, there were other signs as well. The PT found itself at the head of an implausibly broad coalition with parties from the center and from the right, doling out posts to coalition members. Some ministry posts were occupied by conservatives from outside the PT, and others by radicals from within. Another worrisome sign was the renewed emphasis on the figure of Lula himself and his close advisors, the so-called "hard nucleus" of the party, which distanced themselves from direct dialogue with bases from the party. These latter two were uncharacteristic of the party, especially the personal emphasis—seldom did successful local PT administrations rely on the charisma or personal appeal of a mayor in campaigns, with public works and governance strategies much more often occupying center-stage.

The national agenda was, of course, also limited by the constant threat of capital flight or a fall in "investor confidence" in the country. The country risk rating that had shot up with Lula's first gains in the polls in 2002 was eventually lowered, and foreign investment in Brazil has continued apace after a relative decline in the first months of the PT administration. The "Argentina scenario" was averted: there has not been a return to inflation, and the Real is holding steady against the dollar. As promised by Lula in the months leading up to his election, Brazil has honored its debt payments, and has exceeded primary surplus targets set by the IMF. As the administration's critics have been quick to point out, economic policies carried out by the PT government have been indistinct from the previous regimes, and at odds with the party's social movements base of support or its programmatic goals of redistribution and social justice.

In the end, Lula's first term was characterized by compliance with IMF orthodoxy, limited government investment in the national economy, and very little social spending on health, education or housing. A protracted corruption scandal hurt the party's image for many. While corruption is not as endemic within the party or the government as the conservative media has suggested, it was nonetheless established that the PT was no longer a party of social-movement activists turned politicians, and that the party's internal machinery is today as complex and opaque as that of any other party. In its search for legitimacy during political difficulties the administration has relied on Lula's direct appeals to the *povo*—the unorganized poor— as a way to garner support during troubled times, a strategy that proved successful in terms of reelection but may be a dubious legacy for the party. We discuss these events in what follows, with attention to the Old and the New in the PT, as we discuss four aspects of the Lula administration: Brazil's foreign policy under the PT, national participatory programs, the government's relationship with social movements, and the administration's income transfer program.

Foreign policy innovations

Even those who have criticized the Lula presidency for its economic policies have praised its achievements in the field of international affairs (Hunter and Power 2005; Sader 2005; Soares de Lima and Hirst 2006). International relations have historically not been a very prominent issue in Brazilian party platforms during elections so it is difficult to track changes, but it appears that PT positions under Lula have remained consistent with earlier PT positions. PT's foreign policy positions have essentially remained the same in its various proposed government programs since the late 1980s—a few paragraphs without much detail. While anti-imperialism was mentioned in a few sentences in founding documents and may have been part of its slogans, proposed foreign policy has always been surprisingly pragmatic, with a repeated emphasis over the years on national sovereignty rather than the internationalism of parties like the Cuban Communist Party. The PT's first government program, written on the eve of the 1989 campaign, called for "an autonomous and sovereign foreign policy without automatic alignments, and guided by the principle of self-determination of peoples and non-interference in internal affairs of other countries," as well as for Brazil to "occupy a position in the international scenario compatible with its socio-economic, geographical, and cultural stature" to contribute to a new economic order that does not only benefit richer countries, with the formation of bodies like a Latin American Parliament (Partido dos Trabalhadores 1989).[6] Lula's 2007/2010 Government Platform calls for defense of multilateralism, initiatives in favor of a fairer economic order, and for respect for the principles of "national sovereignty, non aggression and non interference in the domestic affairs of other states" while "strengthening South–South relations."

Foreign policy under the PT has been quite different than under previous administrations in Brazil, with a renewed emphasis on building up Brazilian influence in regional politics, on South–South ties and a stronger defense of national interests. It has not been without its ambiguities (for example, the definition of national interest could at times mean national industry but not its workers), and at times seemed orchestrated to barely avoid a collision course with its powerful neighbor to the North, but it represents something new in terms of pragmatic innovations that escape leftist rigidity while advancing multilateralism and the sovereignty of nations of the global South. One of the guiding principles has been to expand Brazilian influence "in regional politics, in Third World agendas and in multilateral institutions" (Soares de Lima and Hirst 2006). This is evident in its active role in efforts to mediate crises in neighboring countries such as Venezuela, Colombia, Bolivia, and Ecuador; its active role in the World Trade Organization (WTO) as well as the Free Trade Area of the Americas (FTAA) negotiations; its efforts to reform the United Nations Security Council (UNSC) to include more developing countries as permanent and non-permanent members as well as a campaign for a permanent seat for Brazil on the UNSC; and its active role in the UN's Action against Hunger and Poverty campaign (Soares de Lima and Hirst 2006; Hunter and Power 2005; Inter Press Service, June 15, 2004).

Two of the most important foreign policy innovations have been the creation and coordination of the G-20 (the Group of Twenty) and the IBSA (India–Brazil–South Africa) Trilateral. The G-20, a "revival of the Third World coalition spirit" (Soares de Lima and Hirst 2006, p. 27) was created during WTO's Fifth Ministerial Conference in 2003 led by Brazil, India, and South Africa, and emerged as a "new force that can act as a counter-weight to the dominant powers in the WTO" to fight against farm subsidies and trade barriers in developed countries to develop fairer trade rules (Inter Press Service, October 7, 2003). It is because of the strong stance taken by the G-20 and its refusal to give in to the demands of the industrialized countries that the WTO talks ended in failure in Cancún. The ensuing Doha rounds have so far faced a similar fate because of the steadfastness of the block of developing countries. It is no longer possible "for the developed countries to get their way with the developing world by a combination of bullying, cajoling, dividing, bribing and threatening" (*Guardian*, July 13, 2006). IBSA, created in the same year, also aims to foster cooperation on issues ranging from the promotion of South–South cooperation, increasing trade between developing countries, the strengthening of multilateral institutions, the reform and expansion of the UNSC, implementation of policies against poverty and hunger, as well as fighting against racial and gender discrimination (Soares de Lima and Hirst 2006, p. 36). As part of one of the initiatives under IBSA, Brazil, India, and South Africa have pledged $1 million each annually "to support South–South initiatives aimed at helping LDCs [Least Developed Countries] to reduce poverty, and fight hunger and disease." The countries have also cancelled substantial amounts of debts owed by "least developed countries" and provided them greater access to their markets (Inter Press Service, December 21, 2006).

While it is true that "Brazil's foreign policy [has broken] with the right wing's attitude of subservience to the United States" (Sader 2005), the PT-led administration has also been careful not to come into open conflict with the United States or with the International Monetary Fund (IMF) (Hunter and Power 2005). While driven by pragmatism, foreign policy has also not been without ambiguity. In terms of the Chávez regime in Venezuela or Castro in Cuba, Brazil has maintained a careful distance. Brazil is Cuba's second largest trading partner in Latin America, and it has officially opposed the U.S. embargo, but Lula has avoided public statements that might be interpreted as anti-American on the question. In his visit to the island, for example, public pronouncements studiously avoided mentioning the United States. Similarly, with regards to Venezuela, Brazil has maintained close ties but Lula has on several occasions publicly distanced himself from Chávez. With the possible exception of the presence in Haiti of some 1,200 ill-prepared Brazilian peacekeepers, Brazilian foreign policy under Lula has been generally creative, pragmatic and free of dogma, and a clear expression of the New in the PT.

Limited participatory programs

In sharp contrast has been the failure of the national administration to translate the novel experiments in governance that defined the party in the

1990s to the national administration. Despite early overtures, the administration has not dialogued with civil society in any sustained way over government policies. The Council for Social and Economic Development
(CDES) was set up to create a state–civil society dialogue to foster a "new
social contract" (SINDPD 2003). Roughly modeled on similar national
councils in social-democratic countries, the CDES includes representatives
from government, business, trade unions, and civil society, in addition to
the presence of twelve ministers. Headed in its first year by Participatory
Budget architect Tarso Genro, the CDES was heralded as an "important
instrument" for making debate surrounding policy questions more democratic (*Gazeta Mercantil*, August 20, 2003). Unlike instruments like the
Participatory Budget, however, the CDES was not vested with decision-
making power and participation in it is limited to a few civil society representatives. It has also been criticized for allowing little room for
participant-initiated agenda items (*Gazeta Mercantil*, August 20, 2003). In
addition to allowing the administration to articulate a coalition to support
its structural reforms, however, the CDES has accomplished little. For
example, after a series of meetings in 2003 on macro-economic policy, the
council proposed "reducing interest rates and increase public investment"
(*Gazeta Mercantil*, October 23, 2003) but its most of its economic proposals
were not taken up (*Gazeta Mercantil*, August 20, 2003).

Similarly, the PPA—the *Plano Plurianual*, or Multiyear Plan—held for
some the prospect of creating a participatory process on national investment
priorities. A process of consultation with civil society took place in all twenty-
seven states, and culminated in a proposed PPA in August of 2003. The PPA
was extensively modified by both the executive and by Congress, and resulted
in a final document that ultimately privileged certain exporting industries,
such as mining and agro-industry, and included dam construction projects
that were heavily criticized by civil society observers/monitors. The executive
branch in fact submitted a 2006 budget to Congress unrelated to even the
modified PPA. Like the CDES, the PPA process invoked the language of participation, but had an unclear mandate as far as linking that participation to
decision-making. Like the CDES, it became a process that included consultation but locked in "technical decisions" such as interest rates or budgetary
priorities as the exclusive realm of government technocrats.

At stake for social movement and civil society actors are these economic
policies. The current political economic regime has done little to ameliorate
social problems. The government's overhaul of an outdated pension system
as a means to balance the books was certainly viewed with suspicion by
some of the left, as was its controversial decision to *exceed* the target primary budget surpluses set forth by IMF conditionalities. Lula's first term
was characterized by limited government investment in the national economy, let alone social spending on health, education, and housing. Not only
did the central bank's high interest rates (meant to attract foreign capital)

stunt growth and limit credit available to small businesses, but it also means that the Brazilian government has paid billions of dollars in interest at the cost of social spending. This is no different than what happened during the Cardoso years, for example, but what makes it worse is that the election of Lula held the real promise of popular input into these kinds of decisions.

Political legitimacy and its bases of support

If in terms of participation the administration did not translate the party's new practices, its relationship to social movements was also a reversal to old modes of engagement. Instead of creative forms of engagement with civil society, the party returned to bargaining and conflict with social movements. Like the first PT local administrations, the national PT government has had its share of difficulties with its former base of support, and this has created rifts within the party. The landless movement, the MST, has been engaged in a back-and-forth contest with the administration, at times threatening a wave of invasions, and at times promising to wait for campaign promises to be fulfilled. In 2005 the MST organized the National March for Land Reform, which resulted in the administration's announcement of a National Plan of Land Reform, which was not fulfilled by the end of 2006. Similarly, an umbrella organization, the National Coordination of Social Movements, was founded in 2003, bringing together over one hundred movements like the MST and the National Student Union (UNE) that they felt were not given a voice in the administration. The movement is in "favor of national sovereignty, development, jobs, income distribution, and social inclusion" (*Brazzil Magazine*, September 16, 2003). It has organized "public hearings" on FTAA, and carried out several actions in favor of a change in the national political economy, in favor of an audit of the national debt, and asking for a voice in the national administration.

In the 2006 election, the MST, like other social movements, did not endorse Lula until the runoff (Marques and Nakatani 2007). Once a trusted ally, the MST change in attitude towards the PT is evident in the statement about the PT's performance:

> Our analysis of the Lula government's policies shows that Lula favored the agribusiness sector much more than family-owned agriculture. The general guidelines of his economic and agricultural policy have always given priority to the export-oriented agribusiness. And agrarian reform, the most important measure to alter the status quo, is in fact paralyzed or restricted to a few cases of token social compensation.
>
> (Stedile 2007, p. 54)

Like the national Coordination of Social Movements, which would also reluctantly endorse Lula's reelection bid only at the second round, the MST and other previously ardent PT supporters have been distanced from the party as a result of the national administration.

The rifts within the party have been severe. Early on in the administration, leaders of the party passed a resolution that bound all PT members to supporting the Lula administration's economic policies. The "radical wing" of the PT nonetheless fought the pension and tax reforms, and consistently criticized the policies of the central bank. These issues came to a head in July and August of 2003 over the struggle to pass the administration's pension reforms. Four parliamentarians who voted against the administration were expelled by the end of the year and eight others suffered sanctions. The expulsions not only led to the founding of a splinter party, the PSOL, but tainted the party's image of being internally democratic. Shortly after the expulsions, a group called Workers' Party Rescue, consisting of approximately 2,200 PT members and "university allies," recently released a manifesto denouncing Lula, saying his policies mirror the IMF more than the PT's socialist traditions. Many prominent PT activists, like PT founder Chico de Oliveira, have left the party since, dissatisfied not only with the administration's economic policies, but also with the increasing decline in internal democracy as well as the distancing of Lula and his cabinet from the party's bases.

As the corruption scandal unfolded on TV during Lula's third year, it seemed briefly that social movements might have a voice again in the administration. Alliance members abandoned the PT, as it seemed, for the first time since the election, that Lula would lose if not being impeached outright before then. The conservative media in Brazil seized on the accusations, and the barrage temporarily destabilized the party. Perhaps surprisingly, some social movements reacted in defense of the president, though with the understanding that the party in a more precarious electoral situation would more likely heed movement claims for a change in course for the administration.

But instead of an opening to bases of support, the last year of Lula's administration saw a renewed emphasis on his persona. From Lula's part, the last year saw a discourse increasingly tinged with populist and social justice themes, and a series of publicized visits and talks in the impoverished Northeast. Lula himself seldom addressed the corruption scandal; while even members of his cabinet were implicated, Lula claimed ignorance of the malfeasance and addressed the poor directly as their protector in speeches that many have compared to those of former populist president Getúlio Vargas. But at the same time there were few changes in the main policies of the government—save for renewed attention to the administration's large income transfer program, started in earnest in the second year of Lula's tenure. Despite the crises of the PT and the national administration, Lula ended his term with high approval ratings in the months leading to the election, particularly among the poor. The fourth year was also marked by a notable absence of enthusiasm among the organized base in Lula's electoral campaign.

The Bolsa Família program

The *Bolsa Família* program is the most ambiguous facet of the administration. It is a novel policy that is redistributive, costs relatively little, and has had real social impact. At the cost of a fraction of a percentage point of the country's GDP, this direct income-transfer program to the country's poorest has pulled some 11 million families out of dire poverty, altering the country's poverty statistics within a short period of time.[7] However, it is also a program that has been central to Lula's reelection, and not a few skeptical observers have viewed it as strategic. Others have criticized its conditional provisions, arguing it is a paternalistic program more in line with populist governments than with the democratic socialism that has defined the PT.

The *Bolsa Família* is today the largest conditional cash transfer (CCT) scheme in the world (Hall 2006, p. 689), reaching about 30 million of the poorest in the country. In Brazil, different cash transfer programs were first initiated at the local level by municipal governments (for example, *Bolsa Escola* was first started in the Federal District under a PT government in 1995) (Suplicy 2006). Some of these programs were extended to the national level under Cardoso's government and consolidated and expanded under Lula. *Bolsa Família*, a national scheme, was initiated in October 2003 with the integration of two existing conditional cash transfer programs: *Bolsa Escola*, *Bolsa Alimentação*, and two other existing cash transfer programs: *Cartão Alimentação do Fome Zero* and *Auxílio Gás* (Soares et al. 2006, p. 4). Under *Bolsa Família* poor families receive a monthly stipend on the condition that the child/children maintain 85 percent attendance at school, children up to age six be immunized, and pregnant and breast-feeding women have regular health checkups (Soares et al. 2006).

While *Bolsa Família* has no doubt been successful as a temporary measure to lift portions of the population out of poverty, it is in itself not enough and probably needs to be accompanied by higher spending on education and health if root causes of poverty are to be addressed (Hall 2006). The conditional cash transfers have also been criticized, not only for the difficulties faced in implementation but also in its paternalism, in that it does not treat financial/social security as an inherent right, but rather makes it conditional (Hall 2006, p. 705). An alternative from within the PT has come from Senator Eduardo Suplicy (Sao Paulo, PT), for example, who has argued for a universal, unconditional Citizen's Basic Income (Hall 2006; Suplicy 2006) which would provide every citizen with a set basic income, regardless of one's socioeconomic condition. In our view, *Bolsa Família* can eventually come to represent the New or the Old in the party. As critics have pointed out, Lula's strength has increased in the Northeast region of

Brazil as result of the program, because the Northeast is home to three-quarters of the beneficiaries of *Bolsa Família* and the poorest region of the country (Hall 2006, p. 705). Insofar as the program remains a part of the party's electoral strategy and does not evolve into a program that promotes broader notions of entitlement and social safety, the critics of Lula will be correct: that this is a program that provides an unquestionable social good at a real political cost. But perhaps the program will evolve and will broaden notions of entitlement. Some within the party see it as an incremental step toward the provision of a national basic income. The government program, for example, sees *Bolsa Família* as an emergency measure that is part of an expanding safety net and set of government programs, including popular credit schemes and job creation programs. There is also promise that *Bolsa Família* can be part of an expanding notion of citizenship, of not just feeding the poor but giving them a voice in the administration as participants and citizens. If the latter becomes true, then *Bolsa Família* will represent the New within the party.

"Lulismo" vs "Petismo"? The New and the Old in the future of the party

The 2006 elections saw Lula reelected for a second term in a runoff election, with a wide margin over his opponent, a candidate representing a center-right coalition, former São Paulo governor Geraldo Alckmin. The debates leading to the runoff were polarized, with Lula adopting an increasingly populist discourse, and emphasizing their different positions on privatization. It was also a highly polarized electorate. According to the polls, Lula had high acceptance rates from the poor, and very high rejection rates from those in upper income brackets. Some of it, no doubt, has to do with a kind of popular appeal that Lula has among the poorest electors, but much of it has to do with seeing the direct benefits of the administration's redistribution programs. Accordingly, regional votes that came in were very different. The South and Southeast rejected Lula (whereas at one point in time, a state like Rio Grande do Sul could have been counted on to vote to the left), but he had very high approval rates in the poorer North and Northeast, where the PT elected four governors in states far from the traditional bases of support of the party, places rather known for the rule of notoriously conservative landowners.

The party that contested the national election in 2006, though, would have been unrecognizable just a few years ago. Internal dissention led to crises and rifts within the party throughout the Lula administration, from the party's first expulsions of parliamentarians in 2003 to the many prominent departures proceeded by it. It was a party more distanced from social movements than at any other point in its history. This distance also expressed itself in the 2004 municipal elections, when the PT was severely punished in several of its politicized strongholds (like Porto Alegre), something that can only be read as a reaction to national policies. Maybe most damning of all was that the once pure party of outsiders now found itself at the center of corruption allegations. Still, many progressive forces which had refused to support Lula in the first round came out in support for the second. *Brasil de Fato*, an alternative newspaper, for example, declared its endorsement of Lula, indicating that

> like the majority of the forces of the left, we break the silence and endorse Lula. For four years we have shown the limits of his government, but we evaluate that a victory of Alckmin would be a defeat for the working classes.
>
> (*Brasil de Fato*, October 10, 2006)

The CUT supported the reelection campaign throughout, though not without internal contention. Frei Betto, a prominent Liberation Theologian, asked for support among progressive Christians in the terms that seemed to capture the mood among activists in Brazil at the time: "Lula still owes us a lot of what he promised throughout his presidential campaigns, like land reform. But Brazil and Latin America are better with him than without him" (*Brasil de Fato*, October 10, 2006).

The PT itself has throughout all of this shown that much of the Old in Brazilian politics remained within it. The lack of accountability of the party's top echelons to its base spoke of vertical organization; the expulsion of members for not toeing the party line reeked of the authoritarianism that the PT was formed to combat. Coalitions based on electoral calculations and not on ideological affinity may seem a natural fit for twentieth-century Brazilian political history, but are at odds with the PT's programmatic orientation. The electoral campaign, rife with populist appeals and centered on Lula, seems the mirror image of a party that from its inception rejected the populist left tradition.

Of course, the very figure of Lula and the fact that he has been the only candidate to run for president from the PT is in itself at odds with the party. An extremely able politician with powerful appeal to the country's poor majority, Lula has always been in at least one way the least qualified of high-profile *petistas* for the job. Unlike other candidates who have at various points been discussed within the PT, Lula had never held public office. Among potential candidates there have been senators, governors, and mayors with records of governance and public service, sometimes associated with a particularly successful policy or position on government. Lula, in fact, had not even been president of the party for many years, holding instead an honorary and lifetime position.

All of these facets of governance mentioned above, that Lula and his advisors embarked on, speak to a way of going about the business of governing that is radically different from the new ways that local-level administrators helped invent in the 1990s. If in the 1980s the party emphasized its organic relationship with movements, and in the 1990s it crafted a way to bring that relationship to bear on governance, it could be said that in the 2000s governance itself supplanted all other priorities for the PT. That the national administration did not adopt the party's trademark participatory schemes is the result of the internal political game within the PT and its coalition. Instead of anchoring its legitimacy on broad participation, as local administrations had done for a decade and a half and as the PT platform for government called for, the PT in national power relied on alliances with practically all ends of the political spectrum. Administrators sought to balance interests within the administration, sometimes yielding to social movement pressure (such as the partial concession to the landless movement), but generally shielding themselves from dialogue with movements or with the party itself.

Many observers in Brazil have come to juxtapose "Lulismo"—Lula's style of charismatic leadership—with earlier PT practices. Commentators as well as activists within the PT have begun to discuss whether Lulismo has actually *overcome* earlier practices. As we have argued here, this type of leadership represents the Old within Brazilian politics—it represents continuity with earlier models of leadership in Brazil—but it has come to be alongside the New. The party, with all its innovations of the last two decades, continues to exist and continues to transparently run local administrations throughout the country. Party structure and leadership continues to be intertwined with social movement leadership, and social movements continue to try to exert pressure on the administration, with varying analyses about when there will be possibilities for exercising voice. In 2005, during the corruption scandals, the party turned out over 300,000 members to vote in internal direct elections, and those elections shifted internal politics to the left. The "Socialist re-foundation" platform did not carry the day, but leftist factions within the PT became more powerful, demanding popular participation of the administration and a change in course.

For some, the runoff election was an opening for a progressive turn within the administration, particularly with regards to participation. The National Coordination of Social Movements, in supporting Lula's candidacy, delivered a thirteen-point plan to the president. In addition to demanding land reform, increased spending in education, better environmental practices, and a change in the country's political economy, it called for the strengthening of popular participation:

> Popular consultations should be stimulated and supported by government policies that increase participation and the decision-making of the population over its problems. Political and social power should be under the permanent control of the population and its social organizations in

order to exert efficient mechanisms of intervention in the local and national realities, aiming at the quality of life and the common good.

(*Brasil de Fato*, October 27, 2006)

It appears at the time of this writing that none of the participatory proposals are being seriously considered by the administration. The composition of the new cabinet for Lula's second term appears similar to the one for his first term—with little emphasis on social platforms and a strong emphasis on the same economic policies. But this second term will be different. A clear base of support among the poor at the same time as the party has a narrower parliamentary coalition could mean new priorities. The regional weight of the North and Northeast during Lula's second term could cause a real shake-up within a party almost always dominated by leaders from São Paulo state. A turn to the Northeast, to address Brazil's longstanding regional disparities in human, economic, and social development, would mean a new set of priorities for the PT and for Brazil's national government, and could possibly fulfill some longstanding desires for equity and social justice in the country. But it would mean more. Social movements in the North and Northeast have for a long time operated with different horizons of possibility—unlike the South or Southeast; being "part of government" is relatively new to the lexicon of social movements there, a basically uncommon occurrence until the last two municipal elections. This, of course, means social movement practices are more likely to be untainted by the bad habits of "being government" and used to more contestatory practices against ruling elites. Today the national leadership of the PT has very few Northeasterners or Northerners. Whether the PT is able to incorporate these new actors into its leadership structure and reshape itself is a crucial question.

In April of 2007 the party held a crucial congress. Part of the agenda revisited its platforms of broad alliances, with many expressing disappointment after three years of a Janus-headed administration that resulted from these alliances. Also on the agenda were discussions for concrete participatory proposals and transparent mechanisms to monitor elected officials. Finally, of course, the administration finds itself in a curious position—having broad popular support but much less support among parties of the center who would otherwise form alliances as well as facing the severest criticism from the social movements that helped elect it at the national level, now twice.

Social movement activists within the PT also find themselves in a curious position—they know they are better off under a national PT administration than under other parties, but much of their experiences these last four years have been disappointing. Just as activists within the PT had the imagination to create a party that did not dominate social movements, social movement activists are now faced with the task of imagining a double game of supporting the administration against more conservative forces while actively opposing some of its policies until real voice is opened in the national administration.

Notes

1 The now-classic English language work on the PT's founding and evolution is Keck's (1992) *The Working Party and Democratization in Brazil*. In Portuguese, Rachel Meneguelo's (1989) *Partido dos Trabalhadores*.

2 The phrase is Paul Singer's, in his recollection of the Erundina administration.

3 Many instances of Participatory Budgeting allow citizens to act as representatives of movements or similar groups in thematic or sectoral meetings (i.e. a meeting on health), but the bulk of participation and investment occurs through geographically organized fora, where citizens participate as individuals. Most also have rules that diminish the proportion of representatives of locales that bring large numbers of representatives to a meeting to protect neighborhoods with little organization.

4 See for example, Silva's (2003) insightful descriptions of Participatory Budgeting in the municipalities near Porto Alegre. The multi-sited study by Silva et al. (2006) uncovers similar patterns throughout Brazil.

5 The literature that documents this is vast. Among the works, see those collected in Baiocchi (2003a) and those by Abers (2000), Avrizter (2003), Guidry (2003), Nylen (2003), and Wampler (2004).

6 It also calls for support of the Palestinian peoples and breaking ties with governments that practice racist policies.

7 Official statistics about the program and its outcomes are available at: http:// brasil. serpro.gov.br/pais/indicadores/cat_assist/categoria_view

Chapter 7

The successful Chilean left
Neo-liberal and socialist

Patricio Navia

The socialist governments of President Ricardo Lagos (2000–2006) and Michelle Bachelet (2006–2010) stand out as notable exemptions of successful and popularly supported leftwing commitments to a social democratic adoption of neo-liberalism in Latin America. As the leader of one of the countries with the strongest economic growth in the region, Ricardo Lagos successfully combined during his six-year term a social democratic rhetoric and practice with an outstanding fiscal discipline. After being elected on a platform of continuity in economic policies and promotion of bottom-up democracy, Michelle Bachelet has forged ahead on the path of neo-liberalism with a human face that has become the trademark of the Concertación, the center-left coalition in power in Chile since the end of the Pinochet dictatorship. In this chapter, I discuss the experiences of the Lagos and Bachelet administrations, highlighting how those two administrations have combined sound market-friendly economic policies with an effective emphasis on economic and social inclusion. I will show how those two administrations have helped to consolidate democracy but have also found ways to deepen it and make it more inclusive. After discussing the international context under which they came to power—and highlighting their leftwing credentials—I analyze how each one of those two leaders sought to implement policies that could bring about more economic growth, reduce poverty, and combat inequality. While the jury is still out on whether Bachelet will succeed in her endeavor, the Lagos administration shows that market-friendly socialists can effectively combine economic growth with more social inclusion.

The Chilean left in the Latin American context

Between December 2005 and December 2006, eleven Latin American countries held presidential elections. Altogether, 80 percent of the Latin American population went to the polls—about 250 million voters. In addition to Brazil and Mexico, the two largest countries in the region, Colombia,

Peru, Venezuela, Chile, Bolivia, Ecuador, Haiti, Costa Rica, and Nicaragua chose new leaders or re-elected incumbents. Among the most populous nations, Argentina was the only large country without an election in 2006. Because some countries are on a four-year cycle and others are on a five-year cycle (with Mexico being on a six-year cycle), only every sixty years can we expect such an active election season. Yet, sixty years ago all but three countries in the region had competitive democracies. Moreover, few would expect the next sixty years to go smoothly without alterations in the electoral calendar in every Latin American country.

With the election season over, some have already noted a tension between a good and a bad political left (Castañeda 2006; Corrales 2006b; Navia 2006b). Others have highlighted the prevalence of populism (Corrales 2006a; Shifter and Jawahar 2005; Schamis 2006; Shifter 2006); some have pointed to the strained relations between the U.S. and Latin America in the aftermath of September 11 (Domínguez and Shifter 2003; Valenzuela 2005). Others have highlighted how incumbency, runoff provisions, and other institutional features have affected the results (Latinobarómetro 2007). Despite having different approaches and emphases, most analyses agree that 2006 showed positive signs of democracy strengthening but also warn about the persistent presence of some worrying threats to democratic stability.

The path of democratic consolidation experienced by Latin American countries seems to be a non-debatable fact. The annual reports produced by Freedom House on civil and political liberties around the world confirm that trend. Figures 7.1 and 7.2 show the advance of civil (Figure 7.1) and political (Figure 7.2) liberties in Latin America since 1972 (lower scores indicate more liberties for a country). The figures show the average level of liberties for twenty-one countries (the largest eighteen continental countries plus Cuba, Haiti, and the Dominican Republic) and those values for Chile, to show how much that country has advanced in relative terms in strengthening

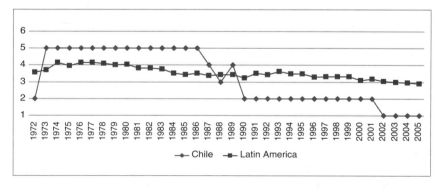

Figure 7.1 Civil liberties in Chile and Latin America (Freedom House), 1972–2005.

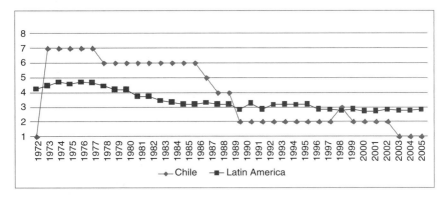

Figure 7.2 Political rights in Chile and Latin America (Freedom House), 1972–2005.

its democracy. While it consistently had worse levels of civil and political liberties than the rest of the region throughout the 1970s and 1980s, after its transition to democracy in 1990 Chile has performed substantially better than the Latin American average. Moreover, since socialist leader Ricardo Lagos became president in 2000, the country has further advanced in securing civil and political liberties to the optimal level, according to Freedom House.

Thus, whereas all of Latin America has experienced a democratic renewal in the last two decades, Chile has consolidated as a country where the values associated with democratic consolidation have strengthened and remained strong. Because that process of democratic consolidation has occurred under center-left coalition governments led—since 2000—by socialist leaders, Chile deserves special attention as a successful case of democratic consolidation.

The socialist government of Ricardo Lagos (2000–2006)

Since 1990, Chileans have voted to keep the same center-left multi-party coalition in power. The Concertación por la Democracia was formed in 1988 by Christian Democrats, socialists and other center and left-leaning parties to oppose the rightwing military dictatorship headed by General Augusto Pinochet (1973–1990). After the Concertación was formed, Pinochet was defeated in a plebiscite in 1988. Democratic elections were held a year later. Christian Democratic (PDC) Patricio Aylwin, the Concertación presidential candidate, easily won the election (Angell and Pollack 1990; Constable and Valenzuela 1991).

The Concertación also won the congressional elections held concurrently with the presidential contest, but constitutional provisions placed by the outgoing dictatorship gave the forces loyal to the military a majority control of the Senate. The Concertación was thus forced to bargain with conservative parties all legislative initiatives and most of the policies it sought to implement during the first democratic government. Because General Pinochet managed to remain in charge of the Army and there were a number of pressing issues on a legacy of human rights violations, widespread poverty, and growing inequality—together with the constitutional constraints—the transition to democracy was difficult. Fortunately, left-leaning parties displayed special restraint in pushing for their social and political demands. Their support for the PDC candidate—rather than attempting to impose one of their own—together with the PDC decision to consolidate an electoral alliance with leftwing parties facilitated the transition to democracy and democratic consolidation (Boeninger 1997; Drake and Jaksic 1995).

The first Concertación government (1990–1994) led an era of impressive economic growth, significant reductions in inflation, unemployment, and—perhaps most importantly for left-leaning parties—poverty. The Concertación showed that it could manage the economy much better than the outgoing dictatorship. It also promoted democratic consolidation and reduced the influence and scope of the protected democracy framework that had been left in place by the deadlock provisions of the 1980 Constitution and other legislation passed by the military before leaving office (Ensalaco 1994; Loveman 1991). As the Aylwin government neared its end, the two main leftist parties, the Socialist Party (PS) and Party for Democracy (PPD), sought to increase their influence by naming socialist leader and PPD founder Ricardo Lagos as their presidential candidate. Lagos challenged the PDC presidential candidate Eduardo Frei for the Concertación's 1993 presidential nomination (Godoy 1994; Navia 2005a).

Although initially formed by seventeen center and leftist parties, by 1993 the Concertación comprised four parties that survived the party merging and fusion that took place during the transition to democracy. The PDC remained the only centrist party in the coalition. The other members were the left-leaning parties PS, PPD, and PRSD (Radical Social Democratic Party). The PPD was formed in 1987 when the PS was proscribed by the 1980 Constitution. Created as an instrumental party, the PPD took a life of its own as many left-leaning voters showed uneasiness to support the PS (Garretón 1995). The PS had undergone a profound ideological renewal in the 1980s, but was still home to many Marxists. Although they had significant differences, the PS and PPD agreed on leftist principles and supported the candidacy of PPD founder and PS militant Ricardo Lagos in 1993.

Lagos had emerged as a natural leader of both parties during the campaign against Pinochet in the 1988 plebiscite. Together with PDC leader Patricio Aylwin, Lagos was the most visible Concertación leader. Having withdrawn his presidential bid in favor of Aylwin, Lagos went on to an unexpected defeat for the Senate in the 1989 elections. After being appointed Minister of Education by Aylwin, Lagos led an aggressive reform aimed at increasing government spending in education, regulating the growing private sector in primary, secondary, and tertiary education and—most importantly for left-leaning parties—significantly increasing government funding for education for the poor and marginalized. Lagos consolidated his position as natural leader of the PS and PPD. Although both parties developed and strengthened autonomous identities during the Aylwin government, Lagos remained de facto presidential candidate of both parties.

In 1993, Lagos again sought the Concertación presidential nomination. Yet, the electoral strength of the PDC and the overwhelming popularity of PDC candidate Eduardo Frei (son of the homonymous president and Senator from Santiago) stood on Lagos' way. Nonetheless, Lagos pushed the Concertación to adopt primaries to elect the candidate. Semi-open primaries were held in May of 1993—with party militants automatically eligible to vote and Concertación sympathizers eligible if especially registered—thus allowing for an open democratic contest between centrist PDC and left-leaning parties within the Concertación. As expected, Frei easily won the presidential candidacy, but leftist Concertación parties were strengthened by the fact that voters, rather than party leaders, chose the coalition candidate.

During the economically successful—but politically weak—Frei government (1994–2000), leftist parties strengthened their position within the Concertación. While the center-left coalition retained its electoral dominance, the left-leaning parties gained a larger share of the Concertación vote. As Minister of Public Works, Lagos masterfully used the post as an effective launching pad for a new presidential bid. In addition to promoting an aggressive public works program, Lagos brought the private sector into infrastructure developments previously funded solely by the state. Through a Build-Operate-and-Transfer (BOT) scheme, the socialist leader helped raised billions of private investment funds to help develop new roads and other infrastructure projects. Private companies built roads and other infrastructural developments and collected government-set user fees. Thus, public projects were built with private funds and paid for with user fees. The government could use its scarce resources to develop infrastructure in areas where private investors would not find it profitable. Thus, not only was much more infrastructure developed, the government also targeted its funds to areas most in need, promoting government spending that could reduce existing inequality (Engel et al. 2000).

Concurrently with his work as Minister of Public Works (1994–1998), Lagos also put together a presidential platform that could make it possible for the left to take control of the Concertación, replacing the centrist PDC. The creation of the Chile 21 Foundation, a leftist think-tank, allowed for the creation of a space where new ideas and policies could be discussed in a setting related to, but independent of, the PS and PPD. Because it was associated more with Lagos' presidential ambitions than with the leftist parties, Chile 21 could freely engage individuals from both leftist parties without undermining political parties and without getting involved in intra-coalition disputes.

In mid-1998, Lagos resigned his cabinet post to pursue a new presidential bid. Just as in 1993, the Concertación parties agreed to hold presidential primaries. However, this time the primaries allowed all eligible Chileans to vote—except those who were militants of non-Concertación parties. The expectations were that more people would participate in the 1999 primaries than in 1993. Thus, preferences reported in polls would be more easily reflected in the results. Lagos' poll ratings had strengthened as a result of his celebrated performance as Minister of Public Works.

Notwithstanding Lagos' overwhelming popularity, the PDC decided to present its own candidate for the 1999 primaries. Senator Andrés Zaldívar—who incidentally had narrowly defeated Lagos in 1989 in a senatorial election race—was named the PDC candidate. He faced Lagos in the May 23, 1999 primaries. Lagos went on to win by a 71.4 to 28.6 percent margin, with almost 1.4 million Concertación militants and sympathizers voting (about 18 percent of the registered voting national population). His impressive victory led many to mistakenly believe that the socialist candidate would easily secure a victory in the December 1999 presidential elections.

In October of 1998, during a private trip to England, former dictator Augusto Pinochet was surprisingly arrested by British authorities after a Spanish judge issued an international warrant for his arrest on charges of crimes against humanity. Pinochet, who had stepped down from power in 1990, had remained as head of the Army until March of 1988. He had immediately assumed a lifetime post in the Senate, according to an existing provision put in place in the 1980 Constitution. Despite his claims of diplomatic immunity for being a Senator and former president, the British government denied a request to release Pinochet. Inevitably, the presidential election was marked by the political implications of Pinochet's arrest. Unexpectedly, the conservative candidate who stood in Lagos' way indirectly benefited from Pinochet's arrest. Joaquín Lavín, a militant of the conservative UDI party, was a strong supporter of the dictatorship in the 1980s, but he had reinvented himself as a moderate conservative. He had been a successful mayor of the most affluent municipality since 1992. His political party, the Independent Democratic Union (UDI), was the most important conservative force in the multi-party Alianza conservative coalition. Yet, after Pinochet's arrest, Lavín successfully distanced himself from the unpopular legacy of the dictatorship and instead reinvented himself as a moderate candidate. Because Lagos was the Concertación presidential candidate and, unlike previous elections, no PDC candidate was in the field, the quest for moderate voters proved to be a far more complicated affair than many in the Lagos camp had initially predicted. Lavín successfully positioned himself as a moderate and captured more support from moderate voters than previous conservative presidential candidates.

In 1999, Chile also experienced its first economic recession after fifteen years of continuous economic growth. The 1999 presidential election was, as a result, the most hotly contested election since transition to democracy. In fact, Lagos, the early favorite to win the election, was surprisingly forced into a runoff by Lavín. The latter proved to be a tough campaigner with an intelligently designed strategy that took advantage of the discontent produced by the 1999 recession. Lagos narrowly edged Lavín by a 48 to 47.5 percent margin, but he was forced to a runoff. Lagos went on to win by 51.3 to 48.7 percent. But he took office as the first post-authoritarian president to win in a runoff election.

Lagos' electoral difficulties had a lot to do with the economic troubles. The Concertación candidate paid the costs of popular discontent. In September of 1999, 58 percent of Chileans believed the country was headed in the wrong direction, according to the much-respected Centro de Estudios Públicos (CEP) poll. Yet, Lagos was also the first Concertación candidate who was not a member of the centrist PDC. As the first leftist presidential candidate since Salvador Allende won the highly contested 1970 election, Lagos had a difficult challenge. Many observers expected that moderate Concertación sympathizers would have a difficult time supporting a leftist candidate. Although moderates had overwhelmingly supported Aylwin and Frei, the presence of a leftist presidential candidate made it easier for Lavín to lure moderate voters away from the Concertación.

Thus, socialist Ricardo Lagos took office as president at a very difficult time in March 2000. Unlike former presidents Aylwin and Frei, who started their terms with the country in good economic shape and with most people sensing the country was heading in the right direction, Lagos began his period as the country was slowly emerging from a recession (see Table 7.1). To top things off, Lagos was inaugurated only a week after former dictator Pinochet was sent back to Chile from his house arrest in London on humanitarian grounds. The Chilean government of President Frei had actively lobbied the British authorities to free Pinochet on humanitarian grounds while promising to try Pinochet in Chile. Crimes committed in Chile must be tried in Chile, the Frei government successfully argued. Among Lagos' immediate challenges, together with promoting an economic recovery, the divisive Pinochet situation and the complicated legacy of human rights violations was one of the most difficult to face.

Although Lagos (born in 1939) did not occupy political posts before the Pinochet dictatorship, he supported the Allende government (1970–1973). After graduating with a law degree from the Universidad de Chile (1962), Lagos obtained a Ph.D. in Economics from Duke University. Back in Chile,

Table 7.1 Selected economic indicators in Chile and Latin America, 2000–2004

Indicator	1998	1999	2000	2001	2002	2003	2004	2005	2006
GDP growth Chile	3.3	–0.5	4.5	3.5	2.0	3.3	5.8	6.3	4.4
GDP growth 21 Latin American countries*	2.3	0.5	3.7	0.4	–0.5	1.9	5.5	4.5	5.3
Unemployment Chile	6.4	9.8	9.2	9.1	9.0	8.5	8.8	9.2	7.9
Unemployment Latin America	10.0	10.7	10.2	9.9	10.8	10.7	10.0	9.1	8.7
Inflation Chile	4.7	2.3	4.5	2.6	2.8	1.1	2.5	3.7	2.1
Inflation Latin America	10.0	9.7	9.0	6.1	12.2	8.5	7.7	6.1	4.8

Source: ECLAC 2006d
*The eighteen most populated continental Latin American countries plus Cuba, Haiti, and the Dominican Republic

Lagos joined the faculty of the economics department at the Universidad de Chile, and was elected the University's Secretary General in 1969, at age thirty-one. Although he was an academic, the post of Secretary General was a political position democratically elected by faculty members, students, and staff. Lagos was the candidate of the leftwing parties, although he was formally an independent. In 1972, President Allende nominated Lagos as Ambassador to the Soviet Union, but he was never ratified by the Senate. Lagos was a professor at the Universidad de Chile at the time of the 1973 military coup. After a period in Argentina working for the different United Nations agencies, Lagos returned to Chile to continue working for a United Nations employment research agency, the PREAL.

Once in Chile, and having formally joined one of the Socialist Party factions that existed during the dictatorship, Lagos became a leading opponent of the Pinochet dictatorship. Because of his affiliation with an international organization and because he was not tainted by the political disputes among Pinochet opponents who had supported or opposed the Allende government, Lagos became a socialist leader who easily gained the trust of PDC leaders. Because the PDC had strongly opposed the Allende government, it was difficult for PDC and socialist leaders to form a unified coalition to oppose the dictatorship. Lagos emerged as a leader trusted by socialists and acceptable to the PDC, a party that had historically opposed the Marxist views of most socialists. In the 1980s, as protests against the Pinochet dictatorship increased, Lagos consolidated as one of the best-known moderate socialist leaders. By 1988, as Chileans were getting ready to vote in a plebiscite to decide on the future of the military regime, Lagos was already the best known and most popular figure from among socialist leaders.

The combination of difficult economic times and the leftward shift in the political party militancy of the Concertación candidate combined to make the 1999 presidential a difficult challenge for the center-left government coalition. Despite having been forced into a runoff election, Lagos became the third consecutive Chilean president from the Concertación. Perhaps more symbolically importantly, he was the first socialist to become president since Salvador Allende. Lagos' challenge as president was, thus, twofold. While he needed to help steer the country out of the economic downturn, he also needed to conduct a successful government that would diminish the argument that Chilean socialists could not govern effectively (Ottone and Vergara 2006).

Lagos' tenure was negatively affected by economic difficulties and surprising corruption scandals that involved government officials and Concertación legislators (Navia 2004). However, his tenure was also positively marked by a number of successful legislative initiatives, by a number of policy initiatives and, perhaps most notably, by the signing of long-awaited free trade agreements with the United States and the European Union. A comprehensive health care reform (which was eventually scaled down to secure legislative approval), a profound labor union reform (which included the adoption of an unemployment insurance scheme), a state modernization initiative (which included the creation of a civil service career independent of changes in government), campaign finance reform (which included government financing for political parties), and a number of economic modernization initiatives made the Lagos tenure a fruitful one in terms of legislative initiatives and policy reforms.

The direct election of municipal mayors and a comprehensive set of constitutional reforms that eliminated most pending authoritarian enclaves from the 1980 Constitution were also among the most noted successes of his tenure. A program aimed at better combating poverty by targeting government resources to those most in need—the *Chile Solidario* program—has also helped further alleviate poverty. In addition to the above-mentioned free trade agreements, a number of other measures to promote exports and eliminate import barriers have helped make Chile's economy more competitive. Finally, Chile's aggressive international commitment to the promotion of democracy and international rule of law (which included Lagos' opposition in the United Nation's Security Council to authorize the United States' request to use force to remove Saddam Hussein from power in Iraq) also gave Lagos a well-deserved reputation as an independent and democratically minded leader, perhaps among the most admired in Latin America today (Funk 2006; Alcántara Sáez and Ruiz-Rodríguez 2006).

As can be inferred from Table 7.1, the Chilean economy performed remarkably better than the rest of Latin America during the Lagos administration. While the 1999 economic downturn affected Chile more strongly than Latin America as a whole, the national economy outperformed the region in the first year of the Lagos administration. While Latin America grew at a 3.7 percent rate, Chile's economy expanded at a healthy 4.5 percent in 2000. In 2001 and 2002, while Latin America stagnated, Chile grew by a modest 3.5 and 2 percent respectively. Finally, as Latin American economies began to recover in 2003, Chile recovered more strongly with a 3.3 percent rate. In 2004, as Latin America experienced its best good year in almost a decade, Chile's economy expanded by a healthy 5.8 percent. In 2005, Chile also outperformed Latin America, with a 6.3 percent growth, higher than the region's 4.5 percent average.

Yet, Chile's economy was not problem-free during the Lagos administration. Unemployment remained high after 1999. Although the economy expanded at a decent rate, the unemployment levels remained almost as high in Chile as in the rest of Latin America. Inflation, on the other hand, was kept under control. In 2003, the country experienced its lowest inflation on record and in 2004 the inflation rate was kept considerably low given the upsurge of economic activity observed in the country.

When compared to Latin America as a whole, the economic performance of Chile during the Lagos administration was patently successful. The country fared better than Latin America. Although there seems to be a regional convergence towards lower inflation levels in recent years, Chile has continued to maintain particularly low inflation rates. Because inflation usually becomes a threatening factor when countries come out of long periods of economic stagnation, concern over inflation pressures in Latin America will surely arise again as the regional economy begins to show signs of recovery. Inflation concerns in Chile, however, remain almost non-existent.

Chilean public opinion apparently agreed with this assessment. While 63 percent of those polled by the highly reputed CEP survey in 1999 believed that the country was headed in a bad direction, that number went down to about 30 percent in late 2004. Similarly, those who believed the country was making progress increased from a low of 22 percent in mid 1999 to 58.6 percent in late 2004. President Lagos' approval ratings also reflect the upbeat feeling among Chileans. While he enjoyed a 43 percent approval rating during his first month in office, in mid-2005 (before the presidential campaign started) Lagos' approval ratings were at 60 percent. Lagos was the first president since transition to democracy to experience a higher approval rating during the second half of his government than during his honeymoon period. As Figure 7.3 shows, Lagos' approval ratings during his fifth and sixth years in office were markedly higher than those of President Frei, even though Frei on average enjoyed better years in terms of economic expansion than Lagos did.

While President Frei's approval ratings decreased as time went by, Lagos' approval ratings declined after a typical honeymoon and then picked up again, starting in 2003. Unlike his predecessors, Lagos completed his term with an approval rating higher than the one he enjoyed when he came in.

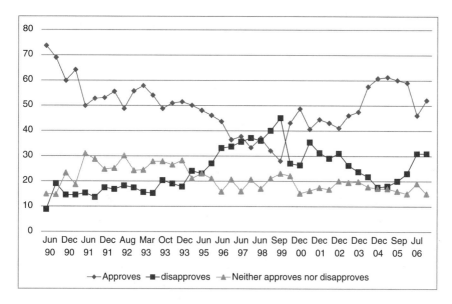

Figure 7.3 Presidential approval ratings in Chile, 1990–2006.

Aylwin, the first democratic elected president after Pinochet, will likely go down in history as the architect of Chile's imperfect and yet successful transition to democracy. Frei, who led the nation through a period of sustained and impressive economic growth, will be remembered—as he initially hoped—for his modernization efforts rather than his democratic consolidation initiatives. But Ricardo Lagos will successfully combine successes in those two fields. The constitutional reforms he championed struck out of the Constitution most remaining authoritarian enclaves, thus making Lagos the president who completed the long-awaited end of Chile's transition away from an authoritarian Constitution. The impressive set of modernization initiatives, which included infrastructure development, state modernization efforts, transparency initiatives, and health and educational reforms, put Lagos on the same footing as his predecessor Eduardo Frei.

Yet, Lagos' legacy seems to reach beyond those of his predecessors. Because he is the first socialist to occupy the presidential palace since Allende, Lagos' electoral and political success as president has finally erased all suspicions about a possible inability of leftwing governments to be successful. After Lagos, no leftwing presidential candidate has to face doubts about the left's ability to govern successfully. In that sense, Lagos' success is impressive, not only because of the actual results but also because it puts an end to an existing debate in Chile about the left's ability to govern.

Both when looking at economic performance indicators and when analyzing public opinion polls, President Lagos' tenure can only be described as successful. Chileans seem to agree. In addition to giving him good marks in polls, the Concertación won all elections held during his term. Yet, the 2000 municipal election left a sour note with the Concertación, as its internal disputes prevented that coalition from transforming its electoral majority into a resounding majority control of municipal governments. Similarly, the 2001 parliamentary election constituted only a partial victory for the Concertación. Although that coalition came up ahead, it lost seats in the Chamber of Deputies. In 2004, however, and partly because of President Lagos' popularity, the Concertación scored an impressive victory in the municipal elections. Although the government coalition fell short of an electoral majority, it widened its electoral advantage over the conservative Alianza coalition. Finally, the results of the 2005 constituted a resounding popular endorsement of President Ricardo Lagos. The Concertación victory meant that it was the first time that a center-left coalition has won four consecutive presidential elections in Latin America. In fact, the only other party to have won four consecutive presidential elections in the region in the last decades is the rightwing ARENA party in El Salvador. But the Concertación tenure will be the longest serving tenure by any democratically elected (beyond questions or special qualifications) party or coalition in the history of Latin American democracy. The fact that such stability, built on the success of economic policies and widespread improvements in the quality of life, has occurred in a country led by a coalition comprising socialists and most recently led by a socialist president himself is, no doubt, worthy of praise and admiration.

When President Lagos left office amid ovations and after ceding power to the first woman president in the country's history, he was also entering history as one of the most successful Latin American presidents in the last hundred years. The fact that he was a leftwing leader, the first socialist since Allende, made his success all the more relevant and more meaningful, not only for Chile but also for the Latin American left. If Salvador Allende remains an inspiration for many, Lagos showed a less heroic but more effective way of going down in history and bringing the country closer to the ideals of social justice and equality that have inspired the socialist left in Chile.

Although the Chilean Socialist Party has championed and defended economic policies that could be easily associated with moderate conservative parties elsewhere in Latin America, it would be unfair to define the PS in Chile as a non-socialist party. Moreover, it would be unfair to label Lagos as a non-socialist government. Many have highlighted—albeit critically—Lagos' neo-liberal policies (Claude 2006; Fazio 2006; Fazio et al. 2006). But Lagos and the Socialist Party define themselves as leftists. In addition, other parties in Chile see them as leftist as well (even though the Communist Party would say that Lagos is more to the right than they are themselves). Analysts and academics also define Lagos as a leftwing leader

(Funk 2006; Alcántara Sáez and Ruiz-Rodríguez 2006; Angell and Reig 2006). To top things off, other leftist parties in Latin America recognize Chilean socialists as their ideological partners.

Admittedly, "left" is a contested concept. It means different things for different people. But precisely because it is contested, we must stay away from attempts at defining what "left" is first and then classifying regimes accordingly. Instead, it is better—and more methodologically sound—to accept self-definitions and definitions assigned by other political actors in each country. Thus, once the map of left-leaning parties is built, we can analyze the characteristics of the left and find commonalities or highlight differences. As for now, socialist and leftwing parties advocate, defend, and promote ideas and ideals of social justice and equality—even if using some tools that are most often associated with moderate conservatives. Using that definition, we can correctly define the Chilean socialists as leftwingers. And, although the Chilean Socialist Party has championed and defended economic policies that could be easily associated with moderate conservative parties elsewhere in Latin America, it would be unfair to define the PS in Chile as a non-socialist party. Because other leftist parties in Latin America recognize Chilean socialists as their ideological partners and because the socialist parties advocate, defend, and promote ideas and ideals historically associated with the left—even if using some tools that are most often associated with moderate conservatives—it is correct to define the Chilean socialists as leftwingers. And its foremost leader since the 1990s can be appropriately regarded as a very successful leftwing government.

The Bachelet government

Although Michelle Bachelet's presidential election victory understandably made news around the world as she became the first woman president in Chile (and the first woman who is not the widow of an important political leader to be elected in Latin America), the fact that she was elected as the candidate of the longest ruling coalition in the country's history sheds more light into recent political developments in the most successful economy in Latin America. Because Bachelet (born in 1951) successfully combined a message of change (based primarily—though not exclusively—on her being a woman) with a message of continuity, she was able to win the runoff election on January 15, 2006, defeating a moderate right-of-center candidate. Yet, without having the idea of *change* as a central component of her campaign, the continuity that she represented would not have sufficed for a victory. Likewise, had she not been a candidate of the ruling and popular Concertación coalition, the fact that she was a woman would not have been sufficient to carry the day.

Certainly, although Bachelet is a lifelong militant of the Socialist Party, her election should not be wrongly included as yet another example of the wave of leftwing victories in Latin America. For one, Bachelet is from the center-left Concertación coalition that has ruled Chile since the end of the Pinochet dictatorship. As the fourth consecutive Concertación president, Bachelet represented continuity much more than change in terms of social, economic, and foreign policies. Because she promised to maintain the economic policies that made Chile the most successful economy in Latin America, her election was as much an approval of the economic and political development model implemented by the Concertación than a call for change in favor of Bachelet's promise of a more participatory democracy.

The first Concertación president, PDC Patricio Aylwin (1990–1994), talked about a "free market social economy" and vowed to give neo-liberalism a human face. True, poverty was dramatically reduced from 40 to 20 percent, and the economy more than doubled in ten years. But the policies adopted by Aylwin and his successor, PDC Eduardo Frei Jr, were squarely in tune with those promoted by the Washington Consensus and international lending institutions. Ricardo Lagos, the third consecutive Concertación president—and a socialist—further deepened neo-liberalism. In addition to signing free trade agreements with the United States and the European Union, Lagos adopted a very conservative fiscal policy, a structural fiscal surplus of 1 percent of the GDP into the national budget. Even in 2005, an election year, and despite the soaring copper prices (Chile's main export commodity), the Lagos administration showed remarkable fiscal spending restraint. The absence of lavish spending did not mean lack of focus on social programs. Ambitious and well-designed programs to promote access to health, education, and infrastructure development have radically transformed Chile under Lagos, who is leaving office with approval ratings of more than 60 percent.

Because she was the candidate of the ruling Concertación coalition, Bachelet's victory should not be seen as yet more evidence of a leftward turn in Latin American electorates. Her rise to power is closely associated with the Lagos government. First appointed Minister of Health in 2000, Bachelet was one of the five women to be appointed in Lagos' first cabinet. She first received wide press attention when, less than a week after his inauguration, President Lagos gave her a ninety-day limit to put an end to physically waiting in line in public clinics. Because health reform had been a major component of his presidential campaign, Lagos decided to announce radical and immediate solutions to a profoundly difficult problem. Perhaps because she was given an impossible task to accomplish—and she duly presented her resignation at the end of that ninety-day period—her popularity grew rapidly. Although her accomplishments as Minister of Health have been widely questioned by the conservative opposition, during the almost two years she served in that position Bachelet became one of the most popular ministers in Lagos' cabinet (Insunza and Ortega 2005).

In January 2002—following a midterm parliamentary election where the ruling coalition lost votes and seats—President Lagos appointed Bachelet as Minister of Defense. Although she was trained as a pediatrician, her personal interests led her to develop a parallel career as a defense expert. The daughter of an Air Force General sympathetic to the socialist cause who served under Salvador Allende, Bachelet was arrested and tortured after the military coup of 1973. Her father died when he was being held by the military and her mother was also arrested and tortured. After her father's death, Bachelet and her mother left for exile, first in Australia and then in East Germany. She married a fellow Chilean there and in the early 1980s returned to Chile, where she completed her medical education. When Pinochet left power in 1990, Bachelet was an active militant of the Socialist Party. Her interests in defense issues led her to take classes in military academies—including a one-year stay at the Inter-American Defense College in Washington, DC—and to obtain a Master's degree in military sciences in Chile. Thus, her appointment as Defense Minister was not accidental (Insunza and Ortega 2005; Navia 2006a).

Yet, as the first woman to be named to that post, her appointment captured wide attention. As the first socialist to serve as Defense Minister since the 1973 military coup—and a victim of political prosecution herself—the symbolic meaning of her appointment cannot be overestimated. It was a historic moment in Chile's successful but difficult process of democratic consolidation. The manner in which she conducted herself as Defense Minister and her ability to personify the national desire for reconciliation and closure quickly made her the most popular minister in the Lagos cabinet. Although the idea of having a woman as presidential candidate had been floated around within the Concertación when Foreign Affairs Minister Soledad Alvear, a Christian Democrat, emerged as a leading presidential contender after Lagos was inaugurated, the thought of having Bachelet, a divorcee, mother of three, socialist, agnostic, and former political exile as the Concertación standard bearer seemed too wild to become true.

However, as time went by and Lagos' term came to an end, Bachelet's popularity continued to increase. By late 2003, she was the most popular Concertación presidential hopeful, after she surpassed Alvear, who had remained on top of the list since 2000. In September of 2004, a month before the municipal elections, President Lagos reshuffled his cabinet and, given their presidential intentions, let Bachelet and Alvear go. They both campaigned heavily for Concertación municipal candidates and contributed to an overwhelming victory by the government coalition in October of 2004. Soon after, Bachelet was proclaimed presidential candidate by the Socialist Party and the PPD (the second and third largest of the four-party Concertación coalition). Because Alvear was proclaimed by the PDC (the largest party in the Concertación) in January of 2005, presidential primaries were scheduled for July 31, 2005, to choose the coalition candidate. Yet, as Bachelet strengthened in polls, Alvear opted to withdraw her candidacy in favor of Bachelet in June of 2005. For the first time in its history, the Concertación had a woman as its presidential candidate (Navia 2006a; Siavelis 2006).

Because of the economic success and political stability of the sixteen-year-old Concertación government, and because the conservative parties overly identified with Pinochet's authoritarian legacy during much of the 1990s and Lagos' superb performance, the Concertación easily won the 2005 election. With more than 51 percent of the vote, the center-left coalition secured its twelfth consecutive electoral victory with a majority in the Chamber of Deputies and the Senate (for the first time comprising elected members only). Yet, Bachelet obtained only 46 percent in the first round (the lowest for any Concertación presidential candidate since 1990). She came ahead of right-of-center candidate Sebastián Piñera (25.4 percent), conservative candidate Joaquín Lavín (23.2 percent) and humanist–communist Tomás Hirsch (5.4 percent). Because she is a woman (which scared some men away) and because she underplayed her proximity to Lagos, Bachelet was forced into a runoff against Piñera (Angell and Reig 2006). She went on to obtain 53.5 percent of the vote to become the first woman to be elected president in Chile.

Despite her electoral troubles, Bachelet successfully attracted voters who had historically been less inclined to support leftwing candidates. Men have supported the candidates of the center-left coalition more strongly than women (in Chile, votes are tallied separately by gender). Although Augusto Pinochet obtained only 44 percent of the vote in the 1988 plebiscite that brought an end to his seventeen-year dictatorship, his support among women reached 47.5 percent. In all elections held since the return of democracy, conservative parties have captured a higher share of women's votes than the Concertación. In 1999, Lagos won the election with 51.3 percent in the runoff. But in the first round and the runoff, conservative Lavín got an absolute majority (50.6 and 51.4 percent, respectively) among women. Lagos became president with a 54.3 percent among men and 48.7 percent among women voters in Chile. In 2005, Bachelet captured 47 percent among women (44.8 among men) in the first round. In the runoff, she won 53.3 percent among women and 53.7 percent among men. Because most of those—primarily men—who had supported the humanist–communist candidate in the first round (5.4 percent) voted for Bachelet in the runoff, she ended up collecting more votes among men. Yet, her ability to attract many women voters constitutes a fertile ground for the Concertación's electoral future. Although it is too early to tell, the electoral prospects of the center-left coalition in 2009 already seem very solid.

Bachelet's bottom-up approach to politics

Although the central focus of her campaign was the strengthening of a social safety net to complement Chile's buoyant economy, Bachelet also made participatory democracy a central component of her campaign. In addition, during the campaign and complementing her call for a more participatory democracy, Bachelet promised that her government would bring about gender parity (an equal number of men and women in top posts). She also promised new faces ("nobody will have seconds," she said). Those four promises were at the core of her presidential bid. Yet, as I discuss in this last section, implementing them from the La Moneda palace has proven a difficult and intricate challenge.

To be sure, Bachelet's central message during her campaign was the strengthening of a social safety net. After sixteen years of successful economic policies that brought about growth and strong poverty reduction, Bachelet shifted the focus to building an adequate network to help those who fall behind and to provide opportunities to those who, having left poverty, fear falling back when they lose their jobs, become ill or grow old. Fortunately for her, other candidates also placed a strong emphasis on issues of inequality and lack of opportunities in Chile. UDI candidate Joaquín Lavín, who narrowly lost to Ricardo Lagos in 1999, campaigned on a platform promising more pro-active measures to reduce inequality.

Because Bachelet centered her campaign on building a strong safety net, some criticized her for not focusing enough attention on growth-related proposals. Moderate rightwing candidate Sebastián Piñera, seeking to court centrist voters, made economic growth central to his campaign. But because the country's economy was expanding rapidly in 2005 and unemployment was decreasing, Bachelet and Lavín successful shifted the focus, for the first time since democracy was restored, away from economic growth into building an adequate safety net of educational, housing, infrastructure, pensions, and health services. More than any other proposal, Bachelet's best known social sector promises were a profound reform to the private pension system and the expansion of pre-school education to low income families.

The mediocre 4.4 percent economic growth that Chile had in 2006—lower than that of all Latin America—has forced Bachelet to partially shift her focus back to economic growth. Although she promised to introduce legislation in 2007 to overhaul the pension system and has moved forward with a comprehensive—and controversial—educational reform legislation, the government has been consumed with calls to help bolster economic growth. The economic slowdown experienced by the country in 2006 has made the goal of building a stronger and more encompassing safety net more difficult. However, if the country does recover a rapid pace of economic expansion, Bachelet will likely make significant progress in building a more comprehensive and complete social safety net in Chile.

Bachelet also attempted to introduce non-economic issues to her campaign. She repeatedly spoke of a different way of doing politics. Because she successfully campaigned as a non-career politician, a physician who had not spent her life working her way up through the political party structure, she made participatory democracy a center theme of her campaign. A citizen's campaign, as opposed to a political party campaign, was one of the high selling points of her unconventional bid for the presidency. She candidly admitted that a good standing in polls—as opposed to political party elites—was the reason behind her candidacy. The people, rather than the politicians, paved her way to becoming a candidate. Yet, in highlighting the role of the people, she also tacitly accepted that she had stumbled upon a political career. When she was appointed minister, she did not have the intention or the expectation that she would end up being the Concertación candidate.

Her campaign sought to promote a bottom-up approach to complement a successful, yet distant, top-down model implemented by Concertación technocrats. "Just as medical treatments will not work if you fail to engage patients, the policies Concertación governments implement will work better if you promote participation, inclusion and diversity," she once said during the campaign. Bottom-up, to complement (if not replace) top-down, seemed to be her motto during the electoral season.

Yet, Bachelet did not have a clear plan to introduce more bottom-up mechanisms of democracy. Although she did express a preference for direct democracy mechanisms (like referenda and plebiscites), her government has not put that initiative (which would require a constitutional reform) at the top of its agenda. Moreover, when Bachelet improvised comments, in mid-2006, suggesting that there should be a plebiscite to decide the fate of the controversial electoral law left in place by the authoritarian government, the so-called binominal law (Navia 2005b; Siavelis 2002), she was widely criticized from within the Concertación and the opposition for blurring the debate and blocking the negotiations already underway to introduce changes to the electoral law.

During the campaign, Bachelet had also spoken of her preference for popular legislative initiatives. She argued that citizens should be allowed to introduce legislation to Congress. Although many favored that idea, the Chilean Constitution gives the executive excessive control of the legislative agenda (Siavelis 2000; Baldez and Carey 1999). The president has the sole power to introduce legislation that implies government spending. Through the use of a constitutional prerogative, the executive can also control the legislative agenda. Thus, introducing mechanisms for popular legislative initiative would empower citizens without directly empowering those with authority to represent citizens. Rather than introduce citizens' legislative initiatives, the government would first need to shift the balance of legislative power in favor of Congress. Yet, because the executive is unlikely to do that, the Bachelet administration has slowly shelved the idea of introducing mechanisms for popular legislative initiatives.

To be sure, the Bachelet government did push on with the idea of participatory democracy and citizens' democracy during its first months in office. Yet, the secondary students' protests in May and June of 2006 challenged her commitment to participatory democracy. Students took to the streets to demand improvements in the educational system and reductions in the unequal access to education enjoyed by those attending public and subsidized schools against those in private schools. Because many students from the well-to-do schools joined in the protests, the movement took on a nation-wide cry for improvements in education. The government was slow to react and lost control of the situation. Streets were filled for days with students, and others, protesting against inequality in education, but eventually also complaining against the government's slow response. Because Bachelet represented a coalition that had been in power since 1990, her government could not easily blame previous administrations for the shortcomings in education. Eventually, Bachelet was forced to sack several ministers—including the Minister of the Interior, the most important post in Chile's cabinet. Her first cabinet reshuffle, occurring only four months after she took office, pretty much buried—for the time being—the idea of participatory democracy.

Indeed, as Figure 7.4 shows, Bachelet's approval ratings suffered as a result of the students' protests in mid-2006. After she sacked her cabinet, her approval ratings increased again over 50 percent in late 2006. When she abandoned the idea of participatory democracy and adopted a more traditional Concertación top-down approach to government, her approval increased. Partially, this was because the Concertación parties felt uneasy about Bachelet's initiative to bring about more popular participation. When Bachelet abandoned that initiative, the Concertación parties also began to collaborate more with her government. True, mistakes were made on

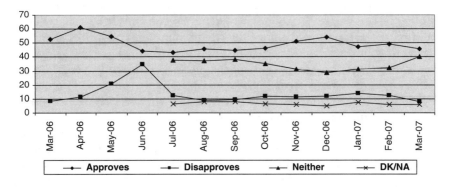

Figure 7.4 Michelle Bachelet's approval ratings, 2006–2007.

Bachelet's side, but the Concertación did not make life easy for the president when she attempted to introduce more elements of participatory democracy to her government.

Another promise related to a more participatory and inclusive democracy was her commitment to gender parity and new faces (ten of the twenty cabinet ministers she first appointed were women). Bachelet actively embraced the idea of gender parity. In part, that initiative was first championed by President Lagos, who appointed five women to his first sixteen-member cabinet. Bachelet was among those women appointed. She was the first woman to head the Ministry of Health in Chile's history. Then, she became the first woman to be appointed to the Defense Ministry in Latin American history. Yet, as president, Bachelet went further in adopting initiatives to promote gender parity.

Bachelet also promised to introduce legislation to provide for gender quotas in Congress, but so far she has not delivered on her promise. She has signaled that she will wait for the binominal law to be modified before she introduces gender quotas legislation.

Despite her strong commitment to gender parity, Bachelet was forced to abandon that principle when she reshuffled her cabinet for a second time in early 2007. In her new twenty-two-member cabinet, there are only nine women. Yet, Bachelet has successfully introduced the issue of gender equality as a permanent item in the public agenda. Although the cabinet is no longer evenly divided between men and women, it will be impossible for Chile to go back to those early 1990s years when there was only one woman in a twenty-two-member cabinet. True, former President Lagos moved decisively to incorporate more women to higher posts, but Bachelet's own inauguration as president and her decisive commitment towards gender equity will give women a more relevant role in future Chilean politics than would have been possible without Bachelet's strong advocacy for gender issues.

Finally, Bachelet also promised to bring about a renewal in the Concertación leadership. In her candid and direct manner, she promised during the campaign that nobody would have seconds. When she appointed her first cabinet, only two among the twenty ministers had served as ministers in previous governments. Her first and second cabinet reshuffles forced her to bring back to power some of the old Concertación leaders. In mid-2007, six of the twenty-two ministers occupied important posts in previous Concertación governments. Yet, Bachelet has successfully forged ahead with the promotion of new faces in government.

True, because the government has faced unexpected challenges (in addition to the students' protests, the troubled implementation of Santiago's new transportation system), its approval ratings were falling as she prepared to complete her first year in office. Partly, the government failures might be attributed to the inexperience—and in some cases incompetence—of the new faces and leadership Bachelet has brought to power.

It is certainly too early to tell whether Bachelet will succeed in implementing the four goals discussed above. Whether a stronger and more comprehensive safety net for all Chileans can be constructed will depend largely on the performance of the economy during the next three years. If the economy grows fast, a stronger safety net will be built. Participatory democracy seems to have a tougher road ahead. Because the government is not clear as to what it means when it calls for more participatory democracy, it is unlikely that institutional changes that promote participatory democracy will be introduced. Gender parity will probably not come back to the forefront in the remainder of Bachelet's term, but the position of women in society will be significantly stronger after Bachelet completes her four-year stint. Finally, the fate of the renewal within the Concertación will depend on the success of her government. If Bachelet improves her approval rating and the government has more successes than failures, the renewal of faces will be permanent. But if the government does not end well, the Concertación will bring some of the more familiar faces (including former president Lagos and the Secretary General of the Organization of American States, José Miguel Insulza) back to leadership positions.

Lessons from Lagos and Bachelet for Latin American leftist leaders

Because it is too early to tell for Bachelet, I will concentrate on whether the Lagos legacy can be helpful for other leftwing leaders in Latin America. As discussed, the circumstances that helped Lagos become such a popular leftwing president in Chile are difficult to reproduce in other countries where left-leaning leaders are also in power. Either because economic fundamentals in those countries are not as solid as Chile's or because the basis of popular support for those presidents does not rest on the combination of good personality traits and strong political party structure on which Lagos built his popularity, it is unlikely that leftwing presidents in other countries can enjoy the same success as Lagos.

Because Lagos' success is partially attributable to the strength of the Concertación, the absence of strong established leftwing parties in other Latin American countries makes it difficult for other leftwing presidents to build personal support without being labeled as populists. Perhaps the leftwing government that could best draw lessons from the Lagos experience in Chile is that of Uruguay, where leftwing leader Tabaré Vázquez was inaugurated in March of 2005 as that country's first leftist president. Facing admittedly harder economic challenges than those faced by Lagos when he first came into office, Vázquez seems headed in the same direction in terms of policies as Lagos. Vázquez enjoys majority control of the legislature. His Frente Amplio Encuentro Progresista Nueva Mayoria (aka Frente Amplio) controls fifty-two of the ninety-nine-seat Chamber of Deputies and seventeen seats in the thirty-one-seat Senate. If he can successfully lead his leftwing multi-party coalition to support his legislative initiatives and fund his public policy programs, Vázquez will be in a position to replace Lagos (whose term ended in March 2006), as Latin America's most successful leftwing leader.

Chapter 8

Uruguay

A role model for the left?[†]

David Altman, Rossana Castiglioni,
and Juan Pablo Luna

Nobody was really surprised by the outcome of the 2004 presidential election in Uruguay. Yet, this will unquestionably be remembered as an historical election. For the very first time in Uruguay's 176 years as an independent state, a party other than the two "traditional" ones (the Blanco and the Colorado) won the presidency. This time the winner was the center-left party Encuentro Progresista–Frente Amplio–Nueva Mayoría (EP–FA–NM), a party composed of Socialists, former Tupamaro guerrillas, Communists, Christian Democrats, and other smaller political groups. Traditional parties have governed Uruguay for 168 years, authoritarian rule being a real exception in Uruguayan history. This change will probably have profound implications for the political life of the country. However, in spite of its scale, this electoral earthquake took place calmly and the transition to the new government was remarkably smooth (Altman and Castiglioni 2006).

While two years do not provide enough leverage to substantiate conclusive arguments about the future of the Frente Amplio (FA) or its government, this small country provides a rich milieu to examine the project's theoretical framework. Basically, given that it is problematic to frame the Frente Amplio as either a "good" or "bad" left (Castañeda 2006), the evidence presented in this chapter seems to support the idea that more than two types of leftist governments co-exist today in Latin America. Moreover, at least for the Uruguayan case, the evidence shows more than two types of left co-existing within the Frente's government.

The road to government: institutions and economic decay

The arrival of the EP–FA–NM to government took place "the Uruguayan way" in the sense that it was not a real surprise and followed institutionalized democratic procedures (Altman et al. 2006). Before examining the path to

[†] This research was financed by FONDECYT's Project #1060749.

power transited by the Frente Amplio, it is necessarily to look at its origins and the context in which it developed. Uruguay has currently four political parties with legislative representation. Two of them are called *traditional parties*—the Colorado and the Blanco—and two belong to the left and center-left of the ideological spectrum—the Frente Amplio and the Nuevo Espacio, respectively. The origins of the traditional parties could be traced back to the Carpitería Battle of 1836 (Pivel Devoto 1942). The other two parties in Congress constitute the heirs of what Uruguayans called *"partidos de ideas"* that have been present in the legislature ever since 1910, with combinations and transformations.[1] Table 8.1 presents the percentage each party held in the Chamber of Deputies since 1942 and Figure 8.1 the evolution of the electoral support using party-families (traditional vs left).[2]

Despite having one of the oldest party systems on earth (Sotelo Rico 1999, p. 138), Uruguay has a very peculiar one, which has been traditionally highly fractionalized and increasingly fragmented.[3] Since the origins of its party system in the early 1830s, political parties have been internally fractionalized, with each fraction having its own name and leadership. The different institutional designs, especially the electoral system, have continued to allow party fractions to compete among themselves without hurting their parties' electoral performances. Since 1942, the Uruguayan electoral system has presented four key characteristics that, in combination, have made it very unusual in the democratic world: (1) concurrent elections for all elective offices every five years;[4] (2) closed lists; (3) double simultaneous vote (DSV) and simple majority for the presidency; and (4) proportional representation (PR) in both legislative chambers and triple simultaneous vote (TSV) for the House.

One of its most unique features was the double and triple simultaneous vote. Citizens elected simultaneously both at the intra-party and inter-party levels. For the presidential election, the double simultaneous vote permitted party tickets (*lemas*) to divide into competitive fractions (*sublemas*).[5] The votes for these fractions were then accumulated according to a party ticket without any possibility of making alliances among them. Consequently, the winner of the presidency was the candidate of the fraction that received the most votes within the party that received the most votes.[6] Thus, Uruguayans elected their president by a simple majority. For the congressional election, the triple simultaneous vote enabled the citizens to choose at three levels: first for a *lema*, then for a fraction, and lastly for a list of candidates.

One of the most relevant consequences of the traditional electoral system in Uruguay was that the elected president was no more than another fraction leader (Buquet and Chasquetti 2004; Buquet et al. 1998) since he was only able to control the internal competition and nominations within his fraction. Thus, he had no capabilities to control the nominations and competition of other fractions, even in his own party (Morgenstern 2001).

Table 8.1 Percentage of seats in the lower chamber, 1942–2004

Party	1942	1946	1950	1954	1958	1962	1966	1971	1984	1989	1994	1999	2004
Colorado	58.6	47.4	53.5	51.5	38.4	44.4	50.5	41.4	42.3	30.3	32.3	33.3	10.1
Blanco	23.2	31.3	31.3	35.4	51.5	47.5	41.4	40.4	35.4	39.4	31.3	22.2	36.4
PNI	11.1	9.1	7.1	3.0	—	—	—	—	—	—	—	—	—
U. Cívica	4.1	5.1	4.1	5.1	3.0	***	***	—	2.0	—	—	—	—
Comunista	2.0	5.1	2.0	2.0	2.0	3.0*	5.0*	—	—	—	—	—	—
Socialista	1.0	2.0	2.0	3.0	3.0	**	0.0	—	—	—	—	—	—
PDC	—	—	—	—	—	3.0	3.0	—	—	—	—	—	—
U. Popular	—	—	—	—	—	2.0*	0.0	—	—	—	—	—	—
F. Amplio	—	—	—	—	—	—	—	18.2	21.2	21.2	31.3	40.4	52.5
N. Espacio	—	—	—	—	—	—	—	—	—	9.1	5.1	4.6	—
Others	0.0	—	0.20	0.0	0.0	0.0	0.0	0.0	0.0	0.0	0.0	0.0	1.0

Notes: * From 1962 the Communist Party votes were within the *lema* Frente Izquierda de Liberación (FIDEL).
** From 1962 the Socialist Party votes were within the *lema* Unión Popular.
*** Since 1962 the name of the *lema* has become Partido Demócrata Cristiano (PDC).
Source: Author's data; Bacigalupe and Marius (1998); Buquet et al. (1998).

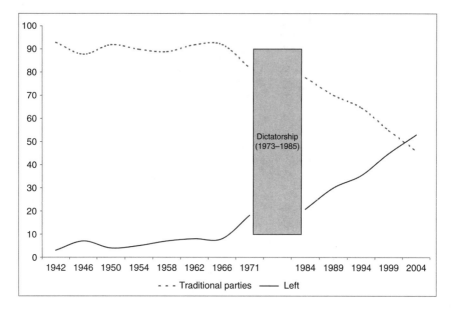

Figure 8.1 Congressional support of political families (1942–2004).

Additionally, political parties' fractions controlled the nomination process and thus were the most prominent political agents. These fractions presented a high level of legislative cohesion (Moraes and Morgenstern 1995) and they were the most important actors when building political agreements in order to govern (Altman 2000; Buquet 1997; Buquet and Castellano 1995; Chasquetti 2003; González 1991; Moraes 2004; Morgenstern 1996, 2001). While parties are macro-electoral organizations that seldom behave as unitary actors, fractions have been responsible for decisions such as choosing to integrate a cabinet, joining the opposition, taking offices in the public administration, and even determining what kind of political lines they are going to promote (Altman 2000).

The Frente Amplio, however, has a different organization than the traditional parties, partially due to its origins. This party was officially born on February 5, 1971. It is currently the largest party in Congress and it comprises nineteen political groups.[7] Since its creation, FA had a dense network of activism closely related to labor unions (especially around the Communist Party). Although each fraction acts as the ultimate decision point, as in the traditional parties, the Frente has central authorities and sophisticated decision-making processes. Each group has veto power, forcing binding decisions among the members of the coalition. This veto power is responsible for an increasing internal fractionalization. Whenever legislators want to increase their political power in the internal political structure of FA, they only need to succeed in creating a new fraction—which is not an easy task—to activate the veto power. Also, unlike the traditional parties, the Frente Amplio always has presented a unique candidate for the presidency of the republic, behaving more as a solid party than a coalition, as it is formally called. This candidate usually was the president of the Frente Amplio and served as a sort of moderator of different interests. However, the president was not always successful in building consensus, as strong tensions arose among the diverse groups of the party. These tensions became evident many times in history; for instance, in 1973 the Christian Democrats left the Frente Amplio and the same occurred in 1988 with the Partido por el Gobierno del Pueblo, the largest sector of the party. Nonetheless, since the mid-1990s FA has been pretty successful in broadening its constituencies and including diverse fractions from the traditional parties and other independent, smaller parties.

In general terms, four main explanations for the left's access to the presidency have been offered. For some analysts, this victory is the result of a historic–demographic trend that has gradually increased the number of adherents of the leftist coalition since its foundation in 1971 (Figure 8.1 shows the relation of congressional support enjoyed by traditional parties and the left). As younger, more progressive generations gained the right to vote, the left enlarged its basis of support (González and Queirolo 2000). For others, this victory reflects the disappointment of Uruguayan voters with the management of the economy by traditional parties. Triggered by the devaluation of the Brazilian Real in January 1999 and exacerbated by the 2001 financial crisis of Argentina, Uruguay has been immersed in one of the deepest, if not the worst, economic and financial crisis ever confronted (see Figure 8.2). The left would thus constitute a source of alternative economic policies voters were seeking. Yet other scholars point to the fact that the increasing moderation and pragmatism of the EP–FA–NM, mainly because of its experience governing Montevideo (the country's largest city) since 1990, allowed it to siphon away center-left voters who have usually supported traditional parties (Garcé and Yaffé 2004). Another argument is that this electoral shift is driven by a natural erosion of the traditional parties, due to the decreasing possibilities of using the State as the national employer and as a springboard for pork-barrel politics (Lanzaro 2004). Perhaps all interpretations are partially correct and should be integrated to offer a comprehensive explanation (Luna forthcoming).

In a broader sense, these explanations probably assume that the Frente Amplio has benefited extensively from social discontent with the traditional parties. Political discontent reflects a gradual historical trend that began in the mid-1950s when Uruguayans started to seek a change by switching first between fractions of the traditional parties and then between parties, leading to significant alternation within the traditional block (González 1995). However, the 2001–2002 economic collapse constituted a catalyst that

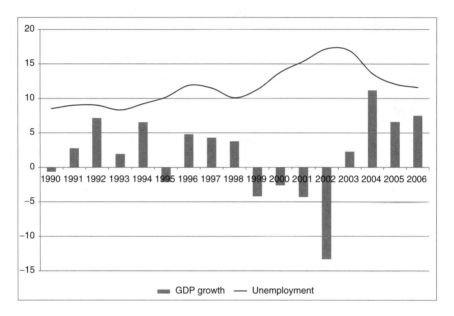

Figure 8.2 GDP growth and unemployment in Uruguay (1990–2006).

affected electoral behavior. While discontented voters became alienated from governing parties as a result of economic decay, the fiscal crisis hindered the ability of both traditional parties to feed their political machines. As a result, not only voters but also traditional party activists, and even some fraction leaders, grew alienated from Blancos and Colorados. As traditional party leaders failed to fulfill clientelistic pacts with their constituents and brokers, the Frente Amplio made inroads with these groups.

As a result, the salience of the economic crisis cannot be overestimated and thus it merits some attention. Triggered by the devaluation of the Brazilian Real in January 1999, the country has been immersed in the worst economic and financial crisis ever confronted. During the second half of 2001, Uruguay's economy was affected even further by the overall weakness of the global economy and, more significantly, by the deepening of the Argentine crisis of 2001–2002. Argentina and Brazil represented more than 45 percent of all the foreign trade of the country as well as over 90 percent of its tourism industry. The Argentinean and Brazilian devaluation reduced the competitiveness of Uruguayan products in the world market.

As a net importer of oil, the country was further weakened by the increase of international oil prices. Moreover, in the year 2000 Uruguay experienced a severe drought and the outbreak of foot and mouth disease in its livestock. These events had devastating consequences for the country's exports. In order to gain competitiveness in the international market, the

Uruguayan government abandoned its policy of maintaining an exchange rate pegged to a crawling target of 12 percent. Although the Uruguayan peso immediately sank, thus making Uruguayan products more competitive in the world market, Brazil also devalued its currency, which deflated Uruguay's competitiveness yet again. As of October 2006, the peso floated against the U.S. dollar.

By mid-2002, Uruguay's GDP had fallen 19 percent from its 1998 level, and the peso was steeply devalued, with the dollar rising to 27—up from 17—pesos after the banking recess. Inflation hovered around 9 percent on an annual basis. The overall public sector deficit by March 2002 represented 4.5 percent of GDP and the official rate of unemployment was 15.6 percent of the economically active population.

Beyond long-term roots and the impact of the economic collapse of the Uruguayan economy, institutional aspects also explain the Frente Amplio's ascent to power. The constitutional reform of 1996, mainly triggered by traditional parties to avoid an electoral victory of the left, brought with it the seed for FA's victory (Altman et al. 2006). Reformers were shortsighted and unable to anticipate the long-term effects of some measures that were introduced jointly with the runoff system to successfully achieve their short-term objective (i.e. prevent FA winning the election of 1999). The 1996 reform had unquestionably negative externalities for (both) traditional parties.

First, the mandatory presidential primaries and the elimination of the double simultaneous vote for the upper chamber restricted the scope for maintaining the traditional "electoral cooperatives" that provided Blancos and Colorados with opportunities to expand their electoral menu by enhancing internal competition between alternative leaderships. Second, the separation of local from national elections hindered the articulation of efficient electoral pacts between regional caudillos and national candidates. This was especially detrimental when mayors were asked to support a national party candidacy that did not coincide with their fraction or when they perceived that actively engaging in campaign efforts to support an unpopular option could hinder their own electoral chances in the upcoming local election. In both cases, they "reserved their political machine for local elections."[8] At the national level, and especially in 1999, this translated into a significant gap between national and local electoral results, with FA being favored in the former.

In sum, a mixture of historic, economic, and institutional variables should be taken into consideration to explain the Frente Amplio's ascent to power. From a comparative perspective, Uruguay's exceptionality within Latin America in terms of its socio-structural configuration (relatively low degrees of poverty and social inequality) and the scope and coverage of social policy entitlements (in spite of declining fiscal capacity and deteriorating quality) in health, education, and especially pensions, should also be taken into account to explain the characteristics, expectations, and interest configurations of the party's heterogeneous social base.[9] Yet, the role of the left as an opposition party and the way in which it related to its social base are also key elements to understand the electoral earthquake seen in Uruguay (see Figure 8.1).

The role of the Frente Amplio as an opposition party

Since the reinstatement of democracy in 1985, governmental authority has been distributed in a rather decentralized manner in Uruguay. Thus, multiple political actors share the process of policy-making in a context in which the rules of the game prevent the concentration of power in a single or a few decision-making units. Given the increasing fragmentation of the party system and the marked intra-party fractionalization seen in the country, Uruguayan presidents have sought to forge intra- and inter-party alliances to secure the passage of their legislative initiatives since re-democratization. The extent to which they succeed has been crucial for the prospects of advancing policy change.

At the same time, this fragmented structure of decision-making has been inimical to the promotion of policies that radically altered the status quo (Castiglioni 2005). This marked dispersion of governmental authority offered both non-governmental actors and the center-left opposition coalition multiple opportunities to block policy change, allowing the Frente Amplio to distinguish itself as a powerful challenger to traditional parties. In this vein, the existence of direct democracy devices has provided Uruguayan interest groups—more often than not with the explicit support of the Frente Amplio—a powerful institutional resource to block policy change (Altman 2002).

Additionally, data on the ideological placement of all major political fractions show that the party system has clustered either around the center or toward the left of the ideological spectrum, with a limited presence of right-wing fractions. This pattern of ideological distribution—in the context of a relative dispersion of governmental authority—has been, and still is, prone to maintaining the status quo.

Partially because of the relative decentralization of governmental authority, the role played by non-governmental actors, and the ideological distribution of the political system, Uruguay did not exhibit a pattern of radical reforms that alienated Latin American voters who turn left to manifest discontent (Castiglioni 2005). This forced the Frente Amplio to articulate its political strategy mainly around two key tasks. On the one hand, it sought to build strong ties with those non-governmental actors who challenged the governing coalition. On the other, it played a role as a relatively responsible opposition that, however, did not participate in the governing coalitions after re-democratization.

The forging of alliances with non-governmental actors was particularly clear in social policy. For example, in the area of pensions, the Frente Amplio actively supported the efforts of the National Organization of Pensioners (ONAJPU) and the Inter-Union Workers Plenary–National Workers Convention (PIT-CNT) to block the reform of the pay-as-you-go pension system. In fact, it even joined ONAJPU and PIT-CNT in the creation of the National Commission for the Defense of the Principles of Social Security and constituted a key actor in promoting the use of direct democracy mechanisms to hinder reform attempts (Castiglioni 2005). A similar picture can be drawn regarding other policy areas, with the exception of macroeconomic policy (especially in terms of trade openness).

Both the Blanco and Colorado governments promoted a social policy that sought to revise the structure of the social protection system rather than promoting new focalized, means-tested policies tailored to low income individuals and families. With the economic crisis of 2001–2002, this lack of focalized social policies became evident. As we previously said, while it is certainly an exaggeration to assert that this crisis alone explains the electoral victory of the Frente Amplio, the magnitude of the economic collapse seen in Uruguay probably accelerated the victory of the center-left coalition.

The 2004 electoral campaign

The 2001–2002 economic crisis deeply affected the electoral campaign of 2004, and consequently economic policy and the urgent need for the country to embrace changes became central aspects. One of the Colorado Party leading political fractions, the Foro Batllista, endeavored to portray the Frente Amplio as a populist party with a dubious commitment to market-oriented policies and democratic politics, and to link some key political figures from the left to the Tupamaro guerrillas who were active in the country during the 1960s and 1970s. The Colorado Party also stressed that the economic recovery the country was starting to experience could be undermined with an electoral victory by the left. These strategies proved fruitless in stemming the massive loss of votes suffered by the Colorados (Altman and Castiglioni 2006).

Although the Blanco Party has been historically identified as center-right, the party's presidential candidate, Jorge Larrañaga, tried to frame his discourse in such a way as to gain the center-left votes that the Colorado Party was losing. Some Blancos even went so far as to claim that the EP–FA–NM's political program was a copy of their own; and Larrañaga criticized Tabaré Vázquez—the FA presidential candidate—for visiting Washington to contact international financial institutions (IFIs) before the election. Indeed, a key leader and former Blanco Party presidential candidate, Juan Andrés Ramírez, even argued: "I feel I am left-wing, and I do not believe that only the EP–FA–NM represents the left" (*La República*, July 26, 2004). However effective this strategy may have been, it was not enough to gain the votes necessary to defeat the center-left coalition.

By contrast, much like the campaigns conducted by Ricardo Lagos in Chile and Luis Inácio "Lula" da Silva in Brazil, Vázquez avoided confrontational issues and moderated his political rhetoric. In one key move, designed to calm the fears of the markets and to gain support from disillusioned center-left voters for the traditional parties, Vázquez asked Enrique Iglesias, then president of the Inter-American Development Bank (IADB), to serve as Minister of Economics. Although most observers believe that Vázquez anticipated that Iglesias would not accept the offer, the proposal helped to convince the skeptical that Vázquez was committed to market-oriented policies. Immediately after Iglesias declined, and months before the election, Vázquez announced during his visit to Washington that, if elected, he would appoint Danilo Astori as Minister of Economics and Finance. Astori is an economist of moderate views, with a good reputation outside the Frente Amplio and who had been contesting Vázquez's leadership within the center-left coalition since 1995.

Even so, all three parties had something in common; in particular, they all claimed they would bring about a true transformation of the country. The Colorados stressed that a new generation was in charge of their party; the Blancos' slogan was that Larrañaga was a president for a new Uruguay. The Frente Amplio campaign took the idea of transformation to its limit, with the simple motto "Let's change" (*Cambiemos*). The center-left coalition even created an animated game on the Internet, where players were required to transform the outlook of the country in a positive, cooperative manner. In sum, economic policy and the need to change were the keystones of the electoral campaign.

Finally, on October 31, 2004, 89.6 percent of Uruguayan citizens (2.5 million) went to the polls to vote in elections to decide the president, vice-president, and Congress to rule the country for the 2005–2009 administration. Tabaré Vázquez, presidential candidate of the EP–FA–NM, defeated Jorge Larrañaga, of the Blanco Party, by almost 17 percent, receiving 50.5 percent of the vote. Presidential candidate Guillermo Stirling, of the Colorado Party, received 10.6 percent of the vote, the worst electoral result in the history of this political party. A runoff election, which would have taken place on November 2004, was made unnecessary because the left surpassed the 50 percent threshold. Also, given the strict proportional representation system utilized in the country at the party level, the Frente Amplio became the largest political coalition of the new Congress (52.5 percent at the Chamber of Deputies and 54.8 percent at the Senate). It is the first time since the 1966 elections that an elected president enjoys a majority in Congress.

The Frente Amplio's government

This section discusses the role of the Frente Amplio as the governing party around four dimensions. First, we deal with the functioning of government, with special emphasis on the organization of the executive and its cabinet; we then move to analyze the most emblematic policies fostered by the Frente Amplio. Third, we give some evidence of the preliminary results of these policies, and finally, we examine the Frente Amplio and the international arena.

Structure of the government

Given traditional parties' electoral debacle in 2004, when the Frente Amplio arrived into office its main challenge was to remain unified in order to assure governance, securing a working majority in Congress. For this reason, it was essential to align the mainstream Frente Amplio's fractions with the executive. To accomplish this, Tabaré Vázquez nominated to the cabinet the heads of the Senate lists of each significant fraction, who were also the most prominent fractional leaders (Buquet and Chasquetti 2005). In doing so, he essentially replicated a strategy that had proven very efficient during his term as Montevideo's mayor and during his years as president of the Frente Amplio heading the "Mesa Política" of the party.

Filling up the executive branch with all relevant Frente Amplio leaders, Tabaré Vázquez sought to circumscribe potential conflicts to the Council of Ministers, in which they could be solved, without risking harsher and more decentralized confrontations in Congress. Once issues were settled in the executive, congressional majorities would be secured through fractional discipline. Again, it is important to underline that political parties' fractions control the nomination process and thus are the most prominent political agents of aggregation and legislative cohesion (Altman 2000; Chasquetti 2003; Morgenstern 1996, 2001, 2004).[10]

Traditionally in Uruguay, distributing ministerial posts echoed the distribution of forces within the winning party (Altman 2000). Nonetheless, in early December 2004, Vázquez announced a new cabinet that clearly deviated from this informal institution. The new cabinet did not reflect the relative share of votes of each EP–FA–NM member. The most obvious imbalance occurred in the case of MPP and AU, which obtained a lower amount of ministries than their vote would have given them (see Table 8.2). Some ministries were entirely given to one fraction (i.e. the newly created Ministry of Social Development was offered to the Communist Party and the Agriculture Ministry to the MPP) and others, usually more central ones, were distributed between different fractions by giving the secretariat to one fraction and the sub-secretariat to another (i.e. Finance, Defense, Foreign Relations, and the Ministry of Interior).[11]

Table 8.2 Frente Amplio's first cabinet

Ministry	Minister	Fraction	Under-secretary	Fraction
Office of Planning and Budget*	Carlos Viera	VA	—	—
Defense	Azucena Berrutti	PS	José Bayardi	VA
Social Development	Marina Arismendi	PC **	Ana Olivera	PC
Economics and Finance	Danilo Astori	AU **	Mario Bergara	Indp.
Education and Culture	Jorge Brovetto	Indp.	Felipe Michelini	NE
Livestock, Agriculture, and Fisheries	José Mujica	MPP **	Ernesto Agazzi	MPP
Industry, Energy, and Mining	Jorge Lepra	Indp.	Martín Ponce de León	VA
Interior	José Díaz	PS	Juan Faroppa	
Foreign Affairs	Reinaldo Gargano	PS **	Belela Herrera	PS
Public Health	María Julia Muñoz	VA	Miguel Fernández G.	PVP
Labor and Social Security	Eduardo Bonomi	MPP	Jorge Bruni	Indp.
Transport and Public Works	Victor Rossi	AP	Luis Lazo	Indp.
Tourism and Sports	Hector Lescano	AP	Alberto Prandi	
Housing, Terr. Plan., and Environment	Mariano Arana	VA **	Jaime Igorra	AU

Notes: * It has ministerial status through the Constitution, its director participates in the Council of Ministers, but formally it depends on the presidency and it is not a ministry in the sense that the director of the office cannot be censured by Congress.
** Denotes fractions' leaders.

Finally, Vázquez also handed out some ministries to previous collabora-tors during his municipal administration, who are seen as "unconditional" supporters of the president (i.e. Health, Public Facilities and Transport, Education). In addition, when debating difficult issues, Tabaré Vázquez usually allowed his ministers to discuss their discrepancies openly—and fre-quently in the press— eventually jeopardizing the career of at least one min-ister. On those occasions, the president acted as an arbiter in the conflict, taking a final position and trying to compensate the losing side, either sym-bolically or through tangible side-payments. The losing side was responsi-ble for securing his or her fraction's discipline in Congress when congressional approval was needed.

In the short run, this formula proved satisfactory and moderately efficient. However, subsequent clashes between Astori and other fraction leaders in the cabinet soon translated into an increasing level of political tension. In particular, during the debate of the five-year budget in September 2005, the stalemate almost broke the cabinet through the con-frontation between several ministers and Astori, who refused to assign the amount promised in the Frente Amplio's electoral platform for improving education. After Astori handed out his resignation to the president,

Vázquez finally convinced the rest of the cabinet to abide by the budget proposal submitted by the Ministry of Finance. In exchange, the latter agreed to include an adjustment formula that—provided economic growth remained steady—would enable the FA government to fulfill its electoral promise by the end of the current presidential term. Nonetheless, Astori has repeatedly stated that until 2008 the government should concentrate on consolidating its financial situation by restricting spending in spite of economic growth. This position explains his capacity to create a good investment climate in the country and to craft a good working relation with the IFIs, both of which are considered centerpieces of Vázquez's government policy. For this same reason, Vázquez cannot afford to risk Astori's departure.

Nonetheless, Vázquez's support for Astori was not exempt of moments of tension. The most evident came about when debating the signing of a Free Trade Agreement (FTA) with the United States. After initially supporting and advocating the initiative, Vázquez switched positions, reacting to internal opposition by an increasing number of FA's fractions. The issue was highly divisive for the Frente Amplio at a symbolic level, which had little to do with the material benefits and costs that this FTA could bring about. FA has always privileged regional integration through Mercosur and it has openly manifested against U.S. imperialism in Latin America since its creation in 1971. After Vázquez's switch, Astori's position in favor of the FTA became unsustainable. This incident was the most recent in a series of significant and public cabinet confrontations between prominent fraction leaders acting as government ministers. Among others, issues have related to agricultural producers' financial debts, tax reform, and education budget appropriations.

Against this backdrop, the continuity of the original cabinet nominated by Vázquez is somewhat puzzling. During the honeymoon period, this imbalance could be maintained. However, as time goes by, internal fractionalization and undisciplined members may pose a challenge to the cohesion of Vázquez's government. Vázquez's decision to form a cabinet that includes the four leaders of the most voted fractions within the EP–FA–NM (PS, AU, MPP, and VA) might help to counteract this possibility. In the context of a highly renovated Congress, where more than 60 percent of legislators are newcomers, this strategy may bestow on the new cabinet a key role in controlling the legislative process.

However, the lack of ministry removals in spite of increasing confrontation and deadlock can be explained by the delicate political architecture underlining cabinet formation. As stated above, Astori's removal could entail definitive damage to the investment climate, essential to providing continuity to the country's economic growth. Meanwhile, in spite of the confrontations produced by his presence, Mujica's continuing in the cabinet has also proved essential for securing the congressional support of the party's strongest fraction. Finally, given that Vázquez nominated his ministers allocating fraction quotas and bringing in fraction leaders to the executive, removing a minister who could not be replaced by another representative of the same fraction (as this would entail a fractional break-up) could break the present balance among fractions within the cabinet. Therefore, the cabinet would need to be integrally refurbished, on the basis of a new series of complex internal negotiations.

Apart from this lack of flexibility, Vázquez's attempts at ensuring party unity and discipline produced two additional externalities. The inclusion of fractional leaders in the executive and the centralization of political negotiations in the cabinet have subordinated Congress and congressional debate to a secondary position. In particular, this is so because major policy packages are designed by the executive and then sent for (automatic) congressional approval. Contradicting a long-standing parliamentary tradition of the left, the FA government has therefore restricted the role of its congressional representatives. Additionally, in some of the few instances in which a proposal was initiated by the Frente Amplio's legislators, it has not been well received by the executive. The most interesting example on this is the proposal for a Law of Reproductive Health, which would legalize abortion. Although the great majority of the Frente Amplio's members would favor the approval of this bill, Tabaré Vázquez has already stated his intention to veto a bill that would contradict his personal position. In this context, congressional representatives show signs of apathy and disenchantment with the executive (*Brecha*, June 3, 2006).

To complement this preliminary overview, we now provide a brief discussion of the main policies enacted or attempted by the Frente Amplio government during its first two years, analyzing their impact on the party's heterogeneous electoral constituency.

Policies fostered by the FA government

Perhaps the most salient policy priority of the EP–FA–NM governing coalition has been related to the implementation of the Emergency Plan (*Plan de Atención Nacional de Emergencia Social*, PANES), a focalized plan intended to attend the needs of the poorest sectors of society.[12] The PANES is structured around a targeted monetary transfer (of approximately US$ 50 per month) that is provided to families living in extreme poverty (covering 320,000 people, a tenth of the country's population) in exchange for family members' enrollment in education and health programs. The decision to adopt this measure and the consideration of this plan as a central component of the agenda has probably to do both with the characteristics of the social policies adopted by previous administrations and the devastating results of the economic recession that plagued the country.

Nonetheless, FA's policies go well beyond the Emergency Plan. Two other governmental policies have enjoyed great popular support: the investigation of human rights violations, and the re-establishment of collective bargaining for wages (*consejos de salarios*). As stated above, the poverty alleviation plan, PANES, is at the top in terms of popular recognition. Being a distinctive trait of this government, it represents the party's commitment to improve the lives of those worst off in society and an attempt to set this government apart from those of the traditional parties. Furthermore, it also allows FA to deliver to a significant segment of the party's emergent constituency. Although PANES suffered from several implementation problems that led to public discontent, the program now seems to be working according to expectations.

With regard to human rights, investigations (many involving the collaboration of the armed forces) led to significant findings on instances of violations during the military dictatorship (1973–1985), while staying within the contours of the Amnesty Law (*Ley de Caducidad de la Pretensión Punitiva del Estado*). This progress on human rights issues constitutes a second accomplishment of the government, which is today widely recognized by Uruguayan citizens, also contributing to setting the Frente Amplio government aside from its predecessors. Furthermore, it satisfies one historical demand of the party's core constituency. This policy partially met the requests of the different organizations that gather relatives of the dictatorship's victims, who also demand the penal prosecution of human rights violators. However, to reach that stage, the government should invalidate the Amnesty Law ratified in a popular referendum in 1989. The party is internally divided on this regard. Nonetheless, thanks to international requests placed by Argentinean judges pursuing trials on *Operación Cóndor* cases, some prominent military officers might be extradited to that country. This would take the pressure from the demand for pursuing not only truth but also justice.

Additionally, the restoration of tripartite collective bargaining among labor, business, and the State (suspended since 1992 in spite of enjoying constitutional status) is the third most consensually supported decision of the government. Mainly in 2005, both labor and business were satisfied with the results obtained in the negotiation rounds, which crystallized in a significant improvement in real wages. Moreover, resulting from this decision, new incentives were created for labor unionization, producing an avalanche of affiliations (almost doubling the existing ones) in the private sector. Through this measure, the government achieved two objectives. First, it satisfied a historical demand of the labor confederation, one of the key pillars within its historical constituency. Second, it contributed to rebalancing the internal distribution of power within the confederation, reducing the relative proportion of state employees through the incorporation of private sector workers who were never unionized or who had lost their unions during the 1990s. Still, in 2005, public sector unions were the ones obtaining greater wage increases. If this pattern continues in the future, with producers of non-tradable goods in a dominant position, the external competitiveness of the economy could be damaged. Moreover, for reasons explained below, the good climate existing in 2005 between business and labor has not been maintained in 2006, leading to significant delays in reaching wage agreements.

Finally, two key reforms proposed in the Frente Amplio platform have met increasing levels of internal and social-movement resistance, inducing at least a momentary gridlock. While different corporations involved have actively opposed the health-sector reform proposal, the tax system reform proposal has also been harshly criticized by FA's members of Congress. The reform, which seeks to implement a more progressively redistributive tax scheme; now needs to accommodate multiple requests for exceptions formulated by, among others, public employees, pension beneficiaries, and rural producers. In fact, this is one of the proposed reforms where distributive struggles among segments of FA's social base will be more explicitly observed.

In sum, during its first two years in office, the Frente Amplio has been able to craft different policies that favored specific segments of its social base, managing tradeoffs by sequentially benefiting different constituencies. In so doing, economic growth has been instrumental in cushioning distributive conflicts. At the same time, and especially when dealing with policies that involved significant resource redistribution or issues traditionally problematic for the party's historical constituency, the government has stalemated. That process has been coupled by increasing conflicts within the party and between the party and the social movement.

Policies and their preliminary results

If measured through objective socioeconomic indicators, FA's performance in office during the first two years of its presidential term is more than positive (see Table 8.3). Although economic growth resumed in 2003 after the greatest financial collapse in the country's history, during 2005, the Uruguayan GDP grew by 6.6 percent. Meanwhile, inflation rates were low, staying at an average of 4.9 percent during that year. Additionally, a primary fiscal surplus (before debt repayment) of 3.6 percent of GDP was achieved. The significant improvement on the efficiency of the fiscal revenue service to monitor and prosecute evasion constitutes a key accomplishment that also facilitated the generation of that surplus.

During the first half of 2006, GDP continued to grow at a rate of 5 percent, while inflation has been kept under 6 percent. Moreover, the country has successfully restructured its external debt-anticipating payments to international creditors (i.e. the IMF) and exchanging short-term IFI-conditioned debt by long-term "sovereign debt" generated on the basis of internationally highly demanded Uruguayan treasury bonds. Market demand for these bonds tripled the amount offered by the Uruguayan treasury.

Table 8.3 Selected economic indicators

	GDP growth (total)	GDP growth (per capita)	Total foreign debt (% of GDP)	Inflation	Unemployment
1997	5.0	4.3	22.8	19.8	11.5
1998	4.5	3.8	24.4	10.0	11.9
1999	−2.8	3.6	39.5	4.2	11.3
2000	−1.4	−2.2	44.3	5.1	13.6
2001	−3.4	−4.1	48.1	3.6	15.3
2002	−11.0	−11.7	85.9	25.9	17.0
2003	2.2	1.6	98.4	10.2	16.9
2004	11.8	11.0	87.7	7.6	13.1
2005	6.6	5.8	68.1	4.9	12.2

Source: Instituto Nacional de Estadística del Uruguay, Banco Central del Uruguay

In terms of social welfare indicators, the FA government's performance is also noteworthy. During the 2001–2003 crisis, unemployment rates went above 20 percent, declining to 15 percent in 2004. One year after FA took office, unemployment was 12.4 percent. Furthermore, although real wages in 2005 were still 17 percent lower than those observed during the 1998–2001 period, in 2005—and after twelve years of continuous decline—real wages went up by 4.6 percent (5.65 percent in the public sector and 4 percent in the private sector). Moreover, during 2005, formal employment has increased by at least 14 percent (as signaled by new pension contributions proceeding from the incorporation into the formal market of former informal workers). Finally, according to preliminary figures from the National Institute for Statistics (INE), poverty was reduced by 10 percent during 2005.

Although sufficiently long time-series of presidential approval are very scarce in the country, extant research is able to document a significant impact of economic performance (measured through unemployment and inflation rates) on presidential approval, in prediction models that include a one-period lagged dependent variable and a series of statistical controls (Luna 2002). Meanwhile, "honeymoon" effects (modeled through different operationalizations) do not show great strength in the country. Against this backdrop and on the basis of FA's accomplishments during its first year in office, one should expect presidential approval to be high and on the rise.

Indeed, Tabaré Vázquez's approval rates outperform those of all other former presidents during their first year in office. Figure 8.3 illustrates this fact comparing Vazquez's ratings to those of the last three presidents. Moreover, during his first year in office Tabaré Vázquez has had the highest approval rating in history since reliable survey research has been available in the country.

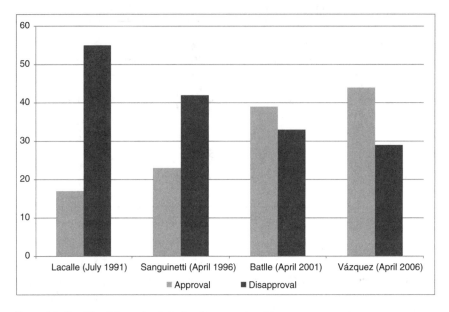

Figure 8.3 Presidential approval during first year in office.

The Frente Amplio in the international arena

Since its very beginnings in the early 1970s FA has had a strong pro-Latin American discourse with significant and recurrent references to the national hero José Artigas. In this way, the rhetoric of FA in regard to the world was structured around a national identity anchored in a regionalist perspective.

Nonetheless, the crisis of the late 1990s disclosed the weaknesses of the Uruguayan economy and its strong dependence on its two major neighbors: Argentina and Brazil. Since then, the country has been immersed in a tension between two apparently contradictory ways of managing its insertion into the world economy. On the one hand, the more centrist voices tend to support the idea of a unilateral opening to the world, signing FTAs with as many countries as possible—the United States included—and following the Chilean way. On the other hand, some voices are still advocating the use of Mercosur as a sub-regional springboard as the most rational strategy in managing the country's economic opening.

There is a consensus, however, on the necessity of diversifying Uruguayan foreign markets. As a matter of fact, Uruguay is currently bargaining with several countries, notably India, China, South Africa, New Zealand, and the United States. With the last, negotiations are much more complicated than simply coordinating economic terms. Unilaterally signing an FTA agreement with the United States would risk Uruguay's eventual expulsion from Mercosur. Meanwhile, Mercosur still remains the country's major trade partner.

Within Mercosur, the first two years of the FA administration were plagued by obstacles. What started as an extremely affable, almost idyllic, relationship between Argentinean President Néstor Kirchner and Vázquez has progressively turned into a very complex and conflictive situation. During the electoral campaign in Uruguay, a high percentage of voters came from neighboring Argentina, where the largest Uruguayan Diaspora resides. Kirchner, who explicitly supported Vázquez's candidacy, gave all Uruguayan administrative workers a two-day leave to travel to Uruguay, thus contributing to the massive electoral participation of Uruguayans living in Argentina. Nonetheless, at this moment the country's relation with Argentina is particularly tense because of the controversy on the installation of two cellulose mill processing plants near the border on the Uruguay River. The conflict was triggered by Argentinean concerns regarding the possible environmental damage that these plants could cause in the neighboring province of Entre Ríos. The confrontation between the two countries has now escalated and is still to be solved, even while one of the plants was relocated to Colonia, on the Plata River basin. Uruguay's refusal to relocate both plants was coupled by a permanent blockade of the bridge that connects both countries. That blockade was set up by environmentalist activists and its removal has not been attempted by either the provincial or the national government, motivating multiple complaints by Uruguay placed at international courts and at Mercosur.

In spite of initial hesitation (particularly in the opposition camp), all political forces and citizens in Uruguay support the government's position in the conflict with Argentina on the cellulose processing mills. This confrontation has eventually served to provide support for the government across the board, distracting attention from the internal problems of the country. In any case, the Argentinean government deserves more credit than the Uruguayan for producing this result, especially taking into consideration its permissiveness over the blockade of the international bridges by some of its citizens and the consequent partial isolation of Uruguay.

Overall, in terms of its international relations, the country

> suddenly finds itself one of the main fronts in the struggle between the United States and Venezuela for dominance in South America. The Bush administration and President Hugo Chávez of Venezuela are jockeying for position here, each trying to undercut the other by winning over Uruguay's left-wing government.
>
> (*New York Times*, September 12, 2006)

Both countries are trying to seduce Uruguay in different ways, the United States giving clear signs of opening the road to an FTA with Uruguay (which has been already declined by FA's government), and Venezuela, on the other hand, offering preferential oil prices, associating financially with some Uruguayan public enterprises, and subsidizing certain social projects in the country. FA lacks a univocal and coherent foreign relations strategy and vision. While some fraction leaders like Astori—the Minister of Economics and Finance from Asamblea Uruguay—tend to portray Chile as a role model, favor an FTA with the United States, and frequently question the utility of maintaining Mercosur membership, others like Gargano—the Minister of Foreign Affairs from the Socialist Party—have systematically opposed an FTA with the United States and would like to deepen the country's relationship with Mercosur and the region.

Conclusions

How can we explain the behavior of the Frente Amplio government fully endorsing an orthodox macroeconomic management while at the same time refusing to sign an FTA with the United States? For some, this could signal a middle-of-the-road way of doing leftist politics in Latin America. For others, however, this apparent contradiction reveals the co-existence of different lefts within the Uruguayan left.

Recognizing that different lefts co-exist in the same government, most analysts would agree in placing the Frente Amplio government among the so-called social democratic Latin American left as opposed to the allegedly populist alternative observed in Venezuela, Bolivia, or Argentina (see Castañeda and Morales in the introduction to this volume). According to this view, the new Uruguayan government went along those of the Brazilian PT and Chile's Socialist-headed Concertación governments. Indeed, as an example, both President Tabaré Vázquez and Danilo Astori have openly declared that Uruguay should seek to emulate the "Chilean model," fully endorsing an orthodox macroeconomic management to attract productive investment while seeking to pay the "social debt" with the country's poor population.

However, even with regard to the cases included in the social democratic group, the Uruguayan experience presents relevant specificities. It would be naïve—and perhaps mistaken—to expect the Frente Amplio to implement the "Chilean model." Although the Frente Amplio is an institutionalized party that underwent a long period of ideological moderation before arriving into office, it differs from its Chilean counterpart in terms of the type of linkage institutionalized between the party and its (heterogeneous) social base. Furthermore, the Frente Amplio governs in a completely different structural and socioeconomic context. Even if Tabaré Vázquez or Lula— heading "reconstructed left governments"—sought to emulate Ricardo Lagos or Michelle Bachelet, they could only produce a cosmetic resemblance.

The effects of both political institutions and socio-structural configurations derived from each country's history would hinder the successful transplant of the "Chilean model." In a nutshell, the Concertación—and especially Chilean Socialists—can implement the policies they pursue because their social bases were drastically dismantled under Pinochet. But also, the economic reforms enacted by the dictatorship hinder contemporary social movements' capacity to organize and link to parties.

The Uruguayan case shows that the historical development and institutional characteristics of the center-left coalition, as well as the evolution of its linkages to different segments of its constituencies, should be taken into account in explaining convergence and divergence in the governmental performance of current Latin American leftist parties. At the least, a path-dependent analysis seems to explain current events better than accounts based either on short-term socioeconomic performance or on simplistic assessments based on the characteristics of presidential leaderships.

The Frente Amplio arrived into presidential office after more than thirty years of existence. During these years, it gradually came to understand the rules of the game and began a process of strategic adaptation to use them in its own benefit. In a way, once the Frente Amplio started to expand its electoral menu by enhancing internal competition between different fractions and concentrating the support of all these diverse groups in a unique presidential candidate, the Frente Amplio took a step forward towards the presidency. The Frente Amplio also capitalized from a clear context of economic crisis (2001–2002). Of course, it would be impossible to answer the counterfactual question of whether the Frente Amplio would have won the presidency without that crisis. The most plausible answer would be "yes," but nobody would know exactly when.

While some disaffected citizens would claim that FA is "more of the same," it has shown a different policy agenda than previous governments. Policywise, the first two years of FA's government were characterized by a set of specific changes: the implementation of an emergency social plan (to ameliorate some of the terrible consequences of the 2001 crisis), the reinstallation of collective wage bargaining (among the government, workers, and business), a proposal to enact a progressive tax reform, and an international agenda that fluctuated between bilateral trade liberalization and the participation in sub-regional alliances.

Despite the evident progress of the Uruguayan economy, the government has been subjected to increasing criticism by civil society organizations, and especially by labor unions. As illustrated by the statements issued by a prominent leader of the National Confederation of Workers, labor is "supportive" but "critical" of a government that is considered as "its own," but which has also "[in only seven months], completely lost its path ... overvaluing international pressures and underrating the social movement."[13]

Notes

1 In general terms, Uruguayan parties are extremely hard to characterize with a single category. The so-called "traditional" parties are not classic Duvergerian mass parties (Duverger 1954), they have weakly institutionalized structures of party leadership selection, stable career paths, or tenure security. Although these parties were defined as "notoriously loosely structured and informally organized" (Gillespie 1991, p. 5), they have yet survived for more than 160 years (Sotelo Rico 1999). Using Kirchheimer's (1966) categories, they have been defined as catch-all parties (Bottinelli 1993; Gillespie 1991; González 1991). And lately, at least in the traditional parties, it is possible to see some characteristics of cartel parties such as state subventions and stratarchy (Katz and Mair 1995).

2 Specialists consider 1942 the year in which the Uruguayan electoral system acquired its maturity in political terms (Bottinelli 1993; Buquet 1997; Buquet et al. 1998; Caetano et al. 1987).

3 *Fragmented* refers to the number of parties in the system, while *fractionalized* refers to the number of fractions within parties.

4 All elections in Uruguay were connected (*vinculadas*) and they were simultaneous. *Connected* means that the voter must cast a ballot for the same party for all offices in dispute. Voters choose for six levels of government: (1) President and Vice-president, (2) Senate, (3) Deputies, (4) Departmental Mayor, (5) Departmental Legislators (*ediles*), and (6) Departmental Electoral Courts.

5 There is confusion on whether to use the concept "fraction" or "faction" in the context of the Uruguayan party system. Some authors have called these political units factions (Coppedge 1994, p. 199; Mainwaring and Shugart 1997, p. 425). Following Sartori (1976), we will not use the term "faction" because it has derogatory connotations: it is deemed "a political group bent on a disruptive and harmful *facere*." Also we consider this definition to be misleading since *sublemas* are more permanent than factions (such as the circumstantial "ins" and "outs" groups formed in Venezuelan parties, Coppedge 1994). Moreover, an important part of people's partisan political identities is directed toward *sublemas* rather than political parties. For a further discussion on this topic see Buquet (1997). On factionalism see also Mershon (2001) and Druckman (1996).

6 A party may present several *formulae* associated with different fractions. Although the Executive power in Uruguay is composed of the president, the vice-president and the cabinet of ministers, the *formulae* represents the presidential and vice-presidential candidates alone.

7 Asamblea Uruguay, Espacio 90 (Partido Socialista, Corriente Popular y Movimiento Socialista); Democracia Avanzada (Partido Comunista y FIdeL); Vertiente Artiguista (Izquierda Democrática Independiente y Artiguismo y Unidad); MPP (Movimiento de Liberacion Nacional-Tupamaros e independientes); Izquierda Abierta. Without parliamentary representation: UNIR (Movimiento 26 de marzo, Corriente de Unidad Frenteamplista, Movimiento Pregón y Unión Popular); Movimiento Popular Frenteamplista; Partido Socialista de los Trabajadores; Partido Obrero Revolucionario (Trotkista); Partido por la Victoria del Pueblo; and the Movimiento 20 de Mayo.

8 Domingo Ramos, Colorado Broker in Tacuarembó, personal interview in Luna (2004).

9 See ECLAC (2006d). According to ECLAC's estimates the country is placed, together with Costa Rica, as the least unequal in the region. Although poverty has dramatically increased as a result of the crisis, the country remains among those showing more favorable ratings in the region. Finally, Uruguay is also among the countries in the region that spend more (as a percentage of GDP) in social provisions.

10 On several occasions, fractions' leaders did not attempt to change the rules and procedures of their own parties and fractions in order to minimize internal dissent or win internal disputes, but instead they tried to change the whole national electoral system and regime of government to fulfill their political desires. Usually changes in electoral system or regime of government were produced by coalitions of fractions belonging to different parties and at the same time they are opposed by a contra-coalition of different fractions from the same parties.

11 This way of distributing the cabinet has reached its maximum expression in Chile, through what Rehren (1992, 1998) calls horizontal integration.

12 See PANES at: http://www.mides.gub.uy/panes/index.html

13 Juan Castillo, Secretary General of the PIT-CNT and leader of the Communist Party (October 7, 2005, interviewed in BRECHA). Diverging from that of 2005, the PIT-CNT May 1, 2006 platform was also characterized by its attempt to confront the government while pressing for better concessions to labor.

Chapter 9

Venezuela, turning further left?[†]

Raúl A. Sánchez Urribarri

I was not well liked in many sectors of the Left or at least among their leadership ... The Left most loyal to its ideals, including the PCV, had differences with me. I remember, for example, that one time a group of workers invited me to a meeting they had in Central Park in order to prepare for the May 1 march ... I arrived at the meeting, and I sat down in a random chair. All the leaders who were there at the head table saw that I had arrived but didn't greet me. I never forgot that ... On the other hand, I knew that in another assembly of those small leftist groups, they had concluded that I was a messianic leader in contradiction with the movement and the interests of the masses.

(Hugo Chávez's comments on his relationship with the political left during the mid-1990s; Chávez 2005, pp. 60–61)

The last fifteen years witnessed the arrival in power of the Venezuelan left. It came first in the form of political parties with little success, such as the Movimiento al Socialismo (MAS) or La Causa Radical (Causa R). These movements had their first victories in the regional arena, and became prominent later on at the national level when they attained a larger representation in the Venezuelan Congress. Subsequently, the definitive dominance of the left in Venezuela arguably breezed in with the victory in the presidential elections of 1998 of charismatic Lt Col. (r) Hugo Chávez Frías, the leader of the coup attempt on February 4, 1992, against then Venezuelan President Carlos Andrés Pérez.

Chávez, his government, and his movement are usually conceived of as the most significant presence of the left in Venezuelan political history. *Chavismo* has also risen as a driving force of the left at a regional scale. The "Bolivarian Revolution" is the first Socialist experiment in Latin America that has relied on a strong and self-sustaining economic bedrock, financed by the revenues of a steadily increasing international oil price. This windfall

[†] I want to thank Julio Ríos-Figueroa for his kind recommendation to the editors of this volume.

allowed Chávez to develop a powerful political platform that has succeeded in winning elections and keeping power, but which still shows a mixed record with respect to achievements in the social, political, and economic realms. Moreover, while Chávez's democratic legitimacy might look solid to many (given the high levels of political support he still enjoys, and the electoral–democratic origin of its government reassured in several elections), the revolution's commitment to democratic values has been objected by the opposition, foreign governments, international organizations, and scholars. Like other charismatic leaders, *El Comandante* Chávez stirs passionate and contradictory reactions among followers and critics, especially in Venezuela's polarized political spectrum. To some, he is a champion of the underprivileged (Boudin et al. 2006), but to others he is just a modern, well-disguised version of a leftist despot (Corrales 2006a).

Although Chávez's regime could be best characterized since 1999 as a populist illiberal democracy, it seems to be taking a more radical path in recent months. After being reelected in the 2006 presidential elections by a generous margin, Chávez now allegedly seeks to implement a socialist regime at a fuller scale. At the time this chapter is written, the talk of the town in Venezuelan politics is a partial constitutional reform proposed by Chávez, "discussed" in the *Chavista*-dominated National Assembly, that would make bold changes to the Venezuelan political system. For instance, it abolishes the limit on the number of terms that Chávez can seek reelection, it gives constitutional character to several social programs (*misiones*), and modifies the concept and protection of private property, while overhauling the state's geo-political structure.

The importance of these changes makes the analysis of the role of the left in Venezuelan politics timelier than ever. It is important to address several questions. What was the role of the organized left in Venezuela prior to the arrival of Chávez to power? What has been the participation of the left in Venezuelan politics since Chávez won the presidency, especially at the onset of the "Bolivarian Revolution"? More importantly, Chávez's government and his project are incontestably leftist, but what kind of left does it represent? Is it a modern and reformist left, a populist left, or a revolutionary left? Do the latest reforms aim for the definitive institutionalization of authoritarian socialism in Venezuela? This chapter provides some initial answers to these questions, looking at the development of the Venezuelan left in recent years.

The Venezuelan left prior to the onset of Chavismo

Although the most important event that has taken place in Venezuelan politics in the last decades is without a doubt Chávez's "Bolivarian Revolution," it is important to analyze the left prior to the definitive downfall of the Venezuelan partyarchy,[1] and to trace its relation with Hugo Chávez's electoral success in 1998. This requires taking a brief look at the role of the leftist political parties in the electoral arena, at both national and sub-national levels, and at their internal organization prior to 1998. But it also requires discussing Chávez's first public political organization, the Bolivarian Revolutionary Movement (MBR-200), and its strategy in the political arena following the February 4, 1992, coup attempt against Pérez. And it is also relevant to dissect how other groups, non-governmental organizations, and social movements, ideologically aligned with the left in specific issue areas, attained a more prominent position in the political arena during these years.

With respect to the political party scene, three leftist electoral organizations played an important part during the demise of the stronghold of Acción Democrática–Comité de Organización Política Electoral Independiente (AD–COPEI) in the 1990s. First, the Movement Toward Socialism (Movimiento al Socialismo, MAS). A splinter of the Communist Party in 1970, MAS was the only political party that represented a viable electoral alternative in the bipartisan context of that decade and the 1980s. It was never a significant electoral force prior to the 1990s, but it was a stable presence. MAS never obtained more than 5 percent of the presidential vote, or 10 percent of the votes for representatives for the two chambers of Congress. But it began winning newly established elections at the regional and local level during the 1990s. These successes, coupled with the uneven political decentralization process that transferred more power to the sub-national authorities, allowed MAS to develop budding regional leaderships. For instance, Aragua state, one of the largest and most important in the country, has been ruled by affiliates or former affiliates of MAS since 1989. The movement also became an important political force in the populous Lara, Sucre, and Portuguesa states. Some of the local and regional leaders simply replicated the clientelist pattern of its AD–COPEI counterparts. Hence, the electoral success of MAS in these regions could not be attributed to skillful programmatic politics, but rather to the individual success of a few politicians who implemented broad clientelism. As a consequence, MAS' regional successes failed to develop a viable progressive alternative to the decaying status quo. The ever divided MAS resembled more and more the worst features of the very parties that it had confronted for so long: stagnation, disconnect with the population, and factionalism. Surely, this was a problem shared by parties across the political system as a whole, but MAS is to a large extent responsible for its own failure.

Perhaps one of its biggest liabilities was pragmatism, which led MAS to team up with odd bedfellows in exchange for positions in government or political influence. MAS was the crucial element in the *chiripero*, the broad coalition of small political parties that supported COPEI's ex-leader Rafael Caldera in his successful presidential bid in 1993. MAS was also an important political actor in the Caldera administration, including the personal involvement of Teodoro Petkoff and Pompeyo Márquez. By the end of

Caldera's term, the party was divided. The masses overwhelmingly supported Chávez's candidacy, but some of its leaders did not, most notably Petkoff (Hernández Márquez 2004). A large portion of the MAS electorate wanted change and saw in Chávez a chance to get it, but part of the MAS leadership was suspicious of him and did not advocate dismantling the current political establishment. Thus, to add insult to irony, MAS ended up backing Chávez, who openly criticized Caldera's government that MAS had sponsored.

Another distinctive representative of the left in Venezuela during the 1990s was La Causa Radical—also referred to as Causa R, with an inverted R. Like MAS, this party was also affiliated with the left from inception as it also came from the Communist Party. It mainly sought to organize the masses to participate directly in government, thus favoring a bottom-up approach to politics. The organization's model was not hierarchical, but a horizontal movement that articulated autonomous mass organizations. From the very beginning, the party adopted a pragmatic anti-establishment approach in which ideology happened to be a secondary issue (López Maya 1998; Salamanca 2004).

Despite the high expectations it raised, the electoral record of Causa R during the 1990s was disappointing. At the local level, the main success of Causa R was limited to the state of Bolívar, where the union movements sponsored by the party enjoyed increasing success during the 1980s. The party obtained the governorship in 1989 and in 1992—electing one of its most emblematic leaders, Andrés Velásquez—and won the local election in Ciudad Guayana, the most important city in the state. Aristobulo Isturiz was elected mayor of Caracas in 1992, a victory that gave national recognition to the party and allowed it to attempt other policy experiments in a different, more challenging setting. Following these partial successes, the party's definitive break into the national electoral arena came in the 1993 presidential elections when its candidate, Andrés Velásquez, came very close to winning the presidency with 21.95 percent of the vote that placed it fourth in the very fragmented election. After this failed attempt, Causa R managed to keep a significant political presence in Bolívar, and even won the Zulia governorship in the hands of former military coupster Francisco Arias Cárdenas. Early analyses show that, once in office, Causa R tried different modalities of participatory democracy, considered promising by political analysts (Salamanca 2004; López Maya 2005). A less distinguished phenomenon was the participation of the leaders of Causa R in the February 4, 1992, coup attempt.[2] According to Salamanca (2004), the failed participation in the aborted coup caused confrontations among the party leadership that contributed to the movement's decay.

Following an alliance in Congress with COPEI and MAS in the late phase of Caldera's term, Causa R fell into greater disrepute. The party split into two different movements in 1997. Some of its leaders decided to create a separate organization that later on adopted the name Patria Para Todos (PPT). Several characteristics prevailed in the ideological orientation of the new party: the importance assigned to the nation's role vis-à-vis the international economy, a claim for a greater regulatory and participatory role for the state in the domestic economy, the protection of human rights, and the pressure for a "radical" version of participatory democracy (López Maya 2004). Perhaps the most important issue to understand the evolution of PPT is its relationship with Chávez and the prominent role it has had on his administration.

Social unrest was characteristic of the 1990s, especially after the 1989 urban riots episode also known as *Caracazo* (López Maya 2005). Some of the social movements that sprang up lacked organization and were characterized by their spontaneity, occasional violence, and lack of concrete demands. However, they clearly rejected the prevailing political parties, and constituted a formidable source of public pressure (Canache 2004). Several of them eventually morphed into issue-driven non-governmental organizations, specialized in advocacy and litigation assistance to underprivileged citizens, the protection of electoral rights, personal security and public safety, monitoring and litigation against police and military abuses, assistance of impoverished Venezuelans living in the vast urban slumps to cater for their basic needs, and so forth. Several of these organizations even suggested that the Venezuelan political system should be overhauled by calling for a far-reaching constituent assembly (García Guadilla 2003). These groups did not usually adopt a leftist stance, or identified themselves with leftist movements, yet they espoused visions that were at odds with the neo-liberal free-market agenda proposed by Pérez and reluctantly pushed by Caldera, which coincided with the agenda of the left. The work of several of these organizations, the mounting public pressure, and an often sympathetic press contributed to creating the impression that socially progressive measures were needed to overcome political instability.

Last, and most important, the 1990s witnessed the consolidation of Chávez's presence in the political arena, along with the transformation of MBR-200 into Movimiento Quinta República (MVR). Although recent studies emphasize leftist elements in MBR-200's proposals, the movement was never formally a part of the organized left. Its military background, populist rhetoric, and emphasis on Chávez's charismatic figure were not enthusiastically backed by many factors of the Venezuelan left. The mid-1990s—the "lost years" of MBR-200—tend to be ignored when analyzing *Chavismo*, but it was a critical period in the formation of the Bolivarian Revolution. During this time, MBR-200 attempted to increase its size and reach, and to become a nationwide movement based on Chávez's popularity. However, it was never a serious political alternative since Chávez was not perceived as a viable presidential candidate (López Maya 1998).

MBR-200 focused on criticizing and confronting the democratic rules of the game, a proposition that was not terribly popular (Pereira Almao 2004). The movement's main proposal was the adoption of a constituent assembly to reorganize the country's political system from scratch, which was not different from what some leftist parties and movements advocated. The organization typically called for abstention as part of its anti-establishment strategy, except when Francisco Arias Cárdenas ran for governor of Zulia under the Causa R label in 1995. Arias Cárdenas' victory contributed to convince MBR-200 that elections were a viable means to attain power. The idea finally gained momentum when the possibilities of a strong show in the 1998 presidential elections became increasingly apparent. It was then that MBR-200 fused into MVR.

Chávez and his arrival to power in 1998

The 1998 presidential elections welcomed Chávez to power. For the first time, Venezuelans elected a president who openly sympathized with leftist views and did not belong to the traditional parties. From that moment on, the role of the Venezuelan left would be tied to Chávez and his movement. Chávez's 1998 bid was centered on his figure and personal appeal. The political movements that supported him contributed to improve his image, creating the impression that he was a politician with a credible agenda and a serious policy platform. However, they aimed primarily at taking him to office, and later to relying on them as their political organization once in government.

It is incorrect to argue that voters supported Chávez *only* because they had moved to the left of the political spectrum, and he represented their views better than any other candidate. It would also be incorrect to depict the Chávez phenomenon as an expression of the retaliation of impoverished masses against the ruling elite, at least when describing the 1998 and 2000 elections (Molina and Perez 2004).

The key element in Chávez's campaign was his anti-establishment stance. There was a growing sensation among the electorate that he would be better able to break with the past. This was probably based on his brief—but impressive—personal record,[3] his fiery rhetoric, and his insistence on several reformist policies. Among other controversial ideas, he advocated a greater role for the military in Venezuelan society, including its incorporation in the fight against poverty. His campaign tried to underplay his radical views, but some of these issues were highly visible and were severely criticized. But he also raised concerns among the opposition from the onset as a result of his close personal ties with Fidel Castro. Despite Chávez's occasional harsh rhetoric and his promise to deliver a dramatic change, the prevailing tone of the campaign evidenced a moderate, reformist left platform. This convinced undecided centrist voters to support his presidential bid and subsequent changes.

MVR formed an alliance with the divided MAS, the PPT, and some minor leftist political parties called Polo Patriótico (Patriotic Pole) between 1998 and 2001. Polo Patriótico sought to provide Chávez with a broader and consistent electoral foundation for his bid. The three movements were all leftist, but the alliance was not ideologically motivated. In fact, a handful of leftist political groups joined the opposition to Chávez, most prominently Causa R. Polo Patriótico proved to be a feeble coalition, with frequent intra- and inter-party disputes which Chávez tended to settle. But it was, in the end, a successful coalition: it got Chávez elected in 1998, it provided support for the process leading to the creation and approval of the new Constitution in 1999, and it managed to get several of Chávez's allies elected in 2000. This was particularly relevant in the final years of the political system inherited from the AD–COPEI regime, when the earlier decentralization process had transferred substantial powers to the regions, and where alliances were critical to push the political project ahead.

In the end, Chávez owed little to the left's ideological contributions. His personality and virtual monopoly of the political scene were the critical factors behind his victory. But the fact that the *Chavista* platform—including its leftist elements—depended upon Chávez to such an extent quickly raised concerns in sectors of the left. Several leaders did not see his project as means to implement the agenda of the left. They feared instead that they would become submissive actors in a Chávez-centered political system. In the end, some sectors of the Venezuelan left would play different roles in Chávez's movement. By joining the *Chavista* files, politicians traditionally aligned with the left had unprecedented access to public office. Leftist parties—especially MAS—offered their local and regional platforms to mobilize voters. *Chavismo* also received the support of professionals aligned with leftist parties and movements, who were subsequently appointed by the new government to elite positions at the top levels of the bureaucracy, the government's corporations, the judiciary, the military, the Central Bank, the national oil company, and so forth.

Although MVR was key to providing support for Chávez's presidential bid, it was not originally devised as a political party but as a precarious organization with the goal of getting him elected (Molina 2004). It lacked ideological coherence and did not have stable connections with different sectors of the population (López Maya 2005), a problem inherited from its parent organization, the MBR-200. Its greatest liability was also its greatest asset: Chávez's powerful and omnipresent leadership. As would be expected, the direct connection between the leader and the masses diminishes the role and importance of the party (see Pereira Almao 2004). Thus, MVR never reached a high level of institutionalization. Its internal composition was always organized around strong factions, which depended on the leaders' specific links with the movement's "boss" (Chávez), a typical feature of dominant parties in populist and clientelistic regimes. Some of its factions were led by politicians aligned with the left, but this never ensured that their ideals would reflect the policy concerns of the Venezuelan left.

Perhaps the most interesting and paradoxical example was Luis Miquilena's role during the beginning of the Chávez administration. An experienced politician from the 1950s, he became the most important organizer of MVR. Very close to Chávez, he was considered his top advisor and mentor. Despite his leftist leanings, he played a moderating role in the early years of the *Chavista* regime. Miquilena developed an establishment of his own, formed by elected politicians, Supreme Court justices, and other formal and informal power-holders. *Miquilenismo* became the strongest civilian faction within the MVR. But Miquilena eventually turned against Chávez and joined the opposition ranks, along with several of his cronies and supporters, in the run-up to the April 2002 coup against Chávez. Miquilena represents a emblematic tale of the many contradictions that the *Chavista* movement has experienced. After Miquilena, there have been several leaders who also achieved prominence thanks to their strong personal connections with Chávez, and formed groups of influence of their own, only to be eventually dismissed by Chávez once they have become too powerful.

The government of Chávez and the path to the Twenty-First-Century Socialism

What kind of left does Hugo Chávez represent? Is it safe to say he represents the *reformist* left, such as that of Brazil, Chile, and Uruguay? Is he just the latest manifestation of a nationalistic, radical, *populist* left, like that of Perón, Vargas, or Cárdenas? Does he represent a contemporary *revolutionary* left, as some of his allies and sympathizers allege? To answer these questions, I delve into some of the most important characteristics of Chávez's government, discussing how they have evolved until the present day.

A fundamental concept to explain *Chavismo* is populism: his government is personalistic, and it relies on a direct connection with the masses, especially vast portions of the most impoverished sectors of Venezuelan society (although it has also enjoyed popular appeal among part of the middle class). Chávez governs on the assumption that he has been endowed with the support of the majority, and allegedly on behalf of its overwhelming interests, often resorting to a confrontational style of government. He has sought to develop a new political identity based on the symbols and images of the Bolivarian Movement, but being careful to emphasize his image as the leader of the revolution. Perhaps the most prominent characteristic of Chávez's populist style is his frequent use of an anti-elitist discourse, a characteristic shared with Latin American populists (Weyland 2001). His rhetoric developed against the Cuarta República leadership (AD–COPEI) and the vested economic interests that blossomed under the previous political establishment. Chávez portrays his struggle as a liberation fight on behalf of the underprivileged against an oppressive group of powerful individuals who ravaged the country's resources for their own benefit. At a later stage, this polarizing rhetoric also turned against the supporters of this elite, the *escuálidos* (the weak ones).

Chavismo is also clientelistic. The extent to which it has relied on informal arrangements to build political support and win elections has not been sufficiently analyzed.[4] However, claims about the use of public funds in exchange for political support abound, along with claims of political discrimination against citizens who signed anti-Chávez referenda petitions and other forms of prosecution and harassment against opposition partisans and leaders. In all fairness, clientelism was not discovered by Chávez. It has been a persistent characteristic of Venezuelan politics that goes back to the AD–COPEI regime and beyond. What changed is the capacity of the government to control the apparatus and make it work for its own benefit. As a result, policy-making and governance have not improved during *Chavismo* and have probably deteriorated (Monaldi et al. 2004). Thus, Chávez's populist style along with his sophisticated clientelist dynamics provide a benchmark to assess the "leftist" character of the Chávez regime.

Four *stages* can be distinguished in the evolution of the "leftist character" of Hugo Chávez: moderate–transitional (1999–2001), confrontational (2001–2003), consolidation (2003–2006), and outset of Twenty-First-Century Socialism (2006–present). These labels have been devised for descriptive purposes, and should serve to distinguish the stages of a protracted transition from a dysfunctional clientelist liberal democracy ruled by different political parties to a new regime of democratic origin but still with some authoritarian traits, organized around a strong executive power headed by Chávez.

The moderate–transitional period (1999–2001)

Chávez was significantly constrained by the disparate will of the political forces in Polo Patriótico throughout this period. Some of these groups had strong links with business and political actors interested in keeping the status quo. Despite Chávez's stunning popularity and AD and COPEI's abrupt downfall, the opposition commanded significant political power, most notably at the sub-national levels. Even if the political arena was ripe for radical transformations, the economic scene was not. Oil revenues were slightly—although not dramatically—increasing and certainly not to the extent they have increased in recent years. Venezuela experienced a deep recession between 1999 and early 2000, due mainly to the uncertainty associated with the political changes taking place.

Perhaps the best examples of "moderation" can be found in the 1999 Constitution, a document that is closer to a representative democracy than many give credit.[5] The new Constitution introduced several elements of participatory democracy, such as different kinds of referenda and the possibility of new associative forms for social and economic ends. But it even maintained elements similar to the institutional framework established in the 1961 Constitution, including the powers granted to the regional and local levels. Even when the institutional design featured a strong executive branch (which suited well Chávez's personal appeal and popularity), it also provided a genuine system of checks and balances, at least in formal terms. Branches of government ended up reflecting the balance of power within *Chavismo,* and the *Chavista* establishment had to agree with an otherwise uncooperative opposition in the designation of the justices of the Venezuelan Supreme Court. The new Constitution established a generous catalogue of fundamental rights and different venues for their protection. It also recognized private property, and allowed for the incorporation of the private sectors in key areas of the economy such as the exploitation and commercialization of natural resources. Despite some controversial incidents—such as the country's increasingly stronger relationship with Cuba, and Chávez's connections with "rogue nations" that caused upheaval in Venezuela and abroad—the government's relations with all countries in the region were, for the most part, trouble-free. Venezuela increased and improved its relations with other oil-producing nations—both OPEC and non-OPEC—to agree on a common strategy with respect to oil production, and to stabilize and increase the prices of this commodity. In the economic realm, Chávez not only showed signs of moderation but at some point even raised hopes among certain sectors that his government was only a variant of *neopopulism* (Weyland 1996). The populist rhetoric of Chávez has been mediated by pragmatism.

Moderation should not be confused with reformism or authentic democratic commitment. Chávez's unilateral approach to policy-making has been a distinctive feature of his government. Since 1999, Chávez has accumulated power beyond the boundaries set by the applicable constitutional and legal framework. During this period, he was nonetheless compelled to refrain from following a more radical approach, because of exogenous and endogenous constraints that forced him to act strategically. Political factions within *Chavismo* that were not ideologically aligned with a radical left served as a moderating influence in the early years of his administration

The opposition, one way or another, struggled for political power, commanded significant support and distracted the administration from enacting radical changes. This uncomfortable equilibrium was altered when *Chavismo* and the opposition engaged in a zero-sum confrontation for power.

The confrontational period (2001–2003)

The period was characterized by increasing threats and counter-threats, numerous mobilizations, frequent violent episodes and chaotic situations that began in 2001 when Chávez started governing by decree using emergency power legislation (*Ley Habilitante*).[6] The *Chavista* discourse portrayed these years as a romantic fight of the left against the entrenched business interests: a zero-sum conflict waged on behalf of the underprivileged population, for the sake of advancing the profound changes proposed by the Bolivarian Revolution. Conversely, the opposition emphasizes the authoritarian features of *Chavismo*: an attempt at reducing basic freedoms directed towards the creation of a Cuban-style communist police state, a view that fueled the motivation to mobilize against Chávez, as the totalitarian revolution needed to be stopped at all costs.

Though there were frequent episodes of violence (including the deplorable and still unclear killings of the April 11, 2002, demonstration against Chávez) and several violations of human rights, repression was not as widespread as it is in typical authoritarian settings. The economy deteriorated rapidly during these years, but the government did not systematically resort to extremist measures—such as a massive wave of nationalizations or confiscations—to restore it, even during the December 2002 *paro petrolero*. Instead, given the cumbersome relations with the vast majority of the private sector, the government started co-opting certain economic groups to keep the economy afloat, including foreign companies. This was crucial to bring the oil industry—and the country—back on track after the conflictive 2002.

There were, nonetheless, several signs of authoritarianism. During these years, Chávez did not show signs of tempering his provocative rhetoric, especially after the clash with the opposition became more intense. The increasing polarization led to an environment where dissidence—within government or in the opposition—was not tolerated, evidencing that *Chavismo* was serious about forming a new political hegemony.

Parallel to the face-off between *Chavismo* and the opposition, several elements of the government's policies evidenced a populist government struggling for consolidation. Chávez became an outspoken critic of the Bush administration, which he blamed for its alleged participation in the coup, or at least for its leniency with respect to the episode in question. This was a handy device to keep the government's supporters in case widespread mobilization was required. Congress was unable to reach consensus during these years, and the judiciary split into two competing factions—one pro-Chávez and another pro-opposition—that struggled to issue decisions to support their respective affiliates.

Chávez emerged victorious and began to consolidate his power. This required perfecting a mechanism that rallied support for Chávez, but did not depend exclusively on his personal appeal or the popularity of his "revolutionary" rhetoric. The defining moment in this process came with the social programs known as *misiones*. Through these programs, the government increased its capacity to deliver what many considered good policy, while channeling oil revenues directly to the impoverished masses.

The consolidation of Chavismo (mid-2003–mid-2006)

During this period Chávez's government—blessed with a remarkable increase of oil revenue, a resulting recovering economic scene, and a decrease in the level of social turmoil, and with a view to winning the recall referendum and the subsequent elections in 2005 and 2006—developed a formal and informal scheme that helped to consolidate Chávez's regime. This process, of course, took even greater force after Chávez survived the recall referendum, and the opposition went into disarray. An important characteristic of this period is the relatively unimportant role assigned to socialist ideology as the driving force of the redistribution plans, and other policies implemented, especially when compared to the present time.

At the beginning of 2003, after the hard times of the *paro petrolero*, the government created and implemented the first *misiones*: programs that catered to the basic needs of the excluded, financed mainly through oil revenues and administered directly by the president, which allowed them greater flexibility and speedier results at the expense of suffering from questionable accountability.[7] The *misiones* were not portrayed as government initiatives, but as a "revolutionary" achievement that generates a direct connection between the benefits received and Chávez as a benefactor.[8] These programs represent the core of the social services provided by the government, and their success seems to be a key element in the evaluation that the Venezuelan population makes of the government, especially among the dispossessed.

Anti-Americanism—best illustrated by Chávez's frequent tirades against U.S. President Bush—became rampant in Chávez's rhetoric during this period. But it also developed into the Bolivarian Alternative for the Peoples of the Americas (ALBA), a regional cooperation mechanism to fight poverty and ameliorate social inequality, based on the endogenous development of the region that does not rely on disadvantageous commercial exchanges which would lead to the enrichment of the continent's economically developed countries. In a word, ALBA is an alternative model to the U.S.-sponsored Free Trade Area of the Americas (FTAA). The initiative has been mocked by opponents as pure "petro-diplomacy." It is difficult to conceptualize ALBA as a tool to disseminate Chávez's socialist ideology, since the adoption of socialism as the government's model happened only recently. ALBA could be interpreted instead as a tool of international statecraft, as it allows beneficiary governments to win key constituencies in each one of these countries and obtain support for politically aligned allies in elections. It also puts pressure in the governments to refrain from confronting Chávez in the international arena. This interpretation puts *Chavismo* at the borderline between unfazed populism and ideologically oriented socialism.

Venezuela has also been active in selling oil at preferential rates to less developed nations in the region, has committed vast amounts of money for permanent investments in oil refineries or factories, and has provided assistance to localities on development projects as varied as the construction of roads, schools, marketing of agricultural products, or health care programs. These investments have been concentrated primarily in countries whose governments are ideologically aligned with Chávez and have provided critical support to his agenda abroad, such as Bolivia, Paraguay, Nicaragua, Ecuador and, of course and most prominently, Cuba.

Seeking to diversify Venezuela's international connections in a "pluripolar" world, Chávez has intensified its participation on international organizations, such as the United Nations (UN)—including an unsuccessful bid for a Security Council seat—or the Organization of American States (OAS). Venezuela has also strengthened its relations with "controversial" bedfellows: China, Russia, Iran, and Belarus. In these cases, the high-profile petro-diplomacy has been fortified through high-scale businesses, including massive purchases of weapons or investment arrangements in the petroleum, construction, and other sectors. But no Venezuelan relationship has been more controversial than that with Cuba. Links between both countries were fully developed during this period. Cubans have provided critical assistance in areas such as health care, sports and, allegedly, intelligence, while the Venezuelan government has provided steady economic and political support to Castro's regime.

This period also witnessed the—unsuccessful—first attempts to redistribute land on a wide scale. The state increased its intervention in the economy, including a comprehensive currency exchange control mechanism and price controls for various products. After the opposition decided not to participate in the 2005 legislative elections, alleging that the conditions for free and fair elections were not met (a decision widely criticized by analysts), the National Assembly ended almost completely in the hands of MVR and other allies of Chávez. Following the approval of the 2004 Organic Statute of the Supreme Tribunal, he also managed to pack the Court with more justices affiliated with the *Chavista* establishment. In sum, this period witnessed a systematic reduction of contestation arenas, diminishing the prospects of democracy. Chávez and his followers are governing virtually unopposed. This, to a large extent, is the result of a flawed strategy of the opposition, but also of a *Chavista* stratagem to create a new hegemony and rule without opposition. Chávez has succeeded, but at the expense of turning the system into what Levitsky and Way (2002) call competitive authoritarianism.

The onset of Twenty-First-Century Socialism (2006–present)

After eight years of *Chavismo*, Venezuela is once again at a crossroads. Chávez has vowed to turn Venezuela into a truly socialist polity, now labeling it Venezuelan Twenty-First-Century Socialism. In theory, the plans devised by the government's policy-makers and ideologues should steer Venezuela further left, following a top-down approach. The times have never seemed more fitting for dramatic reforms: Chávez was reelected president of Venezuela in December 2006 by a broad margin, he enjoys an overwhelming control over the country's institutions (including the National Assembly's recent approval of a law that allows Chávez to rule by decree for eighteen months), even when the economic outlook is ambiguous, the government continues to benefit from sustained high oil prices, and the opposition's capacity to challenge Chávez has been dramatically reduced, particularly after the 2005 legislative elections.

Twenty-First-Century Socialism is still work in progress. It remains an incoherent model, difficult to pin down and subject to several modifications at the current stage. Perhaps the best known theoretical approach is that of Dieterich (2006), who emphasizes participatory democracy as the model's pivotal idea. However, we are compelled to wait until the project is more developed, and further implemented, to really determine whether and to what extent this is different from other types of socialist initiatives attempted in the region (most distinctively, Cuba) and at a global scale. The burden is on *Chavismo* to prove that it can genuinely achieve social justice without suffering from chronic authoritarianism. This is not a mere academic disquisition; it is perhaps the most important question that Venezuelans are asking themselves in the present times.

Thus far, the main aspects of Twenty-First-Century Socialism in Venezuela have been sketched out in the Plan for Social and Economic Development for the 2007–2013 presidential term (MINCI 2007)—presented by Chávez himself—that provides the road map for years to come. The main guidelines of this project are: (1) the creation of a "new socialist ethos"; (2) "supreme social happiness"; (3) the creation of a protagonist and revolutionary democracy; (4) the development of a socialist economic model; (5) a new national geopolitical scheme; (6) Venezuela as a global energy power; and (7) a new international geopolitical scheme.

The "new socialist ethos" implies new ethical principles based on social justice, equity, and solidarity. A "new man" who embraces a revolutionary ethical spirit must be created for the new regime to blossom. Thus far, the education system reform, especially the adaptation of the curriculum to socialist values, appears as the clearest—and most controversial—policy linked to this paradigm, along with measures to eradicate the competing "evil" capitalist ethos through fostering social responsibility in the private industry sector. The "supreme socialist happiness" seeks the creation of a social structure based on equality and inclusiveness that can only derive from transforming the social relations of production. To achieve this goal, the government seeks to devise different types of socialist ownership schemes—different from private property—as well as institutionalizing and expanding the *misiones*. The plan also calls for the expansion of health coverage, housing, social security, the protection of the environment, strengthening of the national identity, and new educational opportunities, all tied to the development of socialism as a whole. It also promotes the direct participation of the citizens through new associative forms via which communities would arguably administer their resources directly.

A "protagonist and revolutionary democracy" implies, for *Chavismo*, social inclusion, majority rule, and direct democracy, as opposed to individual rights, the protection of the minorities in a highly polarized context, and the virtues of representative democracy which are dismissed as "contradictory to society's general interest" (MINCI 2007, p. 17). In Twenty-First-Century Socialism, public participation extends to areas such as budgeting and public accountability, and entails people's participation in the media (an idea that was used to justify the recent closing of the private TV station RCTV and the opening of its government-sponsored substitute, TVES).

The socialist economic model emphasizes production rather than "reproduction of wealth," with the state controlling all areas of strategic importance. To facilitate the transition towards socialism, the government is promoting the creation of companies of social production of goods and services (*empresas de production social*, EPS), formed by workers in a relationship of parity with each other who split the benefits in proportion to their labor input (see Rivero Ramírez and García Soto 2006). These organizations are sponsored by government funds, or result from the transformation of formerly public or private-owned corporations. A critical role for the creation of the model, especially in its early years, is the oil industry, which would rely on EPS to provide the goods and services required for its activity. It also involves promoting endogenous economic development, in particular with respect to the industrial and agricultural sectors, the consolidation of agrarian reform (with a renewed vow to eliminate *latifundio*), the creation of incentives to foster cooperative and other productive associations of workers, and the development of a more vigorous scientific sector to depend less upon the know-how and knowledge coming from other countries or the private sector.

The modification of the geo-political organization of the state is necessary to promote the development of areas with less population density or higher poverty levels, the recovery of urban areas, and the development plans to achieve sustainable growth. Notably, the development of the energy sector does not add anything significant to those that are already in place. The same is true for the foreign policy agenda, as it would only continue the goals and guidelines that characterize Chávez's government, including its anti-imperialistic, nationalist, and regionalist orientations. The document explicitly mentions that the government should continue sponsoring the development of a South American Community of Nations and the expansion of ALBA.

A good number of the measures to implement Twenty-First-Century Socialism are not innovations, but extensions of policies already implemented. There are, however, some significant changes. First, Twenty-First-Century Socialism is presented as a coherent social, political, and economic effort to develop a socialist polity. It is not unusual to hear Chávez talk about "five engines" of Twenty-First-Century Socialism, which include the constitutional reform, ruling by decree, and other initiatives recently put into practice. Despite this fact, many observers still consider it to be empty rhetoric, and have not given it enough credit. But some recent cases suggest that might not be the most accurate interpretation: the re-nationalization of the once-privatized telephone company CANTV and the decision to refuse RCTV a public broadcasting license, setting up a communal TV station (TVES) to replace it. The facts about the run-up to the definitive ceasing of RCTV transmissions are somewhat unclear, especially regarding RCTV's supposed lack of compliance with the procedure to renew its broadcasting license. Furthermore, the decision was upheld by other branches, most notoriously the judiciary, in a way that evidenced their lack of autonomy.

Second, the "rationalization" of the Bolivarian Revolution is being translated into legislation. It is within this context that the extraordinary decree powers granted to Chávez and the constitutional reform he proposed to the National Assembly should be understood. This process seeks to fulfill not only a mere formalistic role, but also a transformational role in the sense of creating a new set of rules to dramatically modify the Venezuelan political, social, and economic structure. Some of the changes proposed in the reform are potentially deeper than those implemented in 1999 when Chávez assumed office. The constitutional reform formalizes the "Popular" branch of power (i.e. communal councils) and the *misiones*, making them financially dependent on the president. It strips some powers from states and municipalities and transfers most of them either to the central government or to the communal councils. All of this substantiates sub-national political units above the states that report directly to the Executive. This effectively reduces the autonomy enjoyed by the regional and local levels of government to a bare minimum. The reform also proposes to increase the presidential term from six to seven years and eliminates presidential term limits. The reform would also grant constitutional character to most of the different economic measures leading to the creation of the socialist economy, including the recognition of new forms of collective ownership, and it would also increase the thresholds required to request recall referenda against public authorities.

Third, some of these changes would be truly radical, particularly the development of a socialist economy and the full recognition of a "Popular" branch of government. The vast majority of the new political and economic elites, despite being affiliated with the government, are disenchanted with the prospects of losing clout as a result of some of these changes. Hence, Chávez risks losing allies and political support on specific sectors. The recent departure of the moderate-left PODEMOS political party, the struggles within the military related to its role in the new political arrangement and, more importantly, the relatively low levels of support for certain areas of the reform among *Chavistas*, evidence that resistance has begun to form.

Chávez has also pushed to institutionalize his movement's power by creating the United Socialist Party of Venezuela (USPV), which seeks to join together the different former MVR factions and small political parties into one hegemonic party. Along with the *misiones*, this provides the government with a direct mechanism to influence electoral behavior and mobilize voters to approve the constitutional reform referendum. It will be difficult to create a coherent political organization without resorting to the same clientelism that privileges a few.

The conjunction of these factors evidences a crucial dilemma. Chávez has managed to accumulate power as a result of a relatively well-administered populist agenda, and has not abandoned pragmatic concerns for the sake of the government's stability. But can he create a truly socialist polity without undermining the very system that has allowed him to stay in power? If so, will *Chavismo* as we know it prevail in the long run, or will it fall prey to mounting factionalism and, eventually, lose sufficient grip to allow a less radical alternative to appear? This issue lies at the heart of the crossroads between populism and revolutionary change, between the wishes of moderate and extremist *Chavista* factions (Ellner 2005). While moderates prefer evolution and a pluralistic political scene, the more radical opt for revolutionary changes and the consolidation of a single political association to organize its masses and leadership. As a result, the *transition* towards socialism is proving controversial, patchy, and uncertain. Twenty-First-Century Socialism may not necessarily be a viable long-term project. The only prediction that can be made about Venezuelan politics is that it will continue being marred by uncertainty.

Final remarks

It would seem natural to affirm that the Venezuelan left went from almost no power to being all-powerful in a matter of fifteen years. Yet, the rising into stardom of Hugo Chávez and the Bolivarian Movement cannot be attributed exclusively to the Venezuelan left. As a matter of fact, the left was plagued by divisionism before and after his arrival to power. Although nobody would contest the leftist credentials of *Chavismo*, its many contradictions and its reliance on populist measures to win elections, accumulate power and refrain from sharing it, might very well represent the kiss of death to the wishes and hopes of those who yearn for social changes in a functioning democracy.

The Bolivarian Revolution now has two faces. On the one hand, several reformists inhabit the movement and push for a moderate approach to politics. On the opposite hand, there is a push for a complete revolution that overhauls the state and pursues Utopia. Both rely on populism, however, to govern. Which side will have the final say? For the time being, recent developments seem to point to a genuine radicalization of the process. A first interpretation suggests that Hugo Chávez wishes to turn his leftist government "further left," or at least attempt to abandon one kind of left—the populist, nationalist left that has so far characterized his government—in favor of another "romantic" left, dedicated to further a new kind of top-down socialist transformation of the state. There are numerous elements following Chávez's reelection in December 2006 that point in this direction. However, many recent developments suggest the opposite: the reform has been tempered in some respects so that the pace of the implementation of some of these new policies has been slowed down (especially when they have failed), Chávez has proved pragmatic in the past and, overall, the fact that the regime still depends on populist baits to move Twenty-First-Century Socialism forward and the relatively limited reach of Marxist ideology among the Venezuelan population, casts serious doubts on whether the government will be able to fulfill its goals without keeping populism alive and kicking.

In any case, since any viable attempt to propose a different leftist alternative in Venezuela seems unfeasible, the fate of the left as a whole seems to be entirely tied to the *Chavista* Leviathan. And, yes, it is the left which depends on Chávez and not the other way round.

Notes

1 This text focuses on the post-1993 developments, but an important work, yet to be carried out, should systematically explore the connections between *Chavismo* and the Venezuelan left in the 1960s, especially the revolutionary left.
2 The role that the party played—or was supposed to have played—on that day, as well as its influence on the young military officers who tried to overthrow Pérez, is still matter of controversy. It is true that Chávez had personal connections with members of Causa R from the beginning of the Bolivarian movement (see, for instance, his own account in Chávez 2005). But competing accounts have been given in this respect by the rebel leaders and by Causa R affiliates.
3 After all, it was he who had orchestrated a coup against Pérez, the staple of the corrupt bipartisan political establishment.
4 An important exception is Penfold (2006).
5 These elements were probably brought in by the more moderate sectors of the *Chavista* alliance. Informal accounts suggest that the constituent assembly was dominated by the Miquilenista faction of the MVR.
6 Chávez issued forty-nine decrees, some of them in key socio-economic topics, such as the regulation of the extraction and commercialization of hydrocarbons, and a new scheme for land reform. These decrees were strongly rejected by business sectors and marked the beginning of the struggle between the government and the opposition.

7 *Misiones* have been portrayed as means to allocate resources aimed at building political support for Chávez (Penfold 2006). To date, nearly twenty *misiones* have been implemented. The first one to appear was *Barrio Adentro* in April 2003, which provided free primary health care to citizens in Venezuelan poor urban communities (*barrios*). It effectively created a parallel health care system, subsequently improved and extended through the *Misiones Barrio Adentro* 2 and 3. On the other hand, the educational *misiones* have been among the most popular. These include *Misión Robinson I* (alphabetization); *Misión Robinson II* and *Misión Ribas* (primary and secondary education, respectively), and *Misión Sucre* (higher education). Some of these programs involved the organization into co-operatives of attendees, who were given a stipend in "exchange" for their participation. Another important program was *Misión Identidad*, which provided national identification cards to Venezuelans and foreign residents in Venezuela. There is not enough room here to discuss in detail whether these and the many other *misiones* are effectively fulfilling their goals. However, their link with the brisk hike in the popularity of Chávez during 2003 and 2004 and his subsequent victory in the 2004 referendum is an important topic that deserves careful study.

8 *Misiones* are, at best, a double-edged sword. On the one hand, if properly devised and carefully executed, they can ameliorate the condition of exclusion of the poor. On the other hand, without careful monitoring by civil society and due accountability, they can be used for strengthening the same clientelist and authoritarian links that ruined the prospects of Venezuelan democracy. Furthermore, the existence of two parallel bureaucracies is unsustainable in the long run.

Chapter 10

The left in Peru
Plenty of wagons
and no locomotion[†]

Martín Tanaka

I analyze the surge, the fall, and the attempts to reconstruct the Peruvian left over the last decades. During the 1980s, Izquierda Unida (IU) became the second most important political force in the country. The source of its success resided in the confluence of strong popular organizations, disciplined parties, and a charismatic leader (Alfonso Barrantes). Yet this very confluence generated particular dynamics: the organizations pulled towards radicalism, the parties towards ideology, and the leader towards moderation. As a result of this tension, IU split in 1989 in the middle of the crisis that led to the collapse of the party system and led Alberto Fujimori directly to power.

Since then, the Peruvian left has not had a leader, and the parties that subscribe to this ideology have remained de-legitimized. The weakness of the organizations that resulted from the decay of the State-based model as well as the effects of neoliberal policies implemented by an authoritarian regime must also be added to this situation. The left followed two paths during the 1990s: on the one hand, the more orthodox sectors that were closer to the social organizations tried to present a class-based profile, which eventually led to their marginalization; on the other hand, the sectors that were aligned with social democratic positions and closer to Barrantes decided to confront the Fujimori authoritarianism and lost their distinctive identities when they decided to integrate broad coalitions. Recently, the surge of the left in Latin America became manifest in Peru with the sudden appearance of Ollanta Humala and his anti-systemic discourse—more so because he won the first round of the April 2006 elections, but lost the runoff to Alan García. Since then, the tradeoff between marginality and subordination remains: some sectors seem to succumb to the temptation of following a leader who is followed by the masses in order to become less isolated, although at the cost of losing their own identity, while others have opted for

[†] This chapter is an updated and reformulated version of a text on the Peruvian left to be published in Spanish in Jorge Lanzaro, ed., *La izquierda en América Latina*, Buenos Aires: CLACSO.

preserving their identity but at the cost of remaining marginal. These two alternatives characterize the Peruvian left.

Even when we can distinguish a "populist traditional" left and a "modern social democratic" left in Peru, they both share the same problems that keep them marginal and politically subordinate. The main challenge for the left, then, is to fine-tune the demands for social and political change. Up to this moment, the lefts are identified with the establishment that Peruvians want to leave behind.

Some precedents

Despite the doctrinal richness associated with José Carlos Mariategui, the Peruvian left was subordinated to the American Popular Revolutionary Alliance (Alianza Popular Revolucionaria Americana, APRA) between the 1930s and 1960s, which incarnated "classical populism" in Peru (Vilas 1994). The overwhelming political weight of the party, as well as the repression and the closed nature of the political system, marginalized the left—which at the time was represented by the Communist Party—as happened in many other countries in the region. APRA became more conservative with the passage of time, which facilitated the development of new variants of the left during the 1960s that expressed the radical and reformist spirit that had no place within APRA or the Communist Party. While all of this happened, hundreds of militants of the left began a process of linkage with the peasants, labor unions, and the general public, which drastically reduced the influence of APRA among these organized sectors by the end of the 1960s.[1]

While this process was underway, a fundamental event for the Peruvian left occurred: the Revolutionary Government of the Armed Forces (Gobierno Revolucionario de la Fuerza Armada) headed by General Juan Velasco interrupted the first administration of Fernando Belaunde (1963–1968) with a coup. The Velasquismo (1968–1975)—unlike previous military interventions in Peru and other military governments in the Southern Cone (Collier 1979)—had a reformist nature (McClintock and Lowenthal 1989; Stepan 1978; Lynch 1992; Pease 1979). It implemented a profound program of changes that signaled the end of the prevailing oligarchic order resulting from the implementation of a series of agrarian and labor reforms, an extensive policy of nationalization, and an education reform, all accompanied by a strong egalitarian rhetoric and fostering of social organizations. The Velasco government implemented an important part of the agenda that the left had advocated until that moment. Not surprisingly, some groups collaborated with the government, but some others actively questioned its reformist character instead of following a revolutionary path (Lauer 1977). By mid-1975, the costs of the international oil crisis became evident, along with the growing frustration of the more conservative groups in the armed forces, which led to a new coup d'état. Velasco was overthrown and control was taken by General Francisco Morales Bermúdez (1975–1980). This government responded to the crisis with an orthodox program of adjustment policies, and engaged in a process that various authors have characterized as the dismantling of the reforms implemented by Velasco.[2]

It is important to note that the left led a vigorous movement of social protests in response to these policies. How to explain what would become one of the most important moments of protest in recent Peruvian history? This is not the place to make an exhaustive analysis, but it would be sufficient to say that most theoretically relevant variables described by theories of collective action and the surge of social movements were present at the time: we find a strong organization (propelled by Velasquismo), resources that could be vested into mobilization (as the crisis was only beginning), strong external groups (the parties from the left), the perception that the political system was closing up to the demands of the people—after an intense period of opening—which created the need to mobilize as means to counter this trend, and a cultural environment that was prone to mobilization derived from years of an official discourse that emphasized rights, social justice, and the revival of popular demands (Foweraker 1995; McAdam et al. 1996).

The left found itself, for the first time in history, heading a wide movement of masses that protested against the policies of the military government. Two national milestones are the national strikes of 1977 and 1978 against economic policy and for the constitution of a "government of the people" (see Figure 10.1).

The military government faced the rejection not only of the organized popular movements, but also of the members of the business class and society in general. This isolation opened a negotiation process with political actors, and finally a process of transition to democracy became possible as a result of the agreements struck between the government and APRA. A Constituent Assembly was called in 1978, and presidential and congressional elections were held in 1980. While the parties from the left initially had doubts as to whether they should present candidates, in the end they did, with two exceptions: the Maoist Red Fatherland Communist Party of Peru (Partido Comunista del Perú Patria Roja, PCP) and a small dogmatic and fundamentalist group, the Shining Path Communist Party of Peru (Partido Comunista del Perú Sendero Luminoso, PCP-SL). And not only did these refuse to present candidates, they announced their transit to armed rebellion against the system.

Despite the fact that all parties from the left—except for SL and later the Tupac Amaru Revolutionary Movement (Movimiento Revolucionario Tupac Amaru, MRTA)—became a part of the political system and accepted liberal democratic rules, together with Red Fatherland (Patria Roja), which

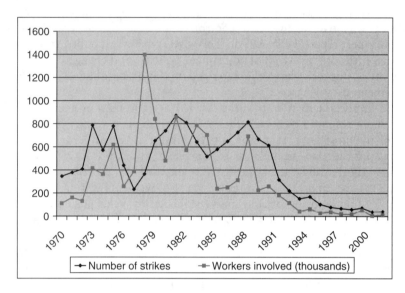

Figure 10.1 Number of strikes and workers involved, 1970–2001

did so in 1980, there were always conflicts involved. The left understood its participation in the Constituent Assembly as a means to score political points during the debates. The left had an impressive success when participating in the "bourgeois democracy." The votes of all five parties from the left in 1978 add up to 29.4 percent, which is slightly higher than the 23.8 percent obtained by the rightist Popular Christian Party (Partido Popular Cristiano, PPC), although lower than APRA's 35.3 percent (see Table 10.1). By 1978, for the first time in its history, the left had become the second largest political force in Peru.

The united left (will never be defeated?)[3]

The participation of the left in the Constitutional Assembly was characterized by its ideological stance and its continuous protests. The left did not actively participate in the deliberations on the most important topics. In the end, it refused to endorse the new Constitution when it was enacted (Sanborn 1991). This left lived a complex paradox: on the one hand, it was wary of the "institutions of the bourgeoisie" but, on the other hand, it achieved substantive advances within these same institutions. Starting with the 1980s presidential and congressional elections, it became possible for the left to accede to power in a sort of repetition of the Chilean way to socialism. The developments in other political parties clearly encouraged this view. APRA, for instance, lived a profound crisis: its historical leader—Victor Raúl

Table 10.1 Percentage of votes for the main political parties, 1978–1995

	AP	PPC	(AP+PPC) FREDEMO	APRA	Left (IU)	Independents
1978 (C)	NP	23.8	(23.8)	35.3	29.4	11.5
1980 (P)	45.4	9.6	(55.0)	27.4	14.4	3.2
1980 (M)	35.8	11.1	(46.9)	22.5	(23.3)	7.4
1983 (M)	17.5	13.9	(31.4)	33.1	(29.0)	6.7
1985 (P)	7.3	11.9	(19.2)	53.1	(24.7)	3.0
1986 (M)	NP	14.8	(14.8)	47.6	(30.8)	7.8
1989 (M)	—	—	31.2	20.4	20.2	28.2
1990 (P)	—	—	32.6	22.6	13.0	31.8
1990 (P)	—	—	37.5	NP	NP	62.5
1992 (C)	NP	9.7	(9.7)	NP	5.5	84.8
1993 (M)	11.6	5.7	(17.3)	10.8	3.9	64.7
1995 (P)	1.64	NP	(1.64)	4.11	0.57	93.7

Note: (C) denotes elections to the Constituent Assembly; (P) denotes presidential election; and (M) denotes municipal elections.

Haya de la Torre—had died in 1979, and the internal fights for succession almost led the party to an insurmountable factionalization. The right was also divided: Popular Action (Acción Popular, AP), which had not participated in the 1978 elections, announced that it would compete in 1980 with Fernando Belaunde—the deposed president in 1968—as its candidate. As a result, AP would compete for the same votes as PPC, splitting the share of votes in the right. Under these conditions, it only seemed necessary for the left to remain united to win the election. By mid-1979, the process to generate a unified front in the left began, aiming at presenting a unified candidacy. The front was conformed under the name Revolutionary Alliance of the Left (Alianza Revolucionaria de Izquierda, ARI), generating hopes and expectations. For many sectors in the left, the country was effectively under "pre-revolutionary conditions" and ARI could become the large political reference for the people. Nevertheless, ARI broke down before the appointed date to register candidacies and the left ran five different presidential candidates with five different lists of congressional candidates.

The consequences of the breakdown of ARI were devastating for the left. Party members were disappointed with their leaders' conduct, which appeared as self- and party-motivated instead of looking out for the interests of the left, the country, or the revolution. The rupture generated a bitter fight to assign responsibility for the failure of ARI. The electoral consequences of this were clear: after the 29.4 percent obtained in 1978 by the left as a whole, these five parties only reached 14.4 percent in 1980.[4,5] With the left out of the way and the divisions in APRA, Fernando Belaunde was able to return to power. Since then, the reminder of division and failure contributed to reunite the left and keep it cohesive during the 1980s. Unity was understood as a moral imperative, and no one would appear as advocating rupture. This can help explain the conduct of political actors when a division was finally produced between January and October 1989.

The failure of ARI quickly led to the reorganization of the left. Hugo Blanco and the Trotskyists were portrayed as responsible for division of the left and thus were isolated. The remaining parties had an easier way to finding the path to unity and created IU in September 1980, seeking to use this label in the municipal elections of November of that same year.[6] The equilibrium between parties was resolved by advocating a personality that was "independent" of all groups. Therefore, a character without much relevance became coordinator, spokesman, and IU's candidate for the municipality of Lima: Alfonso Barrantes.

Unity quickly demonstrated some positive effects: the left recovered many of the lost votes in the municipal elections of 1980, in part due to the leadership of Barrantes. Unlike other leaders of the left, he deployed a special type of provincial charisma. This quickly transformed him into a national figure who garnered the support of public opinion, finding in him an affable and capable personality able to generate confidence and foster cohesion on non-ideological grounds. This contrasted with the traditional leaders of the left, who were typically ideological and reliant on confrontation.

The success of IU was based on the confluence of a charismatic personality, disciplined political parties, and popular movements. Despite the tensions, it was possible to integrate a positive-sum interaction between them. The leadership of Barrantes generated a wide appeal that was easily translated into votes. IU became the second most important political party during the 1980s (see Table 10.1). IU won the mayorship of Lima in 1983, thus making Barrantes the first "Marxist mayor of the city." In the same election, IU obtained 29 percent of the votes at the national level, effectively becoming the second most important political force in the country after APRA.[7] In the presidential and congressional elections of 1985, IU was again second to APRA, securing this position. But the consolidation of the left did not only take place at the polls: it was fairly efficient in Congress and also displayed skill when administrating local governments. To achieve these outcomes, IU recruited a large number of progressive professionals with no political affiliation, and also gained the support of intellectuals and the cultural sphere in Peru.

Even when the parties that conformed IU were ideological and always found it difficult to assume the values of the liberal-representative ("bourgeois") democracy, they nevertheless played by the rules of the system and even acted by the political pact that supported the 1979 Constitution, which they had refused to endorse. This is an even more significant fact if we consider that IU had to coexist with the Shining Path and MRTA,[8] which increased political tension and forced the left to detach from the armed way, but at the same time the repression and militarization of the country as well as the crisis of state pushed the left toward more radical positions.

By the second half of the 1980s, the polarization in Peru evidenced the difficulty to maintain a positive-sum relationship between the different factions within IU, as we will see.

Polarization, rupture, and the disappearance of the left (along with the whole party system)

APRA solved the leadership problem that resulted from the death of Haya with the consolidation of Alan García. He was able to give the party a renewed and active image, as well as a social democratic profile. García's charisma led APRA to the presidency in June of 1985 for the first time in its history. After being elected president, García developed his own rhetoric based on revolutionary and reformist appeals, social justice to favor the poorest, workers and those who had been excluded. And this was coupled with a buoyant economy and a notorious reduction of inflation.[9] All of this led García to have very high levels of approval between 1985 and mid-1987, leaving the left in a position that increased the tensions within, and caused contradictions to surface.

One side was composed of those who advocated a "critical collaboration" with APRA, seeking to consolidate the social democratic–socialist hegemony in the country and avoid the reconstitution of the right which suffered a sever setback in 1985 (see Table 10.1). This strategy had the electoral arena at its core, pursuing average voters that sought center-left alternatives and limit to the confrontation. The visible leader of this side was Barrantes himself, a close friend of Alan García. This strategy presumed that IU would succeed APRA in power, and this required the continuation of the constitutional rule, which required distance from the Shining Path in order to avoid the military veto. At the other end appeared those who proposed a face-on confrontation with APRA, wanting to underscore the limits of the reformist strategy, reaffirm an alternative revolutionary identity, and prepare for the possibility of pre-revolutionary phases in the medium term. From this point of view, it was necessary to strengthen the structure of the party and insert it back into the social movements, especially those located in "strategic" sectors.

The tensions reached their highest levels when Barrantes was not reelected as mayor of Lima, losing to the APRA candidate in the November 9, 1986, election with numerous claims of fraud. The growing conflicts with APRA increased the difficulty of enacting the "critical collaboration" and made it necessary for IU to keep its distance from APRA. The more confrontational positions within the left became more reasonable, as García's honeymoon had come to an end by mid-1987, and critics started to openly voice their concerns. On November 14, 1986, IU called for a public protest against electoral fraud, but Barrantes was harshly scorned when he started his speech with soft words for APRA. Months later, on May 27, 1987, during the inauguration of the IX Congress of the Peruvian Communist Party, Barrantes was scorned again by the Communist youth. These and other incidents exemplify the conditions that led Barrantes to resign the presidency of IU (but not its leadership) on May 31, 1987. He accused those who questioned him of seeking his "political annihilation" from an "overt pro-terrorist position." IU's leadership became collegiate. The internal tensions increased between 1987 and 1988, precisely at the time García's government began to lose its capacity to control the economy, leading the country into a high-inflation situation that was coupled with the collapse of public finances.[10]

The internal armed conflict evidenced the growing process of crisis within the State. By 1988, the number of subversive actions and the number of deaths clearly increased after a slight decrease in 1987 (see Table 10.2). This only added to the tensions within IU.

During this political juncture, the problems that IU would need to address and the definitions it needed to make became clear. First of all, it needed to define its political leadership. After Barrantes resigned the IU presidency, its leadership became collegiate under the National Directive Committee, composed of the Secretaries General of the parties that conformed IU, with a bimonthly rotational "Coordinator in turn." IU convened its first National Congress in January 1989 to define its organizational structure, an immediate plan of action, and the strategy for

Table 10.2 Peru, dynamics of political violence, 1980–1994

Year	Subversive actions registered by the National Police	Victims of political violence
1980	219	3
1981	715	4
1982	891	170
1983	1,123	2,807
1984	1,760	4,319
1985	2,050	1,359
1986	2,549	1,268
1987	2,489	697
1988	2,415	1,986
1989	3,149	3,198
1990	2,779	3,452
1991	2,785	3,180
1992	2,995	3,101
1993	1,918	1,692
1994	1,195	652

the 1990 elections, and to elect a new national leadership that improved upon the system based on representatives from each party.

The call for the Congress brought life back to a relatively paralyzed IU, generated large expectations, and made it grow considerably. By July 1988, 130,000 people had become members of IU. Several surveys taken between 1988 and January of 1989 showed that IU with Barrantes as presidential candidate was ahead of Mario Vargas Llosa as the Democratic Front's (Frente Democrático, FREDEMO) candidate for the 1990 presidential election. By January 1989, IU engaged in a long process of division during its Congress, which progressively undermined its political and electoral clout. The tension between "reformists" and "vanguard-militarists" propelled the rupture.[11] The trouble began as the result of disagreements on the registration of delegates to elect the front's leadership and to determine the role of Alfonso Barrantes. On this matter, I would like to emphasize a seldom noted—but crucial—aspect to aid understanding of what happened: it was not the division that destroyed the electoral prospects and credibility of the left as a whole; in the end, it could have been even better for each group to follow its own path with consistency. The real problem came in the manner in which the division occurred: with a lot of confusion, and with calls for unity confronted by harsh criticisms from all sides that began in January 1989 and ended in October of that year, when the period of registering presidential and congressional candidates ended. Then, IU registered Henry Pease as its presidential candidate, and Alfonso Barrantes was registered as the candidate of the recently created Socialist Left (Izquierda Socialista, IS).

Why go through such a tortuous and complicated division? I think two reasons account for it. The first derives from the myth of unity within the left, which was a necessary idea after the rupture of ARI. None of its members would want to appear responsible for the rupture, which made this matter especially confusing for the militants and the average voter. The second derives from the fact that the rupture was long and complex, given that both sides faced crossed incentives that simultaneously led them to unity and rupture. IS had the candidate (Barrantes), a valuable asset in the electoral arena, but lacked the links with the main parties and social movements, with the "people's movement."[12] Between January and October 1989, IS tried to convince PCP to join the IU dissidence, as PCP held considerable power over the largest workers' union in the country, the General Peruvian Workers' Confederation (Confederación General de Trabajadores del Perú, CGTP). But PCP was also going through a process similar to that of IU, and aligning with Barrantes could effectively mean rupture since the majority of its militants rejected him. The link of IU with the stronger parties and the "people's movement" was solid, but it needed a leader who could compete at the polls. This would explain why Pease himself, along with the more "moderate" sectors in IU (which included the PCP leadership), would advocate the nomination of Barrantes as presidential candidate. But Barrantes did not think it proper to head such a heterogeneous political front with such radicalized sectors.[13]

In the end, centrifugal tendencies prevailed. Each of the members had reasons to see the future with a certain degree of optimism. For IU, the link to the social movements was important and played a key role in defining its identity. Even after the rupture, Henry Pease could still state that "IU gathers basically all sides of the organized people's movement." But the groups within IU failed to perceive the profound weakness and isolation prevailing in the organized groups, as well as how disconnected they had become from society. Therefore, and despite having "basically all sides of the organized people's movement," IU obtained a meager 8.2 percent of the vote in 1990. However, there was initially some hope for Barrantes and IS, since surveys had consistently shown him during 1989 as the natural candidate for a runoff with Vargas Llosa, even after the division of IU in October. Barrantes' leadership was seriously damaged during the campaign, especially near the election. He was perceived as responsible for the rupture and got even less votes than Pease (roughly 4.7 percent). The 1990 elections were disastrous for the left, especially considering the scenario at the beginning of 1989. But its "strategic defeat" would come later, between 1991 and 1995.

The winner of the 1990 elections was not Vargas Llosa's FREDEMO but an outsider, Alberto Fujimori, who was the unexpected beneficiary of both the division of the left and Vargas Llosa's campaign gaffes. Surprisingly, a political system that had an acute problem with ideological polarization and effective government ended up creating a problem of representation, where the left was forced to take the side of the "traditional" forces: system versus anti-system.

Fujimori created a multipartisan Council of Ministers at the beginning of his administration (July 1990–February 1991) which was to be coordinated by Juan Carlos Hurtado. Several conspicuous technocrats, affiliated with IU and IS, who had clearly social democrat positions participated in this cabinet that was forced to implement a stringent stabilization program in August 1990.[14] Since the program was perceived as inevitable, 49 percent of the population supported it—as reported by an APOYO survey for the metropolitan area in Lima published in August 1990—and no social turmoil arose in the country's capital city.

The left clearly opposed the Fujimori administration after Hurtado Miller left the cabinet and was replaced by Carlos Boloña as Minister of the Economy. Hurtado had suggested the stabilization plan, given that no other alternative was available. But Boloña was an individual with neoliberal leanings who also advocated structural reforms to which the left was strongly opposed. Throughout 1991, the reformist left that was excluded from the government lost its luster, which was gained by the more radical and mobilization-based left. These sectors of the left engaged in mobilizations to stop the structural reforms. Conflicts throughout 1991 at times suggested that Fujimori would be defeated, as the opposition not only gathered the left and APRA, who questioned the reform program, but also the parties in FREDEMO, who questioned the authoritarian character of the government.

In the end, Fujimori prevailed over the opposition, and the key to his success was managing to stabilize the economy, a feat that became evident by the second half of 1991. As a result, Fujimori was able to stand as the guarantor of stability which "traditional" parties—the left included—had not been able to accomplish. This also brought about the support of the armed forces, which proved decisive in the self-coup of April 1992. Why couldn't the mobilizations and the left defeat the government? It became clear throughout 1991 that the mobilization strategy had ceased to be as decisive as it had been during the 1980s. This was mostly due to profound structural changes that became evident only by the 1990s. Starting in 1998, with the final adjustments of the APRA administration, two related events happened. On the one hand, an unexpected fall in wages reduced the power of mobilization to nurture protests; on the other hand, the growth of an informal economy rapidly isolated organizations and weakened the ties between the "people's organized movements" and society in general, which translated into a public opinion that supported Fujimori and wanted control of inflation over any other outcome.

In sum, since the left opposed the political and social restructuring advocated by Fujimori, it ended up being bundled up with the institutional order that prevailed in 1979, which was the political system that he was set to destroy, along with all other political parties, during the 1980s. The left became an indistinguishable part of the system that an outsider like Fujimori rejected as a whole, and the success of Fujimori affected it as much as the rest of the system. He engaged in a coup d'état in April of 1992, which was widely supported by the citizenry. Its success implied the consolidation of an anti-partisan rhetoric that liquidated the left, as it was perceived as part of the establishment.

The 1990s, the new century, and the disappearance of the left: between marginality and political subordination

After the self-coup of 1992, and because of international pressure, Fujimori was forced to accept a new Congress which would simultaneously work as a Constituent Assembly: the Democratic Constituent Congress (Congreso Constituyente Democrático, CCD). The divisions in the left became evident once more: only one group decided to participate in the November elections under the Democratic Movement of the Left (Movimiento Democrático de Izquierda, MDI), which grouped the Socialist Affirmation Movement (Movimiento de Afirmación Socialista, MAS), the Revolutionary

Mariateguist Party (Partido Mariateguista Revolucionario, PMR)[15] and some others. This group, descendant of the reformist side of IU, gambled on maintaining visibility and participating in the democratic space. Meanwhile, the leftist parties that were stronger, more ideological and more linked to social organizations (PCP, UNIR, and PUM) gambled on boycotting the elections, arguing that their actions were based on principle, and also avoiding the risk of an electoral defeat while seeking refuge in the social movements.[16] In the end, neither of these strategies was successful. MDI obtained only 5.5 percent of the vote and four seats in the eighty-member CCD. Between 1992 and 1995, MDI became a public figure as a result of denouncing and opposing the constitutional project of Fujimori's majority, but always within the boundaries of institutions and legality. The movement-based left did not succeed in restructuring using social protests, which, as can be seen in Table 10.2, decreased notoriously during the economic and political restructuring undertaken by Fujimori.

The "Command for the No" was created to fight the new Constitution designed by the majority in the CCD. It united leaders from the left with a broad group of "democratic" forces (including some personalities from APRA, PPC, and AP) that fought to defend the rule of law and against the authoritarian rule of Fujimori. The new Constitution was approved by a referendum held in October of 1993 by a small margin—52.25 percent voted yes, and 47.75 percent voted no—surrounded by a series of claims of fraud that were never explained. This led many to think that a unified candidate in the 1995 elections could be a way to defeat Fujimori. As a matter of fact, some polls suggested that Javier Pérez de Cuéllar, the former UN Secretary General, could be an alternative to successfully institutionalize democracy. The candidacy did in fact happen, giving birth to the Union for Peru (Unión por el Perú, UPP).

It is interesting to see that the 1995 general election reproduced the divisions that the left had shown at the end of the 1980s, although this time not as a drama but as a comedy, to use Marx's phrase from his *Eighteenth Brumaire of Louis Bonaparte*. A group on the left chose to align to a centrist coalition, gambling on a more viable way to accede to power, and joined the UPP. Nevertheless, the UPP ended up as a conglomerate of very diverse characters whose incoherence weakened the project as a viable electoral alternative. As a result, the personalities from the left became isolated, without any possibility of imposing an agenda from the left on the organization. At the same time, the movement-based groups in the left proposed to resuscitate IU. They criticized the candidacy of Pérez de Cuéllar as conservative and advocated the creation of a "people's" candidacy. IU registered a presidential formula in October of 1994, with Alfonso Barrantes as its presidential candidate. IU gambled on ideological principles justified by its opposition to Fujimori's neoliberalism, but in practice it only contributed to fractionalizing the opposition vote, thus paving the way for Fujimori in the first round. Furthermore, Barrantes resigned as presidential candidate in January of 1995, in the middle of a bitter confrontation regarding the list of congressional candidates. IU had lived the tragedy of division in 1989; by 1995 it had divided again in a sort of comedy of errors, when it was already an insignificant political actor. Barrantes' substitute, Agustín Haya, obtained only 0.58 percent of the vote and IU's list for Congress only 1.67 percent, thus producing just two representatives, Javier Diez Canseco (PUM) and Rolando Breña (Red Fatherland), although it lost its registration as a political party since it obtained less than 5 percent of the vote.[17]

Between 1995 and 2000, the left practically disappeared from Peruvian politics. So long as politics were determined by the fight against the authoritarianism of Fujimori and a defense of democratic institutions discourse, the left and its demands were bound to be lost before the liberals. This became painstakingly clear in the 2000 and 2001 elections.

The 2000 elections gave way again to center-left personalities in organizations such as UPP, We are Peru (Somos Perú) and National Solidarity (Solidaridad Nacional), as well as in movements like the Democratic Forum (Foro Democrático), among others, while the radical leftists found no space.[18] The 2000 election again showed the extreme weakness of all parties that had existed since the 1980s: Abel Salinas, APRA's presidential candidate, obtained 1.38 percent of the valid votes, and Víctor Andrés García Belaunde, AP's presidential candidate, only 0.38 percent. The frontrunners in the election were candidates who ran under non-partisan labels, such as Fujimori, Alejandro Toledo, and Alberto Andrade. Congress was no different: APRA obtained 5.52 percent of the valid votes, and AP got 2.44 percent.

With the fall of Fujimori and the transitional government led by Valentín Paniagua, the situation changed somewhat (although not for the left) as a result of the opening of spaces that would allow an increased level of political competition. This allowed the return of Alan García to the country— he had been in exile since 1992—and his presidential bid in the 2001 elections. Alejandro Toledo, under the Possible Peru label, won in the end (with 36.51 percent in the first round and 53.08 percent in the runoff), which can be read as a natural result of the ongoing distrust of the more ideological and programmatic parties. Yet Alan García obtained a surprising 25.71 percent in the first round and 46.92 percent in the runoff, with Lourdes Flores of National Unity obtaining 24.3 percent.[19] In Congress, APRA obtained 19.71 percent of the vote, National Unity 13.8 percent and AP 4.14 percent. It is interesting to note the relative recovery of some parties that had existed since the 1980s, and that the left—in all its variants—wasn't able to field its own candidates. The country supported the candidates who were identified with democratic causes and center-oriented in 2001, which again marginalized the left.

During the transition process and the Toledo administration, we observe a similar pattern for the left as that of the 1990s. Many personalities from the "reformist" left were in power because of their technical credentials and expertise, but were unable—and reluctant—to frame a proposal from the left, which made them subordinate to the center-right policies. During the Paniagua administration, there were, among others: Marcial Rubio as Minister of Education, Diego García as Minister of Justice, Susana Villarán as Minister of Women's Affairs, and Alberto Adranzién as an advisor to the president. With the Toledo administration, some other personalities from the left reached power: Nicolás Lynch as Minister of Education, Cecilia Blondet as Minister of Women's Affairs, Diego García as Minister of Foreign Relations, Fernando Rospigliosi as Minister of the Interior, and Ferando Villarán as Minister of Labor. Many others held key positions as well: Juan de la Puente was an advisor to the president, Henry Pease was the President of Congress and President of the Committee on the Constitution, along with Oscar Dancourt and Gonzalo García in the Board of Directors of the Central Reserve Bank, among many others.

The ubiquitous presence of individuals linked to the left in the Toledo administration can have many interpretations. On the one hand, it could be said that it is the natural consequence of the process of maturation in the left, which abandoned its ideological vision to undertake the making of "real life" politics by providing pragmatic solutions, so that the presence of the left is the result of the technical quality and professionalism of its members. As Edward Bernstein would say, it's the path that counts, not the final goal. On the other hand, from a more orthodox position it could also be said that the presence of leftists is an expression of the fragmentation, the resignation to the ideals of change, of an innocuous political stature that cannot produce a leftist perspective, resulting from being in government but not being in power. As a result, there were important improvements in the institutionalization of democracy during the Toledo administration, but there was also a noted continuity regarding the neoliberal economic policy.

But the problem of dispersion and fragmentation also affected the more radical left, which points to the limits of the purely confrontational strategies. The Paniagua and Toledo administrations clearly opened the political system and generated further receptivity to social demands, along with the appearance of multiple domains for dialogue and agreements with social organizations that sought to institutionalize the participation of civil society in the formulation of policy (Remy 2005).[20] But also, the government called for regional government elections in November 2002 and started a decentralization process that gave way to mobilization to achieve the demands of the provinces (Tanaka 2002). This generated the necessary incentives to reactivate many social organizations and protests which are led, for the most part, by people who were members of the more radical left. As a result, and after a long absence, the CGTP, the Unique Syndicate of Peruvian Education Workers (Sindicato Único de Trabajadores de la Educación Peruana, SUTEP), and some other movements linked to the

Red Fatherland Party reappeared. IU gave national political clout and pro-grammatic coherence to the demands of these groups in the 1980s, but as of lately they had just appeared, leading isolated protests that merely sought to vindicate their causes, and were usually of a limited scope which lacked an alternative proposal for the country. Even when the protests during the Toledo administration were not very powerful (at least, not as they were in neighboring countries such as Ecuador or Bolivia during the same years), they were still visible and important, as they were voicing opposition to a government with very low levels of approval.

The reactivation of social protests, which became clear from the very beginning of the Toledo administration, motivated those groups linked to the more radical left to reevaluate their return to a center-stage position in politics, but this never happened. The regional and municipal elections of November 2002 saw only one party from the left presenting candidates: the New Left Movement (Movimiento Nueva Izquierda, MNI), which is actu-ally the new name of the Maoist Peruvian Communist Party—Red Fatherland. MNI obtained only 2.8 percent of the regional vote, 1.9 percent of the provincial vote, and 1.7 percent of the district-level votes. Some lead-ers of the regional movements who had a more confrontational perspective also presented their candidates, but were also seldom successful.[21] Many other candidates from other branches of the left presented their candidacies either under these labels or as "independents," with some success. But again, these are only cases of some "legitimate" personalities that are unable to articulate a program from the left (Meléndez 2003).[22]

In preparation for the general elections of 2006, many groups within the left sought to stage their return to the national scene. The Toledo adminis-tration achieved a higher institutionalization of democracy, which required reconstructing the party system. A new law to regulate political parties was approved in 2003, which sought to produce more representative political organizations. At first, the traditional parties with a national constituency seemed to hold an advantage over the new organizations that surged in the 1990s. If this were to be the case, APRA, PPC, and AP, along with the left, had an important new chance to consolidate. Additionally, new winds were blowing over the region, propelled by the now limited effects of policies associated with the "Washington Consensus" that generated high expectations for the Peruvian left. At some point before the 2006 election, it was feasible to conceive the reconstitution of the party system on the basis of the party system of the 1980s with Alan García, who had amassed a substantive amount of votes in 2001, with AP's new legitimacy after the successful transitional government of Valentín Paniagua, the PPC and the National Unity Front headed by Lourdes Flores, and the new parties on the left.

Again, two dividing tendencies characterized the left. On one side, some more moderate sectors with a social democratic discourse created the

Social Democracy Party (Partido de la Democracia Social, PDS),[23] which ran its candidates under an alliance, Decentralizing Agreement (Concertación Descentralista, CD). On the other side, the more radical sectors attempted unification, which resulted in two competing organizations: the MNI and the Socialist Party (Partido Socialista, PS), which bundled together groups formerly linked to PUM. These groups engaged in a more class-based, anti-imperialist, pro-Cuba, pro-Venezuela, and State-controlling discourse. The results were disastrous: CD obtained only 0.62 percent of the vote in the presidential election, PS 0.49 percent, and MNI 0.27 percent for their respective candidates Susana Villarán, Javier Diez Canseco, and Alberto Moreno. In Congress, PS obtained 1.24 percent of the vote, MNI got 1.23 percent and CD 0.85 percent, which led them to have no representatives. As a consequence of these results, all these groups lost their official registration as political parties. This happened in stark contrast with the performance of the traditional parties. On the first round, APRA's Alan García obtained 24.32 percent of the vote, UN's Lourdes Flores got 23.81 percent, and Center Front's Valentín Paniagua got 5.5 percent.[24] In Congress, APRA achieved 21 percent of the vote, UN 15 percent, and FC 7 percent.

Was it the case, then, that discontent with the political system had no outlet in the 2006 election, as it did in every other country in the region? The answer is that it had an outlet, but it was not the traditional left. In the 2006 election, the anti-system vote, angered by the result of neoliberal policies, was channeled mainly to the candidacy of Ollanta Humala, candidate of the Union for Peru. Who is Ollanta Humala? He is a commander of the Peruvian Army who, along with his older brother Antauro Humala, led a minor insurrection in October 2000 against then President Fujimori. The Humala brothers were granted amnesty in December 2000, during the transition government of Valentín Paniagua. Antauro Humala then founded the *etnocacerista* movement, which became public knowledge through a weekly publication, *Ollanta*.[25] By the end of 2004, Ollanta Humala was discharged, and by the beginning of 2005 he had publicly stated his intentions to enter politics.

Since then, he has followed a peculiar alliance-based strategy, and started by distancing himself from *etnocacerismo*. After many swings that included conversations towards becoming MNI's presidential candidate and the failed attempt to create a party of his own, the Nationalist Peruvian Party (Partido Nacionalista Peruano, PNP), he finally secured an alliance with UPP, the party that ten years earlier had presented Pérez de Cuéllar, but that had become a label controlled by some regional leaders of the left. Humala had an unexpected surge in the polls that started in the southern mountains and ended giving him the highest amount of votes on the first round of the presidential election, with 30.6 percent of the vote, followed by APRA's Alan García and his 24.32 percent of the vote. In Congress,

UPP obtained 21.5 percent of the vote and APRA 20.58 percent. García won the runoff election, with 52.62 percent of the vote facing Humala's 47.37 percent. García managed to move on to the second round by defeating Lourdes Flores, accusing her of being "the candidate of the rich" and then, in the runoff, becoming the candidate of "change with responsibility" in order to defeat Humala. But Humala had become the vehicle of anti-system, anti-political and institutional establishment sentiments, as well as discontent with the results of the Toledo administration in terms of income redistribution and poverty eradication, despite having presided over good economic growth. Humala won in nearly every region in the country, except for Lima and some coastal areas. He obtained very high percentages of votes in the poorest regions of the country, especially in the Andean south. This only highlights the high degree of disarticulation that the economic growth of the last years had produced. Humala's discourse emphasized nationalism, anti-imperialism, State intervention, and opposition to the United States, and sought—and obtained—the support of Hugo Chávez in Venezuela and Evo Morales in Bolivia.

The left was not able to leave the political margins during these elections, neither in its social democratic version nor in its radical one. Of the traditional political forces, only APRA, PPC, and AP managed to become important political actors anew, and managed also to achieve representation in Congress. But citizens developed a new common sense that made them receptive to a critical rhetoric that proposes some alternatives to the neoliberal discourse, and this was capitalized by Ollanta Humala. What happened to the left? I think that both of its versions appear as ineffective forces that are part of the traditional order, which impedes them from capturing the anti-systemic votes. As dispersed and unviable alternatives, they have a small chance of seducing the centrist voters. The reformist version clearly appears as part of the establishment, since many of its most visible personalities were linked to the Fujimori opposition and as members of the Paniagua and Toledo administrations. At the same time, since they never managed to construct a clear identity that was distinguishable from the other alternatives that were part of the same processes, they appear as disperse, unviable or lacking political consistency, and more closely characterized by opportunism. The radical alternative appears, given its association with eroded social organizations, as part of a traditional and corporative order. And after having been linked for so long with the opposition from the political margins, they cannot appear as viable alternatives to the current government.

In other words, fifteen years of failure of both the group-based ideological and radical alternative and the center reformist alternative made it hard for them to make a credible comeback in the 2006 elections. But their rivals on the right and in APRA managed to accomplish this feat, despite their limitations.

Some perspectives

What are the prospects for the left today? In the short run, the results of the 2006 elections prompt a dilemma that repeats the two paths that have been referred to earlier. On one side, there are those who think that the left must be aligned with the nascent Humala movement, assuming that the popular will expressed itself through him. But it implies the repeated risk of losing an identity, not having any real influence in the movement, paying the price of the errors of Humala, and remaining without its own political capital. On the other side are those who think that the left must continue with its successful gamble, using a social democratic perspective (the PDS) and questioning the neoliberal model and the effects of globalization (the PS and the MNI). The risk resides in remaining as a marginal political force. Sinesio López has recently formulated this dilemma rather clearly:

> If the left ... is over, those who want to have a political force on the left have but two alternatives: they can either begin from scratch with new people, or they can go to Humala. I think that there is a bridge; there are the masses of the left. If I want a political project, I cannot just do it inside my head and from an ivory tower. I have to do it facing the people I intend to represent. That can only happen in the *Humalista* space.
>
> (*La República*, June 23, 2006)

The risks associated with each one of these alternatives are considerable. Ollanta Humala is an outsider who lacks previous political experience, which makes him unpredictable. He is a military man facing very serious accusations of human rights violations regarding his years in the Army during the internal conflict period. He is not prone to dialogue, negotiation or the formation of lasting alliances. Thus far he has followed a logic of short-term circumstantial agreements and alliances.[26] He comes from a family (from which he is supposedly distanced) with an extravagant political project which is both authoritarian and racist—the *etnocacerismo*. So far he has only oscillated between a quasi-loyal and a disloyal opposition, which could seriously erode the democratic regime. But judging from the poor electoral results, it is also clear that the alternative of building a different alternative is full of obstacles in the short run and seems to require large doses of resignation by the historical leadership, and renovation.

The success of the Peruvian left during the 1980s depended on the confluence of social movements that were able to express the people's interests, the political parties and the political front that aggregated and processed demands and turned them into a viable program of government, with a charismatic leader able to call upon the average citizen and do so from the media. Currently, we have some particularistic movements and weak parties, and traditional leaders with experience who cannot detach themselves from their past errors and new leaders without experience who are unable to construct credible images for themselves. Despite all this, there are some alternatives for the Peruvian left. APRA, which has historically competed with the left to include those groups at the margin, has been following a center-right orientation while in power, thus leaving social distress up for grabs. García attempts to separate himself from the sour memories of his first presidency by following a very liberal and orthodox economic policy that includes, for instance, the completion of a Free Trade Agreement with the United States. *Humalismo* is still a very weak movement, and it is not unlikely that it will become fragmented and further weakened in the medium term. Will the left be able to fill this vacuum? With which of its currents? We will have to see if the Peruvian left remains at the margin in the following years, despite being in a region that shows a favorable juncture for its viewpoints.

Notes

1 On the development of class-based ideology, see Balbi (1989), among others. It is important to note also that extending the "class-based" discourse by the left also impeded the development of ethnic movements like those existing in Ecuador or Bolivia (Tanaka 2003).
2 On the policies of adjustment between the 1970s and the 1990s see Iguíñiz et al. (1993). On the second phase of the military government, see Pease (1981).
3 This section is based on Tanaka (1998a).
4 The candidate with the highest vote share, Hugo Blanco from the Trotskyist Revolutionary Labor Party (PRT), obtained only 3.9 percent of the total valid votes.
5 Furthermore, with the mechanism to distribute seats in Congress, the left had only nineteen seats out of 240, that is 7.9 percent. The breakdown is ten deputies out of 180, and nine senators out of sixty. See Nieto (1983).
6 IU was composed, most of the time, of the Peruvian Communist Party (PCP), the Socialist Revolutionary Party (PSR), the National Union of the Revolutionary Left (UNIR), the Mariateguista Unified Party (PUM), the Communist Revolutionary Party (PCR), the Workers', Peasants', Students' and People's Party (FOCEP), and Political Socialist Action (APS). Usually, a "radical bloc" was formed by PUM, UNIR, and FOCEP, a "reformist bloc" with PSR and PCR, leaving PCP, APS, and the independents in the center.
7 After 1982, APRA suffered a period of reorganization under the leadership of Alan García, which effectively overcame the death of Haya de la Torre.
8 A detailed description of the Shining Path is beyond the scope of this text. But it should suffice to point out that it was a dogmatic, sectarian, and blood-thirsty organization that never sought alliances with other groups of the left, which it categorized as "revisionists." The Tupac Amaru Revolutionary Movement was inspired by Che Guevara and engaged in terrorist activities like the Shining Path. It began operations in 1984, but despite some of its spectacular actions, it never became as strong as the Shining Path. See Comisión de la Verdad y Reconciliación (2003).
9 Inflation reached 158 percent by the end of 1985, but was lowered to 62.9 percent in 1986. GDP grew by 2.3 percent in 1985 and grew to 8.7 percent in 1986.
10 In terms of inflation, 1987 reached 114.5 percent, 1988 reached 1,722.3 percent and 1989 reached 2,775.3 percent.

11 The "moderates" were led by the PCP, the "radicals" were the bloc formed by PUM, UNIR, and FOCEP. On the process of rupture see Taylor (1990) and Cameron (1994).

12 During the 1980s Peru had gone through a "movement"-based political dynamic: that is, power derived from the ability to mobilize groups that were organized in strategic sectors (Tanaka 1998b). The movement-based dynamics would prove to be unsuccessful throughout 1991.

13 An interesting testimony of this process, voiced by one of the PCP leaders, can be found in Herrera (2002).

14 According to a Weekly Note from the Peruvian Central Bank published on August 5, 1990, the Net International Reserves were $150 million and the fiscal deficit was close to 8 or 9 percent of GDP. The Peruvian government had not served its external debt on time, and had no alternative sources to finance it. Inflation in the previous twelve months of the APRA government (July 1989–July 1990) was 3,029.8 percent, according to the National Institute for Statistics. The tax burden was barely 6.5 percent of GDP by the end of 1989, while it had reached 12.5 percent in 1985. The adjustment program of August 8, 1990, was based on an increase of the cost of public services, since the public deficit was the main problem to be solved, and increased the rate of inflation to 397 percent in that month. See Iguíñiz et al. (1993).

15 PMR was a spin-off of PUM.

16 Other parties, like APRA and People's Action, boycotted the election as well.

17 To be fair, let us remember that APRA's presidential candidate, Mercedes Cabanillas, obtained only 4.11 percent of the vote and the People's Action candidate, Raúl Diez Canseco, 1.67 percent. APRA obtained 6.53 percent of the vote for Congress and eight members; AP obtained 3.43 percent of the vote and four members; PPC only had congressional candidates, where it obtained 3.09 percent of the vote and three representatives.

18 For instance, Gustavo Mohme was elected under We are Peru; and Henry Pease, Gloria Helfer, and Danel Estrada under the UPP label. But Javier Diez Canseco was not able to appear on any list despite his explicit desire to run for reelection.

19 National Unity (UN) is an alliance of parties, in which PPC is the most important.

20 For instance, the creation of the Negotiation Tables for Fighting Poverty, the National Labor Council, the National Agreement, among many others.

21 For example, the candidacy of Washington Román, the national coordinator of the regional fronts, obtained only 2 percent of the vote for the presidency of the region of Cusco.

22 This is the case, for instance, of the presidents of the Apurímac, Lambayeque, Puno, Loreto, Moquegua, Cusco, and Huancavelica regions.

23 Inspired by the "third way" or "alternative path." See Bresser et al. (1993); Giddens (1998); Gomes and Unger (1998); and Castañeda and Unger (1998).

24 Center Front (FC) was an alliance led by AP.

25 *Etnocacerismo* is based on some propositions elaborated by Antauro Humala as well as the brothers' father, Ulises Humala, which are based on extreme—sometimes extravagant—nationalism. The name refers to nationalistic and ethnic vindications (of the "copper" race) that is symbolized by Andrés Avelino Cáceres, a member of the military who led the resistance to the Chilean invasion during the Pacific War, later becoming president (1886–1890 and 1894–1895).

26 It is noteworthy that after the presidential and congressional election in April 2006, the Nationalist Party of Humala, far from consolidation, has shown clear signs of weakness. Their representatives in Congress have not formed a common front, and the party only managed to get 8 percent of the vote in the November 2006 regional elections.

Chapter 11

The evolution of the Mexican left

Kathleen Bruhn

The importance of roots

The Mexican left in 2006 in many ways still bears the scars of its peculiar childhood as the bastard offspring of the Mexican Revolution, raised in the shadow of its legitimate heir, the Institutional Revolutionary Party (Partido Revolucionario Institucional, PRI). Its current incarnation, the Party of the Democratic Revolution (Partido de la Revolución Democrática, PRD), is the convergence of three strands of leftist organization, all profoundly influenced by interaction with that extraordinary hegemonic party which governed Mexico from 1929 to 2000. Despite the best efforts of many of its members, the PRD has been dominated by populist *caudillos* in large part because of these circumstances, particularly its long exclusion from free elections, its isolation from mass organizations, and an intellectual heritage linked to one of Latin America's great populist figures: Lázaro Cárdenas.

The first strand that converged in the PRD came out of independent left parties. The oldest and most important of these was the Mexican Communist Party (Partido Comunista Mexicano, PCM), founded in 1919. For much of its existence, the Mexican Communist Party was banned from elections and purged from labor unions. The public legitimacy of the Mexican Revolution made it difficult for the PCM to argue that another revolution was necessary. Indeed, at least until the 1960s key leaders of the PCM accepted or even cooperated with PRI presidents (Carr 1985, p. 10). The decision of the Mexican government to recognize Fidel Castro further set the PCM apart. In exchange for recognition, Castro kept his hands off Mexico. At a time when Castro was a key source of funding for Latin American revolutionary movements, the Mexican Communist Party was cut off from external support.

Its isolation contributed to its preference for non-violent change. The PCM jumped at the chance to compete in elections after 1977 reforms legalized the party. Immediate results included a reduction in the number of left parties. By 1981, the PCM was gone. The Unified Mexican Socialist Party (Partido Socialista Único Mexicano, PSUM), a merger of the PCM and other parties, replaced it (Martínez Verdugo 1985; Bruhn 1997).[1] In 1987 the PSUM in turn disappeared into another merger, forming the Mexican Socialist Party (Partido Mexicano Socialista, PMS).[2] Participating in elections also brought about significant ideological moderation. By 1988, the independent left had reached its present center-left ideological position and participated in three national elections.

A second strand of leftist political thought, identified with Lázaro Cárdenas, survived within the PRI. During his presidency (1934–1940) Cárdenas profoundly affected the development of the Mexican left. First, it was Cárdenas who originally brought labor unions and peasant organizations inside the PRI. In exchange for financial support, monopolies, and representation through the PRI, they accepted state controls over leadership and legal registration. The result was a system which excluded independent left parties from influence within class-based mass organizations. The poverty of the left's ties to mass organizations increased its vulnerability to the predations of populist leaders and left it without a reliable base.

The second legacy of Cárdenas was *cardenismo*. Its central principle of a working partnership between the state and "the people" against foreign interests and the rich is a hallmark of populism everywhere. Cardenas' political style also fits the pattern of populist "common man" leadership. He refused to live in the presidential palace, started his presidency by cutting his salary in half, and held open public receptions in the National Palace. Cárdenas remains idealized in the popular imagination as a president who served "the people." His son became not only the key founder of the PRD but also its dominant *caudillo* for the first ten years of the PRD's existence.

The third strand of leftist organization stayed outside party politics. The capture of unions and peasant organizations by the PRI served as a cautionary tale about the dangers of close cooperation with parties. Popular organizations were also affected by the 1968 student movement, which ended tragically in the massacre of hundreds of students. Some student leaders came away disillusioned with peaceful protest; they ended up in guerrilla movements. Others, belonging to a Maoist group known as the Organization of the Revolutionary Left–Mass Line (Organización de Izquierda Revolucionaria—Línea de Masas, OIR–LM), began organizing popular movements. Their hostility toward parties, however, remained. Until 1988, relatively few of these organizations had participated in electoral coalitions.

The political earthquake of 1988

These three strands converged around the presidential candidacy of Cuauhtémoc Cárdenas in 1988.[3] The merger was made possible by independent trends within all three. For the independent left, legalization had led to little electoral success. It began to seek support from popular organizations through electoral alliances, helped by ideological moderation that put it closer to the public. At the same time, popular organizations had become more interested in participating in elections, largely through their perception that the PRI was increasingly unresponsive to popular pressure. The economic crisis of the 1980s left the PRI unable to pay for popular subsidies or to address infrastructure demands made by the movements. The earthquake that struck Mexico City in 1985 drove this lesson home. The federal government seemed unconcerned, ordered residents back into buildings that collapsed in aftershocks, provided little help to residents trying to dig friends out of the rubble, and mismanaged the millions in financial assistance that poured in from abroad. Residents of Mexico City organized self-help groups and began to seek new ways to hold the government accountable.

However, the trigger that set the merger in motion originated in the *cardenista* wing of the PRI. During the 1980s, the *cardenistas* felt increasingly excluded from power by neoliberal technocrats. They opposed the direction that economic reforms were taking, toward privatization and free markets. They also worried that economic crisis had weakened the PRI's legitimacy. Led by Cuauhtémoc Cárdenas and Porfirio Muñoz Ledo, a small group of prominent *priistas* demanded that the next PRI candidate address these concerns. When another neoliberal technocrat was chosen, Cárdenas launched an independent presidential campaign. Urban popular movements quickly endorsed him, especially in Mexico City. Toward the end of the campaign, the presidential candidate of the Mexican Socialist Party also withdrew in favor of Cárdenas. One year later, the PMS, the *cardenistas*, and some urban popular movements founded the PRD.

The PRD thus began life in 1989 as a "salad" of contrasting currents, united mainly around opposition to the PRI and the electability of Cárdenas. Factionalism has been a constant and at times destructive feature of party life. To keep the party from flying apart, Cárdenas assumed a central role in strategic decisions and conflict mediation. Though he would step down as party president in 1993, he remained the main point of reference for *perredistas* until 2000. His influence operated informally and outside institutional channels. While perhaps necessary for party cohesion, Cárdenas's centrality slowed the party's institutional consolidation.

Two other consistent features of PRD identity developed in these early years. The first is a commitment to internal democracy. The party has experimented with various selection mechanisms, but the trend has been generally toward more open processes, including primaries for plurality posts and national elections for the leadership. In the process of competing against each other, internal divisions were frequently deepened, sometimes resulting in resignations from the party. Even worse, many internal elections were marred by accusations (often true) of fraud. These failures hurt the party's electoral results, but despite the costs the PRD persisted in using voting as the normal mechanism of competing for power within the party. As a result, powerful leaders of the party can and do end up on the losing side of issues, checking tendencies toward centralized leadership and enabling the party to process at least some conflicts without party splits.

The second consistent feature shaping PRD identity was the experience of repression and the parallel association of the PRD with obstructionism and anti-government mobilization. Evidence of widespread electoral fraud in 1988 led Cárdenas to refuse to acknowledge Salinas as the president of Mexico. He called for a strict policy of non-cooperation with the federal government. Meanwhile, Salinas and the PRI saw Cárdenas as the main threat to their power. The result of this mutual hostility was six years of confrontation and violent repression. The experience fed attitudes of distrust toward institutions and the state that still persist among PRD veterans.

The year 1994 was another turning point for the left. Cárdenas ran for president again, and lost. In fact, he came in third. For six years, his influence had been sustained by the conviction that if only the party could watch the polls more effectively, he would be elected in a landslide. Now the PRD began to re-evaluate the confrontational strategy that had taken them to electoral defeat after electoral defeat. The same year also saw the emergence of a guerrilla movement in the southern state of Chiapas. The Zapatista Army of National Liberation (Ejército Zapatista de Liberación Nacional, EZLN) challenged the neoliberal model and captured the imagination of Mexicans and the world. In the first two years of the rebellion, the EZLN was vastly more popular than the PRD itself. The PRD needed to produce results in order to justify its existence. It could not out-protest the EZLN. But given the EZLN's rejection of elections, the PRD could occupy the institutional politics niche.

Additional incentives to focus on elections came from the changed focus of the PRI itself. Suddenly, the PRD was not the biggest threat to continued PRI rule. The National Action Party (Partido Acción Nacional, PAN) had more votes and the EZLN had more guns. Hostility toward the PRD diminished. The challenge posed by the EZLN, together with the PRI's increased sense of electoral security after victories in 1991 and 1994, contributed to its willingness to sponsor several critical reforms that transformed the electoral environment. Most important was the creation of the Federal Electoral Institute (IFE) to monitor the fairness of elections. For the first time, elections would not be controlled by the PRI, but by an autonomous agency. Public funding for opposition parties and access to media also increased dramatically. Finally, the PRI announced that it would allow popular election of the mayor of Mexico City in 1997. Cárdenas decided to run.

The president of the PRD at the time was another former long-time *priista* and Cárdenas protégé from the oil state of Tabasco. Andrés Manuel López Obrador argued that the party would have to present a less confrontational face to the electorate in order to win. The softer, happier image paid off. Cárdenas won handily and the PRD's share of seats in the Chamber of Deputies went from 16.7 percent in 1994 to 25.7 percent in 1997. The PRD also started winning more elections at state and local levels. In 1994, the PRD won just 6.6 percent of municipal elections and held no governorships. By 1999, the PRD regularly won 12 percent of municipal elections and controlled four state governorships. Most people credited López Obrador with the turnaround.

The dark side of López Obrador's success was that it grew out of an opportunistic strategy to offer the PRD label to PRI members who failed to get their party's nomination. Because they had name recognition and connections, these candidates often won. Over time, however, they turned their electoral victories into power in the PRD. As *perredistas*-for-profit, they were distrusted by ideologically driven activists who saw them as less committed to democracy and social change. They also owed their success to López Obrador. As they rose in party leadership, they enhanced his authority.[4]

The positive side was money. Because the Mexican state funds political parties based in part on their previous electoral support, PRD wins translated into a larger share of what was by then a much larger pie. With these new resources, the PRD was able to improve its organizational infrastructure and mount much more sophisticated campaigns. Winning elections also made it possible for the PRD to consolidate special relationships with popular movements by offering public resources and support. The process went farthest in Mexico City. Former activists of urban popular movements came to dominate the party. However, the PRD failed to build on these successes to become a national party. It remained a highly regional party based in the center and south of the country.

The changing of the guard

The 2000 elections had a galvanizing effect on the PRD. Andrés Manuel López Obrador won election as mayor of Mexico City. Cuauhtémoc Cárdenas lost his third bid to become president of Mexico. He would never again wield the kind of decisive influence within the party that he did in the early years of its existence. Over the next six years, this role would be assumed by his one-time protégé. López Obrador parlayed his position as mayor into a virtually unchallenged control of the party. Because they saw in the popular mayor a chance to reverse their losing streak in presidential elections, even *perredistas* who disagreed with his management of Mexico City tended to defer to him.

One of the issues driving internal criticism was López Obrador's populist style. Populism historically has come from the right as well as the left, from an agrarian or an urban base, from a relatively well-structured relationship to unions or an unmediated appeal to the people. What these versions share is a philosophy opposing the interests of the "common people" to those of a narrow and selfish elite. The state must be wrested away from this self-serving elite and used for the benefit and advancement of the people. Classic communist thought also argues that power must be taken from the few and given to the many. But where communism identifies these groups in class terms, populism makes more general appeals and claims to represent the nation as a whole. The economic model set forth in communism is missing or intentionally vague in populism. And where communism demanded the dictatorship of the proletariat and the withering away of the state, populism views the state as an essential tool to be employed—often by a charismatic leader—*on behalf of* the people rather than *by* them.

López Obrador's administration in Mexico City fits this model in several respects, starting with his announcement that he would hold a plebiscite in the third year of his government to determine whether he would remain in office. The "revocable mandate" was an attempt to forge a direct connection between López Obrador and "the people." Essentially, he promised to remain accountable to them rather than to his party or, for that matter, Mexican electoral law. While in office, he held plebiscites on various issues, from whether to raise the price of a subway ticket to whether to adopt daylight savings time, in each case bypassing the local legislative process to appeal directly to the people.

Second, López Obrador initiated a series of highly inclusive social programs aimed at broad demographics. The most well known was the pension for senior citizens. Any Mexico City resident over sixty-five, regardless of income, qualified for a modest stipend of a little less than $80 dollars per month. Outreach specialists went to homes to sign people up. By 2005, most people in Mexico City either were enrolled or had a relative or friend enrolled. The pension was too small to support anyone, but did restore a sense of dignity to older people who felt themselves a burden on their families. Similar programs served single mothers, the handicapped, and schoolchildren. These programs were a major reason for the growing popularity of the mayor. But they were populist because they extended social services as a matter of popular rights (rather than targeted and justified functionally) and because they were not institutionalized. The programs were linked to López Obrador and operated at least implicitly as conditional upon continued PRD government.[5] Decisions about which groups would get benefits were not a matter for public or legislative debate; they came at the personal initiative of López Obrador.

Third, López Obrador embarked on a program of job creation through public works. The two most publicized projects were the construction of a second freeway level to ease traffic congestion, and the revitalization of Mexico's historic downtown. One estimate suggests that the public works projects created some 658,000 new jobs, contributing to a growth rate in Mexico City of 3.2 percent per year—much greater than the national average of 1.6 percent (Grayson 2006, p. 221). While not specifically populist in nature, the fact that he justified these projects with a public plebiscite (the highway) and appeals to national identity (the historic center) gave them at least populist overtones. His proposal in 2006 to construct a bullet train to the border, though dismissed as wacky and unrealistic by most experts (including some of his own economic advisors), made sense to López Obrador in terms of the jobs it would create in the Mexican economy.

Finally, López Obrador cultivated a humble "man of the people" image. He lived with his sons in a modest apartment in a middle-class neighborhood. He arrived at his office in an older model Tsuru rather than a luxury car. And he got there early. Where most Mexican politicians might arrive at work around 11.00 a.m., López Obrador was famous for his almost daily 6.15 a.m. press conferences. Grayson (2006) reports that between May 31, 2001, and April 10, 2005, López Obrador held 1,316 morning press conferences, missing only ninety-one days (p. 185). His reputation as an honest, hard-working man not only set him apart from most politicians in Mexico, but also helped him survive a corruption scandal midway through his term that might have tainted a politician with more visible signs of living beyond his means.[6] It is also a classic populist style.

Even at the height of López Obrador's popularity, however, the PRD could not be reduced to the personal tastes and preferences of one person. It remains internally diverse and factionalized. Ironically, internal democracy contributed to the formalization and consolidation of organized factions. Belonging to a faction improved the members' chances of mustering a coordinated vote that would win them leadership positions or candidate nominations. Early in the party's development, factions were organized mostly according to the previous political history of the members. By 2006, the nature of factions had changed at least somewhat, to reflect regional political bases rather than distinct ideological differences. In Mexico City, for example, two of the most important factions—Izquierda Democrática Nacional and Nueva Izquierda—were based largely on clientelistic relationships with urban popular movements in specific districts. A third—Unidad y Renovación—was headed by two key leaders of the activist union of teachers at the National Autonomous University (UNAM).

By 2006, the PRD had also held office in a growing number of municipal and state-level governments, providing leadership for new factions or mergers with old ones. In the state of Zacatecas, for example, Amalia García was elected the nation's only woman governor in 2004. Amalia García attracts support and respect from many women in the party, as well as many of the former Communist and Socialist Party members, through her long-standing support of women's rights; she is one of the few ex-presidents of the PRD who was never a member of the PRI, though she is the daughter of a PRI governor of Zacatecas. Similarly, the governor of Michoacán has provided another nucleus around which *perredistas* loyal to Cuauhtémoc Cárdenas gather: he is Cárdenas's oldest son, Lázaro.

The PRD has also governed the states of Guerrero, Baja California Sur, and of course Mexico City. Each of these governors has the opportunity to gather a personal following or to dominate the faction to which he or she belongs. At the municipal level, the PRD won 445 municipal elections from 2004 to 2006, out of 2,211.[7] Since municipal elections are held every three years (on a staggered schedule), the PRD over these three years won control of roughly 20 percent of Mexican *municipios*. More importantly, the party has dominated Mexico City continuously for nearly ten years. Small-town mayors can leverage their positions into advancement within the party. But governors and the mayor of Mexico City are potential presidential candidates, and factions form around them depending on the strength of their performance in office.

López Obrador's populist program has also been contested within the party. Nevertheless, the party is basically on board with its essential outlines. Using a method developed by the Comparative Manifestoes Project, I analyzed the electoral platforms of four Latin American left parties: the PRD, the Brazilian Workers' Party (2002), the Chilean Socialist Party (2001), and the Argentine Peronists (2003).[8] The 2006 PRD platform scores well to the left of all of the other platforms. The cause appears to be two-fold: (1) a weaker than average emphasis on conservative themes like the need for balanced budgets, strong state authority, and support for police; and (2) a stronger than average emphasis on welfare spending and spending for basic education. These are, of course, classic populist emphases, as is a second finding: of the four parties, the PRD is the least likely to include favorable mentions of labor or peasants, preferring to couch its appeals in terms of non-class demographic groups like women or youth. It is, of course, the only party of the four to lack a strong relationship to unions.

Its weak relationship to mass organizations also helps explain why the PRD's strong emphasis on democracy and decentralization at the rhetorical level has not translated into experiments with direct democracy, the creation of formal channels for citizens to make decisions on local issues outside representative institutions. Due to the PRI's far more successful penetration of civil society, transferring government decision-making to "popular councils" effectively would give the PRI more influence, as PRD mayors I interviewed in Michoacán in the 1990s pointed out. In Brazil, where participatory democracy has gone farthest, studies show that new participatory institutions are dominated by PT-affiliated organizations, making the risk more tolerable.

On more specific issues, the 2006 PRD platform focuses most strongly on social justice, social welfare spending, and support for non-economic demographic groups, followed by democracy. Prior to the victory of the PAN in 2000, PRD platforms typically put much more emphasis on democracy and political reform, particularly the need to strengthen legislatures and the separation of powers, but support for social welfare spending as a top priority consistently characterizes the PRD. By way of comparison, the top priority of the Argentine Peronists in 2002 was technology and infrastructure, and market incentives, market regulation, and government efficiency all outranked social welfare spending. Lula's 2002 platform places a similar level of emphasis on social welfare and social justice as the PRD's, but much higher emphasis on productivity increases (more than four times as much) and technology and infrastructure development (twice as much). Indeed, the PRD platform pays relatively little attention to *any* aspect of macroeconomic management: only 14 percent of its platform mentions economics at all, compared to 36 percent of Lula's, and 46.8 percent of the Peronists' platform.[9] Ironically, López Obrador's *personal* platform (issued separately from that of his party) is significantly more conservative. It emphasizes economic incentives, productivity, efficiency, and neoliberal economic policies much more than that of the PRD, and it emphasizes social justice and social welfare spending much less.

These platform emphases are confirmed and enriched by a telephone survey of PRD majority district candidates for Congress carried out just prior to the 2006 national election.[10] We received telephone contact lists from the PRD with numbers for 250 candidates, 188 of them proposed by the PRD.[11] Of these candidates, we were able to complete interviews with sixty, for a response rate of 32 percent—quite respectable considering the generally low response rates of elite surveys and the hectic time period in which we conducted the survey. Because we used plurality district candidates for the survey rather than candidates from the national proportional representation list, our results reflect opinions that are widely shared by PRD activists across Mexico, not a potentially insular Mexico City elite.

These candidates identified jobs as the most important problem facing Mexico, followed by crime, poverty, and economic management. Their solutions to these problems were far more likely to involve state intervention than those of candidates from its coalition partners or the PAN (the other party included in the survey). When asked whether government or individuals should be responsible for the economic welfare of individuals, 73 percent of the PRD candidates thought the government should be partly or primarily responsible for individual economic welfare; only 25 percent of PAN candidates agreed. PRD candidates were also significantly more likely to prefer a big government (more services and more taxes) over a small one, and to believe that the electricity sector ought to remain "almost entirely" in government hands (by 68 percent). On social issues, they were no less liberal. Of PRD candidates, 72 percent thought that abortion should be legal in cases of rape and 83 percent opposed the death penalty for homicide. Interestingly, despite generally negative evaluations of George W. Bush, 77 percent thought that commercial relations with the United States should increase. Although significantly more skeptical than PAN candidates

(95 percent of whom wanted to expand relations), they share at the very least a recognition that Mexico's future economic development depends on the United States. This recognition may also help explain the general neglect of U.S.–Mexican relations in the public discourse of the candidates. Only one candidate from Hidalgo emphasized migration in their personal campaign; nobody emphasized the North American Free Trade Agreement (NAFTA) or other U.S.-related themes. This is consistent with the PRD's electoral platform, which mentions the United States in just 0.6 percent of statements—half positive and half negative.

Demographically, the average PRD congressional candidate is a forty-five-year-old man who has been a member of the PRD for eleven years, has lived in his electoral district for thirty years, made his career in local and state politics, and considers himself to be "very" or "somewhat" leftist. He probably has *not* belonged to any other political parties (only 45 percent of PRD candidates listed prior party memberships), but if he has, he is most likely to have belonged to the PRI: 48 percent of those who had previously belonged to another political party came out of the PRI, compared to 37 percent who came out of other leftist parties.

The 2006 presidential election—and beyond

Inevitably, Andrés Manuel López Obrador became the PRD candidate for president in 2006. No one in the PRD even bothered to run against him in a scheduled primary. At the start of the campaign, he had a commanding lead over both of his rivals, Roberto Madrazo of the PRI and Felipe Calderón of the PAN. He maintained this lead until March 2006, just over three months before the election. Initially, López Obrador attempted to campaign from the center, presenting himself as someone who could champion the poor and still work with business. He tried to distance himself from radical elements in his party by issuing his own electoral platform, at once more moderate and more specific than that of the PRD.

However, the dynamics of the campaign changed dramatically when PAN strategists began to air a series of ads calling López Obrador another Hugo Chávez, a dangerous zealot who would bankrupt Mexico, expropriate private property, and stimulate violent mobilization. Initially, López Obrador tried to ignore the attacks. When it became clear that his poll ratings were slipping, he went on the offensive, accusing his opponents of lying, but not going so far as to deny that there were profound differences between his platform and that of Calderón. In this, at least, he had no choice. He would have alienated his own base—and not convinced others—by claiming to be a centrist. In any case, it was his ambition to speak for the people against the rich and the corrupt politicians that he said were behind the attacks. López Obrador began to recover the ground he had lost. By election day, Calderón and López Obrador were in a dead heat.

It was still too close to call after the voting ended. On election night, the IFE announced that it could not declare a winner based on the votes counted so far. The candidates themselves had no such hesitation, each proclaiming himself president of Mexico within minutes of the IFE's announcement. A few days later, the IFE reported that with the count completed, Felipe Calderón had been elected president, albeit by a razor-thin margin. López Obrador refused to accept defeat and charged that the PAN had stolen the election.

And so the trouble began, the end of which is not yet clear. A week after the election, López Obrador mobilized half a million people in the center of Mexico City to call for a recount. Later, he upped the ante by occupying the main street through Mexico City's financial district, Paseo de la Reforma. The tent city he and his supporters set up blocked traffic for weeks. They engaged in physical confrontations with police guarding the Congress. They prevented President Fox from giving his final state of the union address in the Congress by using PRD congressmen to take over the tribunal. They forced Fox to move his Independence Day declaration out of its traditional location in Mexico City. The next day, a large crowd proclaimed López Obrador the "legitimate president of Mexico." In his acceptance speech, he promised to set up a parallel government and vowed never to give up the fight against Calderón.

Whatever these actions tell us about López Obrador, they also tell us something about the PRD. No matter what their private doubts, top party leaders closed ranks behind him in public. Post-electoral polls do not demonstrate a major erosion of support among *perredistas*, though negatives for the party and its candidate have increased among other groups. Indeed, support for radical tactics is foreshadowed in a pre-electoral poll of PRD and PAN congressional candidates.[12] PRD candidates were significantly more likely than PAN candidates to doubt that the election in their district would be clean. They were significantly less likely to define Mexico as a democracy. And they were significantly more favorable toward protest than their PAN counterparts: 64 percent of PRD candidates said that they would participate in protests if their presidential candidate announced that there had been fraud, versus 48 percent of *panistas*.

It is too soon to tell whether the antics of Andrés Manuel will sink the party or save it, whether his personal stock will continue to hold steady or whether he will end up splitting the party and forcing a thorough re-foundation of the Mexican left. Likewise, it is too early to come to definitive conclusions about the effects on Mexican democracy. In the short run, public confidence in institutions has declined. The contempt expressed in López Obrador's new favorite slogan—"to hell with your corrupt institutions"—could presage the withdrawal of the Mexican left from institutional life and a turn toward the kind of praetorian politics that has characterized Bolivia, Venezuela, and Ecuador in recent years (*Los Angeles Times*, September 6, 2006).

A good deal will depend on what the "lessons of 2006" turn out to be, for Mexico and for the PRD.

Nevertheless, whatever survives of the electoral left in Mexico is likely to retain strong populist overtones. The internal fragmentation and ideological heterogeneity of the party, combined with weak institutional development, creates fertile ground for populist leaders around whom these currents can converge. In turn, the emergence of each new populist leader further retards the development of institutions, as formal rules are bent to accommodate the wishes of the leader. Andrés Manuel's downfall might give the party a chance to develop stronger internal institutions, but it might also clear the way for the next aspiring *caudillo* to seize his (or her) chance to fill the vacuum.

Second, populism's oppositional framing of politics—little guys versus corrupt elites—resonates well with the PRD's own image of itself. The PRD was formed outside and against the political institutions of the 1980s. Its first experiences involved brazen electoral fraud that targeted the PRD specifically. Over the next six years, many of its activists were imprisoned, beaten, or murdered in the course of their political activities. They have been spied on, investigated, and threatened. In addition, many PRD activists come from clandestine or independent popular movements. They had grown accustomed to protests as their only means of making demands on a government that was institutionally closed to them. Given all of these precedents, it would be remarkable if most *perredistas*—and particularly those early risk-takers who founded the party—did *not* see themselves as scrappy underdogs fighting a dark conspiracy against them.

Finally, populist strategies may be more appealing because of the PRD's isolation from organized labor. European social democracy offers a mechanism for peak organizations of business and labor to negotiate directly the division of the costs of adjustment to globalization. The opportunities for social democracy are limited everywhere in Latin America, but are particularly out of reach for the PRD. The nature of the PRD's main civil society allies—urban popular movements oriented toward consumer demands—contributes to its fondness for broad non-class appeals and its focus on providing state services. The Latin American nations that developed a "good left" tend to have strong union–party ties. This dynamic may be one of the keys to their success: they can afford not to make as many populist appeals because of their strong and mostly loyal organizational base. The PRD has no such luxury.

Standing up for the little guys is not a bad thing; indeed, it is the raison d'être of the left. Moreover, to stand up for the little guys in deeply unequal societies like Mexico, it is necessary to confront the rich. A left that is adored by economic elites is probably not much of a left. The problem is that populism's style lends itself to a more confrontational and polarizing dynamic than other leftist models, such as social democracy. The oppositional quality of populism may limit the left's ability to harness the energies of at least some business and productive sectors to improve the living conditions of ordinary people. It certainly seems to have contributed in Mexico to the savageness of the struggle between two political forces who seem increasingly to feel that they cannot share power with the other. Even prior to the election, the PAN's eagerness to portray the PRD program as dangerous and the PRD's haughty dismissal of concerns about its program as persecution contributed to an environment of intolerance and distrust. Only in such a context could López Obrador sustain claims of a massive fraud and be believed, at least by his own base, despite the lack of solid evidence.

Mexico's non-electoral left is if anything less trusting and more confrontational than the PRD. The EZLN is the best-known example, but there are troubling indications that they are not alone in their utter rejection of institutional politics. Over the summer of 2006, for example, a large movement calling itself the Popular Alliance of the Peoples of Oaxaca (Alianza Popular de Pueblos de Oaxaca, APPO) developed in support of a teachers' strike that began in May. They held demonstrations and marches, then escalated to occupy the central square of Oaxaca for months. Several people were killed during confrontations with police. Even after the teachers made a deal to return to classes in exchange for a pay increase, APPO continued to occupy the square and demand the resignation of Oaxaca's governor. Federal police eventually cleared the square by force, but APPO retreated to the university campus, where it continues to protest as of this writing. In June 2006, another group of protesters in San Salvador Atenco confronted police. In the ensuing riot, two people were killed. And in November 2006, a guerrilla group known as the Popular Revolutionary Army (Ejército Popular Revolucionario, EPR) claimed responsibility for setting off four bombs in Mexico City that targeted the Federal Electoral Tribunal, foreign banks, and the PRI headquarters. All of this took place during an election year. The pervasive threat of violence calls out for the construction of institutional ways to process conflict, but it is not clear that the PRD or any existing party can play that role. Mexico's young democracy desperately needs a strong, institutional left party to offer the poor and the marginalized an avenue of expression. It may be a populist party; indeed, it probably will be. But it must be an institutional party, not one that puts programmatic goals or personal ambition ahead of institutional consolidation.

Notes

1 The most important of these groups were the Movement of Popular Action (MAP), the Movement of Action and Socialist Unity (MAUS), the Party of the Mexican People (PPM), and the Socialist Revolutionary Party (PSR).
2 Specifically, these groups included the Revolutionary Patriotic Party (PPR), the Popular Revolutionary Movement (MRP), the Mexican Workers' Party (PMT),

and Communist Left Unity (UIC). Only the PMT had national electoral registry at the time (Bruhn 1997, pp. 319–324).

3   For a more thorough account of this process, see Bruhn (1997).

4   The current PRD president, Leonel Cota Montaño, is an example. He was recruited by López Obrador to run for governor of Baja California Sur (success-fully) then promoted to top leadership of the national party.

5   Opponents from rival parties accuse the PRD of *explicitly* threatening voters that they would lose their money if the PRD lost.

6   The scandal erupted when a videotape was aired on a morning variety show depicting one of López Obrador's top aides accepting bundles of money from an Argentine businessman, who had several construction contracts with the city. The aide claimed he was just receiving a legal campaign contribution, but resigned from the PRD and spent time in jail. López Obrador denied knowing about his aide's actions. He also charged that political enemies were trying to smear his reputation with a set-up videotape of dubious origin, arguing that the businessman knew he would be taped and tried to make the PRD aide look as dirty as possible by giving him cash and then handing over the tape to PAN operatives.

7   According to data from Mexico's National Institute for Statistics, Geography and Information (INEGI), available at http://www.inegi.gob.mx/est/contenidos/espanol/rutinas/ept.asp?t=mgob06&c=1902.

8   The method I use to code the platforms according to left–right positions is bor-rowed from the Comparative Manifestos Project. The method is based on con-tent analysis of electoral platforms. Coders assign each sentence in a platform to one of fifty-six common categories, according to the sense of that sentence (or part of a sentence, if it contains multiple ideas). The data is expressed in per-centage terms as the relative emphasis for each category with respect to the length of the platform. Coded sentences can be grouped according to issue areas ("domains"), or summed together to create scales on specific dimensions (e.g. left–right placement). The left–right scale developed by Budge and Robertson (1987) on the basis of the European party platforms includes thirteen "right emphasis" items and thirteen "left emphasis" items from the list of categories. To calculate the left–right position of any party, one sums the total percentages of the "right" items and subtracts the total percentages of the "left" items. Positive scores indicate more conservative ideological placements, while negative scores indicate more leftist ideological placement. To enhance the comparability of the data, I obtained the full code books and training manuals from the Comparative Manifestos Project and passed their intercoder reliability test. In the initial phases of coding, I received assistance and advice from Dr Andrea Volkens as I came across problems. I wish to thank the Comparative Manifestos Project and Dr Volkens in particular for their generous assistance.

9   At that, the PRD still does better than the Chilean Socialist Party, which mentioned economics in only 7 percent of its platform sentences, perhaps because everyone already understood fairly clearly the kind of economic policies it—as an incumbent party—would support.

10 Co-principal investigators Kathleen Bruhn and Kenneth F. Greene. The project was funded by the University of Texas at Austin and the University of California, Santa Barbara. We split the sample into a telephone survey and a web survey, but I draw only from the results of the larger telephone survey here. The telephone survey was administered by Data OPM, in Mexico City.

11 The PRD ran in coalition with two other parties in 2006. Of the 300 district candidacies, thirty-nine went to the Workers' Party (PT) and forty-five went to Convergencia.

12 The survey included only candidates for majority seats, as we believed that this would get us the largest national diversity of PRD activists. The PRI was invited to participate but declined to provide the necessary contact information for its candidates. The co-principal investigators in the candidate survey are Kathleen Bruhn and Kenneth F. Greene. The project was funded by the University of Texas at Austin and the University of California, Santa Barbara. The telephone survey was administered by Data OPM, Mexico City.

Part IV

Prognosis

Chapter 12

Where do we go from here?

Jorge G. Castañeda

If one looks back on the early 1990s, just after the fall of the Berlin Wall and the collapse of the Soviet Union, with socialism disappearing, Cuba disintegrating, and China fully engaged in a dynamic model of authoritarian state capitalism, the left today in Latin America is in surprisingly good shape. At the time, not only was the paradigm of a progressive road to development in the region being destroyed by events elsewhere in the world, but its opposite—the so-called neo-liberal, Washington Consensus, free-market option—seemed to be the only game in town. It was popular, successful, and omnipresent: from Menem in Argentina to Salinas de Gortari in Mexico, from the Chilean Concertación to Cardoso's center-right coalition in Brazil, from Peru's Fujimori to the hailed "technopols" from the Economics Departments of U.S. universities, the single path seemed to be the right path. Conversely, anything that smacked of economic statism, social redistribution, subsidies, and anti-globalization movements was perceived as anachronistic and mistaken, in good faith or with a hidden agenda.

The situation now is a mirror image of that recent past. As we have seen throughout these pages, the self-defined left is stronger than ever everywhere in Latin America, whether it is in power or in opposition, whether it is populist, radical, authoritarian, and viscerally anti-American, or social-democratic, moderate, globalized, and intent on dealing with Washington in a pragmatic fashion. Currently, it is the neo-liberal paradigm that is discredited and apparently a failure; poverty eradication, inequality reduction, redistribution, and national sovereignty over natural resources—in the midst of a commodity boom—are the buzzwords and keys to development. Even democracy and human rights are taking a beating: while much of the left is democratic, in power or not, it is increasingly reluctant to criticize those of its components who resort to authoritarian procedures in order to achieve their aims. All in all, the left in Latin America today, which many thought was on the verge of extinction the morning after the end of the Cold War, is, prima facie, on a roll.

As stated, this seems true from whatever perspective one adopts. If the observer adopts the vantage point of the old Cuban Castro–Guevarist dream of spreading revolution throughout the hemisphere, there are grounds for jubilation. Never have our men in Havana had such a presence in the region. Unlike the 1960s, when each attempt at setting up a new guerrilla *foco* failed in part because of meager manpower (Che Guevara died surrounded by fewer than a dozen Cuban comrades), today there are thousands of Cuban doctors, sports instructors, literacy teachers, security cadres, and advisors in country after country: in Venezuela, of course, but also in Mexico—in the states of Michoacán and Coahuila—in Nicaragua, in Bolivia and Ecuador. Contrary to the 1960s, when the Soviet Union refused to bankroll Cuba's Latin American adventures, today there are billions of Venezuelan petrodollars available to spread the gospel across the hemisphere. And in contrast to those years when weapons were scarce and had to be seized from the enemy, or unlike the late 1970s and early 1980s in Central America, where automatic assault rifles had to be brought all the way from Vietnam, now Chávez can count on at least 100,000 AK-47s purchased from Moscow, and soon, it seems, on a Russian manufacturing facility at Maracay to produce these guns himself. Moreover, and perhaps most importantly, the Cuban discourse of today has found a nice fit with much of the rest of Latin America: the United States is more unpopular than ever, and the issues of poverty and social policy are much more salient now than thirty years ago.

If viewed from a less geo-political, and more traditional, Latin American populist and nationalist stance, the current course of history also seems to be favoring the left. As late as 1994, the accent in the region's politics seemed to fall on globalization, open economies, pro-U.S. policies, human rights, and a reluctance to engage in the rhetorical exercises of the past; today, the opposite is strikingly evident. Until 2000 at least, the Free Trade Area of the Americas (FTAA) was the umbrella notion under which hemispheric international relations evolved; today, FTAA is dead in the water, and a significant number of countries are violently opposed to any type of free trade arrangement with the United States. The nationalistic, populist language of the past resonates in Bolivia, when Evo Morales nationalizes his country's gas reserves, seeing himself as a latter-day Lázaro Cárdenas; in Venezuela, when Chávez nationalizes the phone company and an opposition TV network; in Peru, where losing presidential candidate Ollanta Humala uses his near control of Congress to publicize rabidly anti-Chilean tirades, and even attempts to "invade" his southern neighbor and reclaim the land and sea surfaces in dispute between the two; in Mexico, where Andrés Manuel López Obrador denounces the rich and powerful and vows to "send their institutions to hell"; in Ecuador, where Rafael Correa promises to shut down the American Drug Enforcement Agency (DEA) and military base in Manta, and wages war on the Guayaquil plutocracy and the

Quito partidocracy; and even in Argentina, where Néstor Kirchner resorted as often as possible to Perón's anti-American stances and antics, either on his own or inviting others (Chávez, Castro, soccer legend Diego Maradona) as his surrogates.

And finally, if one views the process through the prism of a moderate, modern, "lite" left, there are also, obviously, reasons for optimism. In countries like Chile, Brazil, and Uruguay, a self-defined reformist left begins to lead ruling coalitions that prove, in practice, that the left can govern competently, responsibly, and in a somewhat different fashion from centrist or right-of-center groups. Lula guarantees macro-economic stability in Brazil, and after four years of an efficient but low-growth first term, is reelected and sets about achieving the economic expansion his country needs. Ricardo Lagos and Michelle Bachelet take over the Concertación's leadership in Chile, and demonstrate they are at least as competent in running the administration as the Christian Democrats were, and more honest and democratic, of course, than the military. And a bizarre coalition of former Tupamaros, Communist Party cadres, and social democrats charts out a course for Uruguay so different from the rest of the region's left that George Bush actually visits the tiny country, because it is one of the few nations in the hemisphere where he is welcome, if not by the protesters, at least by the government.

What this evolution implies is that three of the basic premises springing from the debates of the early 1990s regarding the future of the left in Latin America proved essentially accurate. The first was that the end of the Cold War, while perhaps leaving the left in the lurch for a while—ideologically orphaned, geo-politically widowed—eventually would be a blessing in disguise, by eliminating the super-power rivalry which had held it hostage for so long. Washington could no longer oppose the advent of a left-wing government on U.S. national security grounds: Nicaragua could not become a Soviet beachhead, because there was no longer any Soviet Union to be a beachhead for. Either the old Cold War argument would be dissipated, or it would ring totally false; in either case, the left profited.

The second premise that turned out to be true was that the combination of secular poverty and inequality and full-fledged representative democracy would inevitably bring to power governments seeking to govern on behalf of the poor and dispossessed. The syndrome reflected in the tragedies of Jacobo Arbenz in Guatemala in 1954, in Salvador Allende's Chile in 1973, and in Uruguay under Liber Seregni and the Frente Amplio in 1972 stopped being the exception, and became the rule. Under conditions of democracy, the left thrived electorally, winning or showing with remarkable consistency and simultaneity. This was especially true in countries where elections acquired a class connotation: in Venezuela repeatedly, in Chile to a large extent, and in Brazil as of 2006. Only that year, after more than a century of what many had called an "elitist democracy," did the poor start voting for the candidate of the poor—Lula—and the middle class for a candidate of the middle class. The change was striking and rapid. As late as 1989, in Lula's first run for the presidency, he had obtained far more middle-class votes than winner Fernando Collor de Mello, who in turn received most of the ballots cast by the destitute of the Nordeste, from which both candidates hailed. The convergence of democracy and inequality was unbeatable, as it had been in Western Europe in the late nineteenth and early twentieth century: the left won more and more frequently.

The third premise was that this success also brought diversity and proliferation: there was no single left, no monolithic left, no left with a unique message, leadership, and Mecca. Havana remained a reference, but for many it was more a matter of nostalgia than of political affinity; there was no Center, as the Cuban capital and Moscow had been from 1917 through 1989. All sorts of lefts emerged and grew: radical, indigenous, single-issue, environmentalist, peasant-oriented, proletarian, populist or Marxist, moderate or extremist. Perhaps the only common characteristic was that, increasingly, all the chapters of the left accepted that the barrel of a gun was the only way not to gain power. Still, the blessing and solidarity extended by the Foro de São Paulo (a loosely binding organization of all of the region's self-proclaimed left organizations, including the Cubans and the Mexicans, as well as the FARC and the Chilean Socialists) for the Colombian FARC, as well as the support received throughout the region in 1994 by the Zapatista uprising in Chiapas, shows that the renunciation of armed struggle may not be as deep-rooted as expected and hoped for. Nonetheless, by 2006, only the FARC in Colombia insisted on it, and it was more of a way of life than a political or ideological strategy. But otherwise, the left in Latin America is more diverse and pluralistic than ever before, although it is like a time capsule: it includes all the garden varieties that have sprung up over the past century, from unreformed Communist parties to centrist social democrats.

But if the left is so successful today in the region, and so powerful, potentially victorious or present in office, why does it continue to leave a bitter aftertaste to many, starting of course with its traditional detractors, but including its own supporters? What continues to plague it? Why is it not really at ease with itself, comfortable with its past and confident in its future? There are many answers to these questions, but four stand out.

First, with a few exceptions, the Latin American left has still to come to terms with issues of human rights and representative democracy. That is not to say either that the entire left is aligned with Chávez in this field, or that the Venezuelan leader is fully aligned with Havana in this regard. Even less does it mean that there are not important, on occasion majority, sectors of the left in Chile, in Brazil, in Uruguay, and perhaps in a few more nations, for whom this question is no longer a matter of debate, division, and disagreement. But for every Ricardo Lagos in the Chilean PPD–PS coalition, there is a Camilo Escalona, who believes that Chile should stand with Cuba at the United Nations' Human Rights Council in Geneva, that it should stand with Chávez on the RCTV scandal in the Organization of American States (OAS), that it should maintain solidarity with the FARC in Colombia, and should never forget that there are human rights and human rights: fundamental ones, but also economic and social ones, and the latter are not more important than the former.

For every Amalia García—the former president of the Mexican PRD and current governor of the state of Zacatecas—in the ranks of the Mexican left, there is a *Subcomandante* Marcos, who at least ostensibly rose up in arms against the government in 1994, and continues to reject its legitimacy and legality. For every Cuauhtémoc Cárdenas, who declined to take power by force in 1988, when the presidential election was almost certainly stolen from him, there is a López Obrador, who took his battle to the streets in 2006, when the election was almost certainly not stolen from him.

For every Lula in the Partido dos Trabalhadores, who is increasingly vocal in the distances he takes from Cuba and Venezuela, and the stances he adopts in regard to the radical elements in the Movimento dos Sem Terra (MST), for example, there is an Eloisa Elena—who left the PT and challenged Lula for the presidency in 2006, and retains significant sympathies within the party—who continues to see the island and their neighbor, not to mention Evo Morales in Bolivia, as models that Brazil—*"país grande"*— cannot emulate, but should condescendingly understand: they cannot afford the luxury of respecting human rights and accepting elections as the only way to gain and conserve power. And for every José Dirceu—Lula's former prime minister—banned from politics because of accusations of corruption, but who was able to separate his personal affection for the Cuban regime from the pragmatic, responsible policies he implemented from the presidential office, there is an MST, which refused to invite Lula to its annual Congress in June 2007, denouncing his government as a pawn of the business community.

In Mexico, in Central America, in Colombia, as well as even in the three Southern Cone nations where the left has traveled furthest along this road, the notion that these issues stand above national sovereignty and the principle of non-intervention is still an alien one. We are still far removed from the European left's acceptance, in the 1970s and 1980s, of the Human Rights Court, of the single judicial space, of rejection of the Haider government in Austria because of its neo-Nazi leanings. Mercosur has a democratic clause in its founding treaty; but no one viewed Venezuela's accession through this prism, if only to say that the clause was valid and applicable, but not relevant, because human rights and democracy were intact in the new member, in 2007. The matter was viewed differently: interfering in Venezuela's internal affairs was not the Latin American way, the democracy clause notwithstanding. So there is a certain superficial nature to the commitment of many on the left to these issues, and those who are committed know full well that many of their comrades are not. The "democrats" are all too aware of the fact that many of their colleagues, if push comes to shove, believe that Chávez, Morales, Correa, Ortega, let alone the Castro brothers, should not relinquish the power they have conquered simply because they lose an election; better not to hold it than to lose it. This tension persists within the Latin American left, and while it is clearly diminishing as the old guard fades away and the attachment to democratic practices grows, it is still a fixture in the left's landscape.

The second reason for the left's ambivalence toward its own achievements lies in the ambivalence of its voters. As has been shown in various chapters of this volume, the electoral performance of self-defined parties and candidates of the left in Latin America since 1999 has been little short of astounding, regardless of the exact meaning of "left" in each case, or the precise explanation for each performance. But in exit polls taken after each election, and in cross-country surveys such as the Latinobarómetro series from Chile, a disquieting pattern emerges. The left's voters don't see themselves on the left; the left's electorate does not consider itself as leftist; and on specific issues, public opinion in general, and the body of support for left candidates in particular, does not coincide very much with typical tenets of the left, with the possible exception of anti-Americanism.

Even in this subject-area—a "slam-dunk," as George Tenet would say—a poll carried out by Latinobarómetro in late 2006—just before President Bush's swing through the region—showed that in some countries (Venezuela, of course, and Argentina, Brazil, Ecuador, and Uruguay) he was less popular than Hugo Chávez, but in others (Colombia, Costa Rica, El Salvador, Honduras, Mexico, Nicaragua, Panama, and Peru) he obtained higher approval ratings than his Latin scourge.

More broadly, of all voters throughout Latin America polled by Latinobarómetro in 2005, and who *voted* left (defined as voting for political parties of the left in each country, i.e. the PT in Brazil, the PRD in Mexico, the Socialist Party in Chile, the Polo Democrático in Colombia to give some examples), only 31 percent self-defined as *being* "left," 53 percent self-identified with the "center" and 15 percent did so with the "right." (See Figure 12.1.) This is a higher percentage for the left than among all voters (only 15 percent of all voters self-identify with the left), but it shows that two-thirds of the left's electorate does not consider itself of the left. And what's even more confounding and frustrating for the left is that the distribution of the left's electorate in these three categories is very similar overall to that of all voters.

The left-wing voter in Latin America today, unlike Communist Party voters in Chile and Uruguay forty years ago, or in Spain, France, and Italy through most of the twentieth century, does not belong to a distinct segment of the electorate, with its own self-identification (and also its own ideological

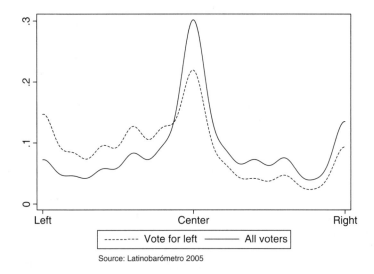

Source: Latinobarómetro 2005

Figure 12.1 Ideological distribution of the electorate in Latin America, 2005.

ghetto, of course), its own geography, and its own attitudes on specific issues, clearly different from the rest of society. It is not, for now in any case, what French scholars labeled a "counter-society" in reference to the Parti Communiste Française (PCF) voters from the late 1920s to the late 1970s.

On issues and attitudes, the situation is similarly unambiguous: 58 percent of those surveyed by Latinobarómetro in 2005 who voted for the left believe their country is governed for the benefit of the powerful—logically enough; but 42 percent believe it is governed for the benefit of the people as a whole—hardly a stance one would expect from left-wing electors. A whopping 73 percent of the left-wing voters believe that a market economy is the only road to development for their country; 40 percent think privatization of state-owned companies has been good for their countries; 70 percent consider that private enterprise is indispensable for the country's development; 46 percent are satisfied with the way the market works in their country; and finally, as seen above with Bush and Chávez, half of all left-wing voters have a positive opinion of the United States, and this at a moment of the American government's greatest unpopularity in the region and in the world since the Vietnam War.

In many cases the left fields better candidates than its rivals; often its policies in government work well (Lula's *Bolsa Família*, for example); this is largely why it now wins elections. But in most cases—the real exceptions as opposed to purely rhetorical ones have only taken place in Venezuela and to a lesser degree in Argentina—its policies are difficult to distinguish from those of its immediate predecessors, and do not seem to explain its victories at the polls. The most obvious examples of this well-studied paradox are Lula and Fernando Henrique Cardoso in Brazil, and the shift within the Chilean Concertación from Christian Democratic leadership between 1989 and 2000 to Socialist leadership since then. In fact, while the two cases are far from identical, the argument can be made that both nations' relative success stems largely from the continuity of now almost twenty years of Concertación government in Chile, and what will be sixteen years of PSDB—PT government in Brazil. If it is not easy for academics to detect the differences separating Lula from Cardoso or Lagos and Bachelet from Aylwin and Frei, no wonder voters cannot either, and thus express the contradictions shown above in the Latinobarómetro poll. The left has been winning or gaining, if and when its candidates, campaigns, and competence in office are simply better than those of the right, but not really because its policies are that different.

This leads directly to the third motive for discomfort. The left in office—nationally, regionally, locally—has generally been forced to choose between two unpleasant options: the populist, nationalist, statist return to the past—what Roberto Mangabeira Unger calls the swashbuckling left—or the competent, mostly honest and responsible, humanized and "kinder and gentler" administration of the present—what he calls the well-behaved left. Neither left has reason to be happy with its own performance, and a growing cohort of Latin America's leftists know it. The swashbuckling left offers a grab bag of social welfare initiatives, boosts to consumption and wages, ad hoc concessions to business interests, and nationalist hand-waving. It succeeds, apparently and for a while, when it follows on an economic disaster and can tap unused capacity and saving (Argentina) or when it can draw on seemingly unlimited oil wealth (Venezuela). It is almost identical in its rhetoric, its policies, and its style to its icons of the past: Perón, Cárdenas, or Vargas. The well-behaved left combines fiscal responsibility as well as bids to win the trust of homegrown and foreign capital with active policy in social welfare, housing, health, education. The two lefts increasingly have the choice of resembling the other colors of the political spectrum, or of progressively resembling a caricature of themselves: Morales copying Chávez, who copies Castro and the Cubans, who invokes increasingly obscure mentors. No one so far has been able truly to square the circle: be truly different from the others, and from the past; from the center and right, and from the command economy, socially subsidized, and hyper-nationalist alternative.

A fourth factor of uneasiness springs from the perennial problem represented by the United States. Absent the Cold War, the geo-political dimension of the left's struggle for power is no longer as crucial as in the past: the United States feels no need to systematically oppose the left in Latin America, whatever it does and whichever it is; nonetheless, there are sufficient conflicts in the world where the United States is involved to provide ample ammunition for the Latin American left's anti-U.S. sentiments, and sufficient mistakes in Washington's policies toward Latin America for those sentiments to appear fully justified. And anti-Americanism in public opinion, while certainly not overwhelming, as we saw, is broad and deep enough to fuel the popularity of those who stoke it constantly.

On the other hand, that same public opinion, business communities, professional elites, and migrant families in many nations (not all, of course) all have a vested interest in their government—left, right, or center—maintaining proper relations with the United States. That is where they export, travel, study, receive remittances from, sell oil to, reproduce life-styles from, etc. The problem is that ideology and the reverential respect for national sovereignty make it difficult to make all of these contradictory objectives simultaneously compatible. Hence, once again, the paradoxes: Lula not only welcoming George Bush at his home in Brasilia, and embracing him during a tour of a Petrobras bio-fuel plant in São Paulo, but also driving through Camp David in a golf cart with the same man who the PT—Lula's party—burns in effigy across Brazil for his policies in Iraq. Dirceu sums up the paradox quite eloquently: it is in Brazil's national interest to work with the United States on ethanol and bio-fuels, whoever is in the White House and whatever his policies elsewhere in the world may be. Except that this approach is the most un-leftist and politically incorrect one that can be found in the annals of the Latin American left, particularly if it leads, as it almost inevitably almost always does, to disagreements with Havana or Caracas. Soon after Lula and Bush's mutual courtship, Fidel Castro devoted one of his now regular columns in the Cuban Communist Party's organ to bash ethanol and alternative fuels, and Chávez, logically enough, followed suit. So Brazilian leftists had to choose—granted, on a rather arcane subject—between Lula, Bush, and Brazil, on one side, and Fidel, Chávez, and their deep-hearted feelings, on the other.

There is no pragmatic left possible in Latin America that does not come to terms with a basic fact of life: the United States will not go away, is a world power, and on occasion—more often than not, though not always—has basic interests that are different from or contrary to those of Latin America, as seen from the left. Any pragmatic stance or negotiation almost always smacks of national treason or betrayal of sovereignty: the latter is by definition non-negotiable. At the same time, though, negotiation and finding common ground, together with encapsulating disagreements and not taking them to extremes is the only way to reconcile contradictory aims. This is not a comfortable place to sit.

And finally, there is the eternal choice: reform or revolution. The Latin American left was never permanently revolutionary; indeed, in its Communist or populist versions, it was eminently reformist, peaceful, electoral, some would say accommodationist, until Fidel Castro and Che Guevara came along in 1959 and radically transformed it. The Cuban Revolution made at least part of the Latin American left revolutionary. This led to profound splits within its ranks (Guevara minimized those differences and paid for his mistake with his life) as well as subsequent reunifications. All students of the left in the region are familiar with the (probably true) anecdote of Castro slamming an AK-47 on the table where he was holding court with the five commanders of the Salvadoran FMLN factions in 1980, and exclaiming they could have his gun if and only if they united.

So for those who followed the Cuban path of revolution, armed struggle, socialism, and radical anti-imperialism, the break with the past and the cost of their metamorphosis was no minor affair. And then barely a few decades later, everyone wanted them to forsake those newly and painfully acquired convictions and abandon the very notion of revolution—not a simple matter. Thus the lacerating choice: resignedly accepting reformism, embracing it, or simply disguising revolutionary beliefs and fervor beneath a moderate coating. Andrés Manuel López Obrador, Mexico's fire-breathing and simultaneously crony-capitalism defender, put it best, perhaps, when he lashed out at Spain's Felipe González, after a long and substantive conversation: "You're just a lousy social-democratic reformist!" Needless to say, López Obrador was right, but González was proud of his reformist credentials, having led his country from authoritarian rule to European democracy and prosperity for more than a decade. For one, reformism was almost an insult; for the other, a source of pride.

For many members of the left—in Nicaragua, in Mexico, in El Salvador, in Brazil and Argentina, obviously in Venezuela and Bolivia, in Colombia— the revolution, the assault on the Winter Palace, is still ever gently on their mind. They are not foolish or unrealistic, and know full well that the prospects for revolution are remote, at best. Even worse, they acknowledge—in private at least—that the definition of revolution is arduous, if not impossible: what would they like their country to look like if, by some miracle, a revolution did take place? Cuba, with or without Soviet support? Venezuela, with or without oil? And yet the stigma of reformism persists, and the attraction of the revolutionary dream endures.

The problem is, of course, that one cannot have it both ways. In some countries the alternative is immediate and explicit: the surprisingly successful Polo Democrático has only thrived to the extent that it has clearly established, maintained, and deepened its distance from the FARC; similarly, many analysts think Cuauhtémoc Cárdenas lost the 1994 presidential elections in Mexico because of the widely and maliciously publicized photograph of *Subcomandante* Marcos and him together in Chiapas. For others, the choice is more abstract; either they are truly reformist, and one day people will vote for them, or they are truly revolutionary, and realize a revolution is an eminently violent, authoritarian event, for better or for worse, but is rarely, if ever, achieved at the ballot box or with the consent of a majority of the people. Lenin had a point. But that doesn't make the dilemma any more comfortable or easier to address.

There are no answers to the left's discomfort other than practice, time, and reflection. This is hardly the place for solutions; they can only emerge on the ground, in the daily work of thousands of activists and intellectuals, in their parties, municipal governments, parliaments, and universities. But some ideas may be in order, just to set down a few benchmarks for future discussions.

The region faces a double challenge in the coming years, and it is almost upon us. The educational deficit, product of poor policy and dramatic demographics in the past, means that there are still millions of children and young people throughout Latin America currently in schools, universities, and technical institutes, and who are not being educated or trained for the global economy, which is the one they will work in, whether they like it or not.

At the same time, however, these countries are also facing a different, but equally crucial challenge, derived from the fact that their population has aged precipitously, and their social safety net—created, as in Western Europe, the United States, and Canada, in close, almost total dependence on having a job—is in shreds, and excludes large majorities of the population. Consequently, Latin America's societies, to a large extent, need to educate their youth and simultaneously to build a system of social protection for their elderly—but also, and as importantly, for that majority of the people who lack health care, housing, professional training, a pension in the future, and a minimum income in the present. This is the first challenge the left must meet.

We borrow on both of these matters from what Roberto Mangabeira Unger, Lula's Long-Term Planning Secretary, and Carlos Ominami, Socialist Vice-President of the Chilean Senate, have suggested in recent years. Bringing education to the top of national priorities means insisting on national minima of investment per child and of performance per school; developing mechanisms for redistribution of resources and staff among richer and poorer parts of each country; creating procedures for localized corrective intervention and reorganization in schools systems when these minima fail to be met. It means involving families in the life of schools and designating a teacher or a member of the community to accompany the progress—and the homework—of each child whose family cannot be involved. It means abandoning a teaching orientation that in the past has been characterized by a focus on shallow coverage and passive information and replacing it with "learning to learn." It means giving every teacher a computer at home, and every student a simplified computer in school hooked up to a national educational network. It means identifying hard-working and gifted poor students at every stage of schooling and showering them with special support and extraordinary opportunities, so that they become a merit-based elite capable of competing with the elites of heirs and protégés that continue to dominate many Latin American countries. On the social protection side, and specifically on the pension and health care side for the elderly, being different without being populist implies creating a single guaranteed pension and elderly health care system (of a non-contributive or pay-as-you-go basis, and financed by a central tax fund), which would complement the individual capitalization pension, and private health insurance for those who have it. But the decisive change must be in guaranteeing the well-being of the elderly, who lived a life unlike that of their peers in the wealthy countries: decoupled from employment in so many cases that they often make up a majority. This must be financed by earmarked taxes, so every tax-payer knows where this specific contribution is going: to address the challenge of a rapidly ageing population that is devoid of the instruments of social protection that other societies have built over the years.

A second area of difference-building for the left lies in constructing the anti-trust legislation, regulation, and enforcement that most Latin American economies and societies sadly lack. Public and private monopolies in business; union monopolies in labor, in both public and private sector in many countries; political parties' monopolies of electoral representation in most countries: all of these excessive concentrations of power and opportunity have become inevitable obstacles to growth and distribution. The right and center cannot be expected to act against the interests that they are so intertwined with; but the left has traditionally—in Latin America—neglected anti-monopoly regulation. First, because it believed in public monopolies, and thought private ones were an inevitable and passing product of monopoly capitalism; and second, because it benefited immensely from union monopolies in the public sector: teachers, government employees, the large unions in the state-owned sector of the economy (oil, mining, steel, electric power, railroads, etc.). It is time for the left that wants to make a difference to embark upon a vigorous anti-trust strategy, introducing elements of competition wherever it is needed, knowing that this will not eliminate "capitalism" (a reformist left does not seek or believe in that goal), but will make it more efficient, and consequently improve living standards and distribution of its benefits.

Third and last in this brief list, the Latin American left must construct an international agenda or program, which it sorely lacks today, given the contradiction between anti-U.S. sentiments and pro-U.S. practices. The left should abandon its last nostalgic ties to the mantra of sovereignty and non-intervention and become a driving force, domestically and abroad, for the construction of a new regional and international legal order, whereby its principles, values, and aims would be enshrined at a supranational echelon. Nothing can level the acutely tilted playing field represented by a one-superpower world as well as an intrusive, ambitious, and detailed legal regime;

no region in the world has more to benefit from this than Latin America. On human rights and democracy; on trade and the environment; on labor rights—where, for example, Latin America has as much to gain by defending itself against child labor in Pakistan as it has to lose by accepting U.S. standards in Free Trade Agreements—and the rights of indigenous peoples; on gender rights and fighting corruption and the drug trade; on small arms traffic and chemical weapons; on just about any issue, a strong regional and international legal order squares the circle for the left. It has to include the United States, but entwines Washington in agreements that eventually bind it. It does not neglect the left's nationalism, but raises it to a higher plane, where it is no longer introverted and archaic but, on the contrary, transforms its passions into laws and principles that can be applied. And most importantly, it acknowledges that in a globalized world, what's not supranational functions less and less effectively.

These are some of the aims the Latin American left might seek to achieve, if it truly wants to emerge from the angst that plagues it, despite its successes. The latter are real, but so is the former. This volume has described some of its advances and challenges, on a country basis or topically. This chapter has attempted to tie these parts together; the reader will judge.

References

Abers, Rebecca. 2000. *Inventing Local Democracy: Grassroots Politics in Brazil*. Boulder: Lynne Rienner Publishers.

Ahmad, Aijaz. 2006. "Radical Promise, Neoliberal Policy." *Frontline* 23(7): 127–133.

Alcántara Sáez, Manuel and Leticia Ruiz-Rodríguez, eds. 2006. *La política chilena: entre la rutina, el mito y el modelo*. Barcelona: Bellaterra.

Alesina, Alberto and Dani Rodrik. 1994. "Distributive Politics and Economic Growth." *Quarterly Journal of Economics* 109(2): 465–490.

Altman, David. 2000. "The Politics of Coalition Formation and Survival in Multiparty Presidential Democracies: The Case of Uruguay 1989–1999." *Party Politics* 6(3): 259–283.

Altman, David. 2002. "Popular Initiatives in Uruguay: Confidence Votes on Government or Political Loyalties?" *Electoral Studies* 21(4): 617–630.

Altman, David and Rossana Castiglioni. 2006. "The 2004 Uruguayan Elections: A Political Earthquake Foretold." *Electoral Studies* 25(1): 147–154.

Altman, David, Daniel Buquet, and Juan Pablo Luna. 2006. "Constitutional Reforms and Political Turnover in Uruguay: Winning a Battle, Losing the War." Presented at the Annual Meeting of the American Political Science Association, August 31–September 3, Philadelphia, PA.

Álvarez Herrera, Bernardo. 2006. "A Benign Revolution." *Foreign Affairs* 85(4): 195.

Angell, Alan and Benny Pollack. 1990. "The Chilean Elections of 1989 and the Politics of the Transitions to Democracy." *Bulletin of Latin American Research* 9(1): 1–23.

Angell, Alan and Cristóbal Reig. 2006. "Change or Continuity? The Chilean Elections of 2005/2006." *Bulletin of Latin American Research* 25(4): 481–502.

Avritzer, L. 2003. "O orçamento participativo e a teoria democrática: um balanço crítico." In *A inovação democrática no Brasil: o orçamento participativo*, ed. Leonardo Avritzer and Zander Navarro. São Paulo: Cortez.

Bacigalupe, Juan and Jorge Marius. 1998. *Sistema electoral y elecciones uruguayas 1925–1998*. Montevideo: Fundación Konrad Adenauer.

Baiocchi, Gianpaolo, ed. 2003a. *Radicals in Power: The Workers' Party (PT) and Experiments in Urban Democracy in Brazil*. New York: Zed Books.

Baiocchi, Gianpaolo. 2003b. "Radicals in Power." In *Radicals in Power: The Workers' Party (PT) and Experiments in Urban Democracy in Brazil*, ed. Gianpaolo Baiocchi. New York: Zed Books.

Baiocchi, Gianpaolo. 2003c. "The Long March through Institutions: Lessons from PT in Power." In *Radicals in Power: The Workers' Party (PT) and Experiments in Urban Democracy in Brazil*, ed. Gianpaolo Baiocchi. New York: Zed Books.

Balbi, Carmen Rosa. 1989. *Identidad clasista en el sindicalismo: su impacto en las fábricas*. Lima: DESCO.

Baldez, Lisa and John M. Carey. 1999. "Presidential Agenda Control and Spending Policy: Lessons from General Pinochet's Constitution." *American Journal of Political Science* 43(1): 29–55.

Benoit, Kenneth and Michael Laver. 2006. *Party Policy in Modern Democracies*. London: Routledge.

Bittar, Jorge, ed. 1992. *O modo petista de governar*. São Paulo: Fundaçao Perseu Abramo.

Bobbio, Norberto. 1997. *Left and Right: The Significance of a Political Distinction*. Chicago: University of Chicago Press.

Boeninger, Edgardo. 1997. *Democracia en Chile. Lecciones para la gobernabilidad*. Santiago: Editorial Andrés Bello.

Boix, Carles. 1998. *Political Parties, Growth and Equality. Conservative and Social Democratic Economic Strategies in the World Economy*. Cambridge, UK: Cambridge University Press.

Bonanno, George A. and John T. Jost. 2006. "Conservative Shift among High-Exposure Survivors of the September 11th Terrorist Attacks." *Basic and Applied Social Psychology* 28(4): 311–323.

Borón, Atilio. 2006. "Vargas Llosa y la democracia: breve historia de una relación infeliz." Available at http://www.iade.org.ar/modules/noticias/article.php?stor yid=754 (accessed December 27, 2006).

Bottinelli, Oscar. 1993. "Estructura y funcionamiento de los partidos políticos en Uruguay." In *Estructura y funcionamiento de los partidos políticos: una reforma posible*, ed. Klaus Bodemer and María Elena Laurnaga. Montevideo: FESUR.

Boudin, Chesa, Gabriel Gonzalez, and Wilmer Rumbos. 2006. *The Venezuelan Revolution: 100 Questions—100 Answers*. New York, NY: Thunder's Mouth Press.

Bovero, Michelangelo. 2006. "La izquierda, la derecha, la democracia." *Nexos* 348: 25–32.

Branford, Sue and Bernardo Kucinski. 1995. *Brazil—Carnival of the Oppressed. Lula and the Brazilian Workers' Party*. New York, NY: Latin America Bureau.

Bresser-Pereira, Luiz Carlos, José María Maravall, and Adam Przeworski. 1993. *Economic Reforms in New Democracies: A Social-Democratic Approach*. New York: Cambridge University Press.

Bruhn, Kathleen. 1997. *Taking on Goliath: The Emergence of a New Left Party and the Struggle for Democracy in Mexico*. University Park, PA: Penn State Press, 1997.

Budge, Ian and David Robertson. 1987. "Do Parties Differ, and How? Comparative Discriminant and Factor Analyses." In *Ideology, Strategy and Party Change: Spatial Analyses of Postwar Election Programmes in 19 Democracies*, ed. Ian Budge, David Robertson, and Derek Hearl. Cambridge: Cambridge University Press.

Buquet, Daniel. 1997. "Partidos políticos y sistema electoral: Uruguay 1942–1994." Facultad Latinoamericana de Ciencias Sociales (FLACSO), Mexico.

Buquet, Daniel and Ernesto Castellano. 1995. "Representación proporcional y democracia en Uruguay." *Revista Uruguaya de ciencia política* 8: 107–123.

Buquet, Daniel and Daniel Chasquetti. 2004. "Presidential Candidate Selection in Uruguay (1942–1999)." Presented at the Pathways to Power: Political Recruitment and Democracy in Latin America conference, April 3 and 4, Winston-Salem, NC.

Buquet, Daniel and Daniel Chasquetti. 2005. "Elecciones Uruguay 2004: descifrando el cambio." *Revista de ciencia política* 25(2): 143–152.

Buquet, Daniel, Daniel Chasquetti, and Juan Andrés Moraes. 1998. *Fragmentación política y gobierno en Uruguay: ¿Un enfermo imaginario?* Montevideo: Facultad de Ciencias Sociales.

Caetano, Gerardo, José Rilla, and Roméo Pérez. 1987. "La partidocracia uruguaya. Historia y teoría de la centralidad de los partidos políticos." *Cuadernos del CLAEH* 44(4): 37–62.

Cameron, Maxwell. 1994. *Democracy and Authoritarianism in Peru. Political Coalitions and Social Change.* New York: St Martin's Press.

Canache, Damarys. 2004. "Urban Poor and Political Order." In *The Unraveling of Representative Democracy in Venezuela*, ed. Jennifer L. McCoy and David J. Myers. Baltimore, MD: Johns Hopkins University Press.

Cardoso, Fernando Henrique. 2006. "Populism and Globalization Don't Mix." *New Perspectives Quarterly* 23(2): 63.

Carr, Barry. 1985. *Mexican Communism, 1968–1983: Eurocommunism in the Americas?* Research Report Series No. 42. La Jolla: Center for U.S.–Mexican Studies.

Castañeda, Jorge G. 1993. *Utopia Unarmed: The Latin American Left after the Cold War.* New York, NY: Vintage Books.

Castañeda, Jorge G. 2006. "Latin America's Left Turn." *Foreign Affairs* 85(3): 28–43.

Castañeda, Jorge G. and Patricio Navia. 2007. "New Leaders, New Voices." *Americas Quarterly* 1(1): 41–51.

Castañeda, Jorge G. and Roberto Mangabeira Unger. 1998. "Después del neoliberalismo: un nuevo camino." *Nexos* 243: 57–64.

Castiglioni, Rossana. 2005. *The Politics of Social Policy Change in Chile and Uruguay: Retrenchment versus Maintenance 1973–1998.* New York: Routledge.

Chasquetti, Daniel. 2003. "Producción parlamentaria: el declive del Parlamento en el 'cuarto año.'" Observatorio Político: Informe de Coyuntura 4: 41–48.

Chávez Frías, Hugo. 2005. *Understanding the Venezuelan Revolution. Hugo Chávez Talks to Marta Harnecker.* New York, NY: Monthly Review Press.

Claude, Marcel. 2006. *El retorno de Fausto. Ricardo Lagos y la concentración del poder económico.* Santiago: Ediciones Política y Utopía.

Cleary, Matthew R. 2006. "Explaining the Left's Resurgence." *Journal of Democracy* 17(4): 35–49.

COHA. 2005. "The Lagos Legacy and Chile's Upcoming Elections." Available at http://www.coha.org/2005/10/11/the-lagos-legacy-and-chiles-upcoming-elections (accessed December 4, 2006).

COHA. 2006. "Uruguay's Tabaré Vázquez: Pink Tide or Political Voice of the Center?" Available at http://www.coha.org/2006/03/04/uruguay%e2%80%99s-tabare-vazquez-pink-tide-or-political-voice-of-the-center (accessed December 4, 2006).

Collier, David, ed. 1979. *The New Authoritarianism in Latin America.* Princeton: Princeton University Press.

Comisión de la Verdad y Reconciliación. 2003. *Informe final*. Lima: Comisión de la Verdad y Reconciliación.

Constable, Pamela and Arturo Valenzuela. 1991. *A Nation of Enemies. Chile under Pinochet*. New York: Norton.

Coppedge, Michael. 1994. *Strong Parties and Lame Ducks: Presidential Partyarchy and Factionalism in Venezuela*. Stanford: Stanford University Press.

Corrales, Javier. 2006a. "Hugo Boss." *Foreign Policy* 152: 32–40.

Corrales, Javier. 2006b. "The Many Lefts of Latin America." *Foreign Policy* 157: 44–45.

Couto, Cláudio G. 1996. *Qual PT? Resenha do livro um governo de esquerda para todos: Luiza Erundina na prefeitura de São Paulo*. São Paulo: Editora Brasileira de Ciências.

Desai, Manali. 2002. "The Relative Autonomy of Party Practices: A Counterfactual Analysis of Left Party Ascendancy in Kerala, India. 1934–1940." *American Journal of Sociology* 108(3): 616–657.

Dieterich, Heinz. 2006. "El socialismo del siglo XXI." Available at http://www.rebelion.org/dieterich/dieterich070802.pdf (accessed November 6, 2007).

Domínguez, Jorge and Michael Shifter, eds. 2003. *Constructing Democratic Governance in Latin America*. Second ed. Baltimore: Johns Hopkins University Press.

Dornbusch, Rudiger and Sebastian Edwards. 1991. "The Macroeconomics of Populism." In *The Macroeconomics of Populism in Latin America*, ed. Rudiger Dornbusch and Sebastian Edwards. Chicago, IL: University of Chicago Press.

Drake, Paul and Iván Jaksic, eds. 1995. *The Struggle for Democracy in Chile. 1982–1990*. Revised ed. Lincoln: University of Nebraska Press.

Druckman, James N. 1996. "Party Factionalism and Cabinet Durability." *Party Politics* 2(3): 397–407.

Duverger, Maurice. 1954. *Political Parties*. London: Methuen.

ECLAC. 2002. "Boletín demográfico no. 69. América Latina y Caribe: estimaciones y proyecciones de población. 1950–2050." Santiago, Chile: ECLAC.

ECLAC. 2006a. *Estudio económico de América Latina y el Caribe 2005–2006* (estadística). Santiago, Chile: Economic Commission for Latin America and the Caribbean.

ECLAC. 2006b. *Panorama social de América Latina y el Caribe*. Santiago, Chile: Economic Commission for Latin America and the Caribbean.

ECLAC. 2006c. *Panorama de la inserción internacional de América Latina*. Santiago, Chile: Economic Commission for Latin America and the Caribbean.

ECLAC. 2006d. *Balance preliminar de las economías de América Latina y el Caribe, 2006*. Santiago: ECLAC.

ECLAC. 2006e. *Statistical Yearbook for Latin America and the Caribbean, 2005*. Santiago: United Nations.

EIU. 2006. Argentina, Bolivia, Brazil, Chile, Uruguay and Venezuela Country Reports. Economist Intelligence Unit, London, UK.

EIU. 2007. Argentina, Bolivia, Brazil, Chile, Uruguay and Venezuela Country Reports. Economist Intelligence Unit, London, UK.

Ellner, Steve. 2005. "Revolutionary and Non-Revolutionary Paths of Radical Populism: Directions of the *Chavista* Movement in Venezuela." *Science and Society* 69: 160–190.

Ellner, Steve and Daniel Hellinger, eds. 2003. *Venezuelan Politics in the Chavez Era: Class, Polarization and Conflict.* Boulder, CO: Lynne Rienner Publishers.

Engel, Eduardo, Ronald Fischer, and Alexander Galetovic. 2000. "The Chilean Infrastructure Concessions Program: Evaluation, Lessons and Prospects for the Future." In *La transformación económica de Chile*, ed. Fernando Larraín and Rodrigo Vergara. Santiago: CEP.

Ensalaco, Mark. 1994. "In with the New, Out with the Old? The Democratising Impact of Constitutional Reform in Chile." *Journal of Latin American Studies* 26(2): 409–429.

Fazio, Hugo. 2006. *Lagos: el presidente "progresista" de la Concertación.* Santiago: LOM Ciencias Humanas.

Fazio, Hugo, Magaly Parada, Hugo Lattore, Manuel Riesco, Gabriel Salazar, Felipe Portales, Horacio Brum, Rafael Otano, Claudia Lagos, and Gonzalo Villarino. 2006. *Gobierno de Lagos, balance crítico.* Santiago: Ediciones LOM.

Fiorina, Morris (with Samuel J. Abrams and Jeremy C. Pope). 2006. *Culture War? The Myth of a Polarized America.* Second ed. New York, NY: Pearson Longman.

Fletcher, Sam. 2003. "PDVSA Workers Oppose Takeover of PDVSA by Chavez." *The Oil and Gas Journal* 101(3): 29–31.

Foweraker, Joe. 1995. *Theorizing Social Movements.* London: Pluto Press.

Funk, Robert, ed. 2006. *El gobierno de Ricardo Lagos: La nueva vía chilena hacia el socialismo.* Santiago: Universidad Diego Portales.

Gaglietti, Mauro. 1999. *PT: Ambivalências de uma militância.* Porto Alegre: Dacasa Editora/Unicruz.

Garcé, Adolfo and Jaime Yaffé. 2004. *La era progresista.* Montevideo: Editorial Fin de Siglo.

García-Guadilla, María Pilar. 2003. "Civil Society: Institutionalization, Fragmentation, Autonomy." In *Venezuelan Politics in the Chávez Era: Class, Polarization and Conflict*, ed. Steve Ellner and Daniel Hellinger. Boulder, CO: Lynne Rienner Publishers.

Garretón, Manuel Antonio. 1995. "The Political Opposition and the Party System under the Military Regime." In *The Struggle for Democracy in Chile. 1982–1990*, ed. Paul Drake and Ivan Jaksic. Lincoln: University of Nebraska Press

Giacalone, Rita. 2006. "La Comunidad Sudamericana de Naciones: ¿Una alianza entre izquierda y empresarios?" *Nueva sociedad* 202: 74–87.

Giddens, Anthony. 1998. *The Third Way. The Renewal of Social Democracy.* Cambridge: Polity Press.

Gillespie, Charles G. 1991. *Negotiating Democracy: Politicians and Generals in Uruguay.* Cambridge: Cambridge University Press.

Gilligan, Michael. 1997. *Empowering Exporters.* Ann Arbor, MI: University of Michigan Press.

Godoy, Oscar. 1994. "Las elecciones de 1993." *Estudios públicos* 54: 301–337.

Goldfrank, Benjamin and Aaron Schneider. 2003. "Restraining the Revolution or Deepening Democracy? The Workers' Party in Rio Grande do Sul." In *Radicals in Power: The Workers' Party (PT) and Experiments in Urban Democracy in Brazil*, ed. Gianpaolo Baiocchi. New York: Zed Books.

Gomes, Ciro and Roberto Mangabeira Unger. 1998. *Una alternativa práctica al neoliberalismo.* Mexico: Océano.

González, Luis E. 1991. *Political Structures and Democracy in Uruguay*. Notre Dame: University of Notre Dame Press.

González, Luis E. 1995. "Continuity and Change in the Uruguayan Party System." In *Building Democratic Institutions: Party Systems in Latin America*, ed. Scott Mainwaring and Timothy Scully. Stanford: Stanford University Press.

González, Luis E. and Rosario Queirolo. 2000. "Las elecciones nacionales del 2004: posibles escenarios." In *Elecciones 1999/2000*, ed. Gerardo Caetano. Montevideo: Ediciones Banda Oriental—Instituto de Ciencia Política.

Gourevitch, Peter. 1986. *Politics in Hard Times: Comparative Responses to International Crisis*. Ithaca, NY: Cornell University Press.

Grayson, George, with Óscar Aguilar Ascencio. 2006. *Mesías mexicano: biografía crítica de Andrés Manuel López Obrador*. Mexico City: Random House Mondadori.

Guidry, John. 2003. "Faith in what will Change: The PT Administration in Belém." In *Radicals in Power: The Workers' Party (PT) and Experiments in Urban Democracy in Brazil*, ed. Gianpaolo Baiocchi. New York: Zed Books.

Hakim, Peter. 2006. "Is Washington Losing Latin America?" *Foreign Affairs* 85(1): 39–53.

Hall, Anthony. 2006. "From *Fome Zero* to *Bolsa Família*: Social Policies and Poverty Alleviation under Lula." *Journal of Latin American Studies* 38(4): 689–710.

Hernández Márquez, Janeth. 2004. "Movimiento al socialismo: su origen y evolución." In *Los partidos políticos venezolanos en el siglo XXI*, ed. Jesús Enrique Molina Vega and Ángel Eduardo Álvarez Díaz. Valencia: Vadell Hermanos Editores.

Herrera, Guillermo. 2002. *Izquierda Unida y el Partido Comunista*. Lima: Termil.

Huber, Evelyn and John Stephens. 2001. *Development and Crisis of the Welfare State*. Chicago: University of Chicago Press.

Huber, John and Ronald Inglehart. 1995. "Expert Interpretations of Party Space and Party Locations in 42 Societies." *Party Politics* 1(1): 73–111.

Hunter, Wendy and Timothy Power. 2005. "Lula's Brazil at Midterm." *Journal of Democracy* 16(3): 127–139.

Iguíñiz, Javier, Rosario Basay, and Mónica Rubio. 1993. *Los ajustes. Perú 1975–1992*. Lima: Fundación Friedrich Ebert.

IMF. 2006. *Balance of Payments Statistics CD-Rom*. Washington, DC: IMF.

IMF. 2007. *World Economic Outlook Database*. Washington, DC: IMF.

Inglehart, Ronald. 1997. *Modernization and Postmodernization*. Princeton, NJ: Princeton University Press.

Insunza, Andrea and Javier Ortega. 2005. *Bachelet. La historia no oficial*. Santiago: Debate.

Iversen, Torben. 2005. *Capitalism, Democracy and Welfare*. Cambridge, UK: Cambridge University Press.

Jost, John T. 2006. "The End of the End of Ideology." *American Psychologist* 61(7): 651–670.

Jost, John T., Jack Glaser, Arie W. Kruglanski, and Frank J. Sulloway. 2003a. "Political Conservatism as Motivated Social Cognition." *Psychological Bulletin* 129(3): 339–375.

Jost, John T., Jack Glaser, Arie W. Kruglanski, and Frank J. Sulloway. 2003b. "Exceptions that Prove the Rule. Using a Theory of Motivated Social Cognition to Account for Ideological Incongruities and Political Anomalies: Reply to Greenberg and Jonas (2003)." *Psychological Bulletin* 129(3): 383–393.

Jost, John T., Jamie L. Napier, Hulda Thorisdottir, Samuel D. Gosling, Tibor P. Palfai, and Brian Ostafin. 2007. "Are Needs to Manage Uncertainty and Threat Associated with Political Conservatism or Ideological Extremity?" *Personality and Social Psychology Bulletin* 33(7): 989–1007.

Katz, Richard S. and Peter Mair. 1995. "Changing Models of Party Organization and Party Democracy: The Emergence of the Cartel Party." *Party Politics* 1(1): 5–28.

Kaufman, Robert and Barbara Stallings. 1991. "The Political Economy of Latin American Populism." In *The Macroeconomics of Populism in Latin America*, ed. Rudiger Dornbusch and Sebastian Edwards. Chicago, IL: University of Chicago Press.

Keck, Margaret. 1992. *The Workers' Party and Democratization in Brazil*. New Haven: Yale University Press.

Keefer, Philip. 2005. *DPI2004. Database of Political Institutions: Changes and Variable Definitions*. Washington, DC: World Bank.

Kirchheimer, Otto. 1966. "The Transformation of the Western European Party System." In *Political Parties and Political Development*, ed. Joseph LaPalombara and Myron Weiner. Princeton: Princeton University Press

Kowarick, Lúcio and André Singer. 1994. "The Workers' Party in Sao Paulo." In *Social Struggles and the City. The Case of Sao Paulo*, ed. Lúcio Kowarick. New York: Monthly Review Press.

Laclau, Ernesto. 2005. *Politics and Ideology in Marxist Theory: Capitalism, Fascism and Populism*. London, UK: Verso Publishers.

Lanzaro, Jorge, ed. 2004. *La izquierda uruguaya: entra la oposición y el gobierno*. Montevideo: Instituto de Ciencia Política.

Latinobarómetro. 2007. *Informe Latinobarómetro 2006*. Santiago: Latinobarómetro.

Lauer, Mirko, ed. 1977. *El reformismo burgués, 1968–1976*. Lima: Mosca Azul.

Levitsky, Steven and Lucan Way. 2002. "The Rise of Competitive Authoritarianism." *Journal of Democracy* 13(2): 51–65.

Llavador, Humberto and Robert Oxoby. 2005. "Partisan Competition, Growth and the Franchise." *Quarterly Journal of Economics* 119(3): 1155–1189.

Lomnitz, Claudio. 2006. "Latin America's Rebellion. Will the New Left Set a New Agenda?" *Boston Review* 31(5): 7–10.

López Maya, Margarita. 1998. "New Avenues for Popular Representation in Venezuela: La Causa R and the Movimiento Bolivariano 200." In *Reinventing Legitimacy: Democracy and Political Change in Venezuela*, ed. Damarys Canache and Michael R. Kulisheck. Westport, CT: Greenwood Press.

López Maya, Margarita. 2004. "Patria Para Todos (PPT): un partido popular en tiempos de dlobalización." In *Los partidos políticos venezolanos en el siglo XXI*, ed. Jesús Enrique Molina Vega and Ángel Eduardo Álvarez Díaz. Valencia: Vadell Hermanos Editores.

López Maya, Margarita. 2005. *Del viernes negro al referendo revocatorio*. Caracas: Alfadil.

López-Moctezuma, Gabriel. 2007. "¿Adios a las ideologías? Un estudio del gasto social en las economías de la OCDE." Ms. ITAM.

Loveman, Brian. 1991. "¿Misión cumplida? Civil Military Relations and the Chilean Political Transition." *Journal of Interamerican Studies and World Affairs* 33(3): 35–74.

Luna, Juan Pablo. 2002. "¿Pesimismo estructural o voto económico? Macropolitics en Uruguay." *Revista Uruguaya de Ciencia Política* 13: 123–151.

Luna, Juan Pablo. forthcoming. "Frente Amplio and the Crafting of a Social-Democratic Alternative in Uruguay." *Latin American Politics and Society.*

Lynch, Nicolás. 1992. *La transición conservadora. Movimientos sociales y democracia en el Perú, 1975–1978.* Lima: El Zorro de Abajo.

McAdam, Doug, John McCarthy, and Mayer Zald. 1996. *Comparative Perspectives on Social Movements. Political Opportunities, Mobilizing Structures, and Cultural Framings.* Cambridge: Cambridge University Press.

Macaulay, Fiona and Guy Burton. 2003. "PT Never Again? Failure (and Success) in the PT's State Government in Espíritu Santo and the Federal District." In *Radicals in Power: The Workers' Party (PT) and Experiments in Urban Democracy in Brazil*, ed. Gianpaolo Baiocchi. New York: Zed Books.

McClintock, Cynthia and Abraham F. Lowenthal, comps. 1989. *El gobierno militar: una experiencia peruana.* Lima: Instituto de Estudios Peruanos.

Machado, Joao. 1993. "Ampliacoes redutoras." *Teoria e debate* 20.

Magalhães, Inês, Luiz Barreto, and Vicente Trevas, eds. 1999. *Governo e cidadania: balanço e reflexões sobre o modo petista de governar.* São Paulo: Fundação Perseu Abramo.

Mainwaring, Scott and Matthew Shugart, eds. 1997. *Presidentialism and Democracy in Latin America.* Cambridge: Cambridge University Press.

Marques, Rosa Maria and Paulo Nakatani. 2007. "The State and Economy in Brazil: An Introduction." *Monthly Review* 58(9): 17–21.

Martínez Verdugo, Arnoldo, ed. 1985. *Historia del comunismo en México.* Mexico City: Editorial Grijalbo.

Meléndez, Carlos. 2003. "Radiografía de una victoria política ¿Adiós a los 'outsiders'?" *Quehacer* 140: 16–23.

Meneguello, Rachel 1989. *PT: A formação de um partido 1979–1982.* Rio de Janeiro: Editora Paz e Terra.

Mershon, Carol. 2001. "Contending Models of Portfolio Allocation and Office Payoffs to Party Fractions: Italy, 1963–79." *American Journal of Political Science* 45(2): 277–293.

MINCI (Ministerio del Poder Popular para la Comunicación e Información de la Republica Bolivariana de Venezuela). 2007. "Líneas generales del plan de desarrollo económico y social de la nación." Available at http://archivos.minci.gob.ve/doc/lineas_generales_de_la_nacion.pdf (accessed November 6, 2007).

Molina, José Enrique. 2004. "The Unraveling of Venezuela's Party System: From Party Rule to Personalistic Politics and Deinstitutionalization." In *The Unraveling of Representative Democracy in Venezuela*, ed. Jennifer McCoy and David J. Myers. Baltimore, MD: Johns Hopkins University Press.

Molina, José Enrique and Carmen Pérez. 2004. "Radical Change at the Ballot Box: Causes and Consequences of Electoral Behavior in Venezuela's 2000 Elections." *Latin American Politics and Society* 46: 103–134.

Monaldi, Francisco, Rosa Amelia Gonzalez, Richard Obuchi, and Michael Penfold. 2004. "Political Institutions, Policymaking Processes, and Policy Outcomes in Venezuela." Available at http://www.iadb.org/res/laresnetwork/projects/pr231finaldraft.pdf (accessed September 11, 2007).

Moraes, Juan Andrés. 2004. "Why Factions? Candidate Selection and Legislative Politics in Uruguay." Presented at the Pathways to Power: Political Recruitment and Democracy in Latin America conference, April 3–4, Winston-Salem, NC.

Moraes, Juan Andrés and Scott Morgenstern. 1995. "El veto del poder ejecutivo en el proceso político uruguayo: 1985–1995." Ms, Instituto de Ciencia Política, Universidad de la República, Montevideo.

Moreno, Alejandro. 1999. *Political Cleavages: Issues, Parties, and the Consolidation of Democracy.* Boulder, CO: Westview Press.

Morgenstern, Scott. 1996. *The Electoral Connection and the Legislative Process in Latin America: Factions, Parties, and Alliances in Theory and Practice.* Ph.D. dissertation, University of California San Diego.

Morgenstern, Scott. 2001. "Organized Factions and Disorganized Parties: Electoral Incentives in Uruguay." *Party Politics* 7(2): 235–256.

Morgenstern, Scott. 2004. *Patterns of Legislative Politics: Roll-Call Voting in Latin America and the United States.* Cambridge: Cambridge University Press.

Navia, Patricio. 2004. "Modernización del estado y financiamiento de la política: una crisis que se transformó en oportunidad." In *Chile 2003–2004. Los nuevos escenarios (inter)nacionales,* ed. Carolina Stefoni. Santiago: FLACSO.

Navia, Patricio. 2005a. "La elección presidencial de 1993. Una elección sin incertidumbre." In *Las elecciones presidenciales en la historia de Chile. 1920–2000,* ed. Alejandro San Francisco and Ángel Soto. Santiago: Centro de Estudios Bicentenario.

Navia, Patricio. 2005b. "Transformando votos en escaños: leyes electorales en Chile, 1833–2003." *Política y Gobierno* 12(2): 233–276.

Navia, Patricio. 2006a. "Bachelet's Election in Chile." *ReVista. Harvard Review of Latin America* 5(1): 9–11.

Navia, Patricio. 2006b. "La izquierda de Lagos vs la izquierda de Chávez." *Foreign Affairs en Español* 6 (2): 75–88.

Nieto, Jorge. 1983. *Izquierda y democracia en el Perú, 1975–1980.* Lima: DESCO.

Novaes, Carlos Alberto Marques. 1993. "PT: Dilemas da burocratização." *Novos estudos* 35: 217–237.

Nylen, William. 2003. "An Enduring Legacy? Popular Participation in the Aftermath of the Participatory Budgets of João Monlevade and Betim." In *Radicals in Power: The Workers' Party (PT) and Experiments in Urban Democracy in Brazil,* ed. Gianpaolo Baiocchi. New York: Zed Books.

Ottone, Ernesto and Carlos Vergara. 2006. *Ampliando horizontes. Siete claves estratégicas del gobierno de Lagos.* Santiago: Debate.

Panizza, Francisco. 2005a. "The Social Democratization of the Latin American Left." *Revista Europea de Estudios Latinoamericanos y del Caribe,* 79: 95–104.

Panizza, Francisco. 2005b. "Unarmed Utopia Revisited: The Resurgence of Left-of-Centre Politics in Latin America." *Political Studies* 53(4): 716–734.

Panizza, Ugo and Mónica Yáñez. 2005. "Why are Latin Americans So Unhappy about Reforms?" *Journal of Applied Economics* 8(1): 1–29.

Paramio, Ludolfo. 2006. "La izquierda y el populismo." *Nexos* 339: 19–28.

Partido dos Trabalhadores. 1989. *Programa de governo do PT.* São Paulo: Partido dos Trabalhadores.

Partido dos Trabalhadores. 1999. *O programa da revolução democrática.* São Paulo: Fundação Perseu Abramo.

Pease, Henry. 1979. *El ocaso del poder oligárquico. Lucha política en la escena oficial, 1968–1975*. Second ed. Lima: DESCO.

Pease, Henry. 1981. *Los caminos del poder. Tres años en la escena política peruana (1975–1978)*. Lima: DESCO.

Penfold, Michael. 2006. "Clientelism and Social Funds: Empirical Evidence from Chávez's *'Misiones'* programs in Venezuela." Available at http://servicios.iesa.edu.ve/newsite/academia/pdf/MichaelPenfold.pdf (accessed September 23, 2007).

Pereira Almao, Valia. 2004. "Movimiento v república: vocación de masas y atadura personalista." In *Los partidos políticos venezolanos en el siglo XXI*, ed. Jesús Enrique Molina Vega, and Ángel Eduardo Álvarez Díaz. Valencia: Vadell Hermanos Editores.

Pivel Devoto, Juan. 1942. *Historia de los partidos políticos en el Uruguay*. Montevideo: Tipografía Atlantida.

Polanyi, Karl. 1944. *The Great Transformation: The Political Origins of Our Time*. New York, NY: Beacon Press,

Przeworski, Adam and Michael Wallerstein. 1988. "Structural Dependence of State on Capital." *American Political Science Review* 82(1): 11–29.

Raby, David L. 2006. *Democracy and Revolution*. Ann Arbor, MI: Pluto Press.

Ramírez Gallegos, Franklin. 2006. "Mucho más que dos izquierdas." *Nueva sociedad* 205: 30–45.

Rawls, John. 1971. *A Theory of Justice*. Cambridge, MA: Harvard University Press.

Rehren, Alfredo. 1992. "Liderazgo presidencial y democratización en el Cono Sur de América Latina." *Revista de ciencia política* XIV(1): 63–87.

Rehren, Alfredo. 1998. "La organización de la presidencia y el proceso político chileno." *Revista de ciencia política* XIX(2): 89–124.

Remy, María Isabel. 2005. *Los múltiples campos de la participación ciudadana en el Perú. Un reconocimiento del terreno y algunas reflexiones*. Lima: Instituto de Estudios Peruanos.

Rivero Ramírez, Gigliana and Carlos García Soto. 2006. "Introducción al régimen de las empresas de producción social." *Revista de derecho publico* 108.

Rodrik, Dani. 1998. "Why Do More Open Economies Have Bigger Governments?" *Journal of Political Economy* 106(5): 997–1032.

Sader, Emir. 2005. "Taking Lula's Measure." *New Left Review* 33: 58–80.

Salamanca, Luis. 2004. "La causa radical: auge y caída." In *Los partidos políticos venezolanos en el siglo XXI*, ed. Jesús Enrique Molina Vega and Ángel Eduardo Álvarez Díaz. Valencia: Vadell Hermanos Editores.

Sanborn, Cynthia. 1991. "The Democratic Left and the Persistence of Populism in Peru: 1975–1990." Ph.D. dissertation, Harvard University.

Sartori, Giovanni. 1976. *Parties and Party System*. Cambridge: Cambridge University Press.

Savarino, Franco. 2006. "Populismo: perspectivas europeas y latinoamericanas." *Espiral* XIII(37): 77–94.

Schamis, Héctor E. 2006. "Populism, Socialism and Democratic Institutions." *Journal of Democracy* 17(4): 20–34.

Shifter, Michael. 2005. "The US and Latin America through the Lens of Empire." *Current History Magazine* 103(670): 61–67.

Shifter, Michael. 2006. "In Search of Hugo Chávez." *Foreign Affairs* 85(3): 45–59.

Shifter, Michael and Vinay Jawahar. 2005. "Latin America's Populist Turn." *Current History* 104(679): 51–57.

Siavelis, Peter. 2000. *The President and Congress in Post-Authoritarian Chile: Institutional Constraints to Democratic Consolidation*. Philadelphia: Penn State University Press.

Siavelis, Peter. 2002. "The Hidden Logic of Candidate Selection for Chilean Parliamentary Elections." *Comparative Politics* 34(4): 419–438.

Siavelis, Peter. 2006. "How New is Bachelet's Chile?" *Current History* 106(697): 70–76.

Silva, Marcelo K. 2003. "Participation by Design? The Workers' Party in the Metropolitan Region of Porto Alegre." In *Radicals in Power: The Workers' Party (PT) and Experiments in Urban Democracy in Brazil*, ed. Gianpaolo Baiocchi. New York: Zed Books.

Silva, Marcelo K., Gianpaolo Baiocchi, Patrick Heller, and Shubham Chaudhuri. 2006. "Evaluating Empowerment: Participatory Budgeting in Brazilian Municipalities." In *Empowerment in Practice: From Analysis to Implementation*, ed. Ruth Alsop, Mette Bertelsen, and Jeremy Holland. Washington: The World Bank.

Simões, Júlio A. 1992. *O dilema da participacao popular*. São Paulo: Editora Marco Zero.

SINDPD. 2003. "Entrevista. Tarso genro, Ministro e Secretário do Conselho de Desenvolvimento Econômico e Social." Available at http://www.sindpd.org.br/noticias/11-11_decisao.asp (accessed December 10, 2004).

Singer, André. 2001. *OPT*. São Paulo: Publifolha.

Soares, Fabio, Sergei Soares, Marcelo Medeiros, and Rafael Osorio. 2006. *Cash Transfer Programmes in Brazil: Impacts on Inequality and Poverty*. UNDP International Poverty Center Working Paper 21. New York: UNDP.

Soares de Lima, Maria Regina and Monica Hirst. 2006. "Brazil as an Intermediate State and Regional Power: Action, Choice and Responsibilities." *International Affairs* 82(1): 21–40.

Sotelo Rico, Mariana. 1999. "La longevided de los partidos tradicionales Uruguayos desde una perspectiva comparada." In *Los partidos políticos uruguayos en tiempos de cambio*, ed. Luis E. González. Montevideo: Fundación de Cultura Universitaria.

Stedile, João Pedro. 2007. "The Neoliberal Agrarian Model in Brazil." *Monthly Review* 58(9): 50–54.

Stepan, Alfred. 1978. *The State and Society: Peru in Comparative Perspective*. Princeton: Princeton University Press.

Stiglitz, Joseph. 2006. "Is Populism Really So Bad for Latin America?" *New Perspectives Quarterly* 23(2): 61–62.

Suplicy, Eduardo. 2006. "The Possible Transition from the Bolsa-Família Program towards a Citizen's Basic Income." Presented at the XI International Congress of BIEN (Basic Income Earth Network), Cape Town, South Africa, November 2–4.

Tanaka, Martín. 1998a. "From *Movimientismo* to Media Politics: The Changing Boundaries between Society and Politics in Fujimori's Peru." In *Fujimori's Peru: The Political Economy*, ed. John Crabtree and Jim Thomas. London: Institute of Latin American Studies.

Tanaka, Martín. 1998b. *Los espejismos de la democracia. El colapso del sistema de partidos en el Perú, 1980–1995, en perspectiva comparada*. Lima: Instituto de Estudios Peruanos.

Tanaka, Martín. 2002. *La dinámica de los actores regionales y el proceso de descentralización: ¿el despertar del letargo?* Working Document 125. Lima: Instituto de Estudios Peruanos.

Tanaka, Martín. 2003. *La situación de la democracia en Bolivia, Chile y Ecuador a inicios de siglo.* Lima: Comisión Andina de Juristas.

Taylor, Lewis. 1990. "One Step Forward, Two Steps Back: The Peruvian Izquierda Unida, 1980–90." *Journal of Communist Studies and Transition Politics* 6(3): 320–331.

Touraine, Alain. 2006. "Entre Bachelet y Morales: ¿existe una izquierda en América Latina?" *Nueva sociedad* 205: 46–57.

United Nations. 2007. *Demographic and Social Statistics.* New York, NY: United Nations Statistics Division.

Utzig, José. 1996. "Notas sobre of Governo do PT em Porto Alegre." *Novos estudos* 45: 209–222.

Vacarezza, Cândido, Marcos Rolim, and Luiz Dulci. 1989. "Administracao Petista em direcao ao socialismo." *Teoria e debate* (6).

Valenzuela, Arturo. 2005. "Beyond Benign Neglect: Washington and Latin America." *Current History Magazine* 104(679): 58–63.

Vilas, Carlos, comp. 1994. *La democratización fundamental. El populismo en América Latina.* Mexico: CONACULTA.

Vilas, Carlos. 2005. "La izquierda latinoamericana y el surgimiento de regímenes nacional-populares." *Nueva sociedad* 197: 84–100.

Wampler, Brian. 2004. "Expanding Accountability through Participatory Institutions: Mayors, Citizens, and Budgeting in Three Brazilian Municipalities." *Latin American Politics and Society* 46(2): 73–99.

Weintraub, Sidney. 2002. "Chile as a Template." *Issues in International Political Economy* 35: 1–2.

Weintraub, Sidney. 2006. "Latin America's Movement to the Left." *Issues in International Political Economy* 75: 1–2.

Weisbrot, Mark. 2006. "Left Hook." *Foreign Affairs* 85(4): 200.

Weyland, Kurt. 1996. "Neopopulism and Neoliberalism in Latin America: Unexpected Affinities." *Studies in Comparative International Development* 31: 3–31.

Weyland, Kurt. 1999. "Neoliberal Populism in Latin America and Eastern Europe." *Comparative Politics* 31(4): 379–401.

Weyland, Kurt. 2001. "Clarifying a Contested Concept: Populism in the Study of Latin American Politics." *Comparative Politics* 34: 1–22.

World Bank. 2007. *World Development Indicators.* Washington, DC: The World Bank.

Contributors

David Altman is Associate Professor at the Political Science Institute of the Pontificia Universidad Católica de Chile, and Editor of *Revista de Ciencia Política*. He works on comparative politics with emphasis on the quality of democratic institutions, mechanisms of direct democracy, and executive–legislative relations in Latin America. He is a winner of the Junior Post-Doctoral Scholars in the Study of Democracy Competition of the Woodrow Wilson International Center for Scholars and the Ford Foundation. His articles have appeared in *PS-Political Science and Politics*, *Electoral Studies*, *Política y Gobierno*, *Revista de Ciencia Política*, *The Journal of Legislative Studies*, *International Review of Public Administration*, *Democratization*, *Cuadernos del CLAEH*, and *Revista Uruguaya de Ciencia Política*.

Gianpaolo Baiocchi is Associate Professor of Sociology and International Studies at Brown University. His most recent book is entitled *Militants and Citizens: The Politics of Participation in Porto Alegre* (Stanford University Press, 2005).

Kathleen Bruhn is Associate Professor of Political Science at the University of California, Santa Barbara. Her research interests include social mobilization, political parties, and democratization. Her most recent book, *Fighting City Hall: Urban Protest in Mexico and Brazil* (forthcoming with Cambridge University Press), discusses the causes of protest and the implications of left party victories for protest. She is also the author of *Taking on Goliath* (Penn State Press, 1997), about the formation of the PRD in Mexico, and (with Dan Levy) has published two editions of *Mexico: The Struggle for Democratic Development* (University of California Press, 2001 and 2006).

Jorge G. Castañeda is New York University's Global Distinguished Professor of Politics and Latin American and Caribbean Studies. He is a renowned public intellectual, political scientist, and prolific writer with an interest in Latin American politics, comparative politics, and U.S.–Latin American relations. He was Foreign Minister of Mexico from 2000 to 2003. He has taught at Mexico's National Autonomous University (UNAM), Princeton, and U.C. Berkeley. Among his many books are *Utopia Unarmed* (Vintage Books, 1993), *Compañero: The Life and Death of Che Guevara* (Vintage Books, 1998), and *Ex Mex: Mexicans in the U.S.* (New Press, 2008).

Rossana Castiglioni is the Director of the Political Science School at the Universidad Diego Portales in Santiago, Chile. She works on comparative politics, with an emphasis on democratic institutions and social policy in Latin America. She was the recipient of the 2003 Eli J. and Helen Shaheen Graduate School Award in the Social Sciences. Her work has appeared in *Electoral Studies*, *Latin American Politics and Society*, *Revista de Ciencia Política*, and *Instituciones y Desarrollo*. Her book *The Politics of Social Policy Change in Chile and Uruguay: Retrenchment versus Maintenance, 1973–1998* (Routledge) was published in 2005.

Sofia Checa is a graduate student in Sociology at the University of Massachusetts Amherst, with interests in social movements, political parties, and social change, especially in Latin America and South Asia.

Pablo Heidrich is a researcher at the Latin American Faculty of Social Sciences (FLACSO), Buenos Aires, Argentina. He specializes in the political economy of trade, regional integration, and financial crises. He recently edited a volume on energy and infrastructure integration in South America, and has written several articles on trade and finances of developing countries.

Juan Pablo Luna is an Associate Professor at the Political Science Department at the Pontificia Universidad Católica de Chile. His research focuses on the quality of representation and party–voter linkages in contemporary Latin America. He is a winner of the Junior Post-Doctoral Scholars in the Study of Democracy Competition of the Woodrow Wilson International Center for Scholars and the Ford Foundation. He is the author of *Desde el Llano: Conversaciones con militantes barriales* (Ediciones Banda Oriental, 2004) and his articles have appeared in *Comparative Political Studies*, *Revista de Ciencia Política*, *Revista Uruguaya de Ciencia Política*, *Cuadernos del CLAEH*, *Latin American Politics and Society*, and *Política y Gobierno*.

José Merino is a doctoral candidate in Political Science at New York University, specializing in political economy and methodology. He is currently an adjunct professor at ITAM (Mexico) and an editorialist for *Excélsior* newspaper in Mexico.

Marco A. Morales is a doctoral candidate in Political Science at New York University, specializing in voting behavior, public opinion, and quantitative methodology. Prior to pursuing graduate studies, he served in various positions at the Mexican Chamber of Deputies, the Ministry of Foreign Relations, and the Ministry of the Economy.

Patricio Navia is a master teacher of global cultures in the General Studies Program and an adjunct assistant professor in the Center for Latin American and Caribbean Studies at New York University. He is also a political science professor at Universidad Diego Portales in Chile. He has been a visiting professor at Princeton, New School University and Universidad de Chile. He has published scholarly articles and book chapters on democratization, electoral rules, and democratic institutions in Latin America. He is a columnist at *La Tercera* newspaper and *Capital* magazine in Chile. His most recent book is *Que gane el más mejor. Mérito y Competencia en el Chile de hoy* (coauthored with Eduardo Engel; Random House, 2006).

Raúl A. Sánchez Urribarri is a doctoral candidate in Political Science at the University of South Carolina, specializing in Comparative Politics. His research and teaching interests are in the field of comparative judicial politics, with an emphasis on Latin America. He holds a law degree from Universidad Católica Andres Bello (Venezuela) and a Master of Laws degree (LL.M.) from Cambridge University. Prior to his doctoral studies, he worked as staff attorney at the Venezuelan Supreme Court, and was a lecturer of law at several institutions in Caracas, Venezuela.

Martín Tanaka is the Director General of the Instituto de Estudios Peruanos in Peru and Professor at the Social Sciences Department at the Pontificia Universidad Católica del Perú. He has been a postdoctoral Visiting Fellow at the Hellen Kellog Institute for International Studies at the University of Notre Dame, Indiana, and Visiting Professor in the Masters in Political Science Program at the Universidad de Los Andes in Bogotá, Colombia.

Diana Tussie is the Director of the Department of International Relations at the Argentine campus of the Latin American Faculty of Social Sciences (FLACSO) and the Latin American School of Social Sciences as well as the Latin American Trade Network (LATN). She holds a Ph.D. from the London School of Economics. Her recent books include *Trade Negotiations in Latin America: Problems and Prospects* (Palgrave Macmillan, 2002) and *El ALCA y las Cumbres de las Américas: ¿Una nueva relación público-privada?* (Biblos, 2003). She has served as Under Secretary for Trade Negotiations in the Argentine government. In 2006, she co-directed an evaluation of the WTO's technical assistance.

Index